SPEAKING OF DUKE

Speaking of
DUKE

Leading the 21st-Century University

RICHARD H. BRODHEAD

DUKE UNIVERSITY PRESS

Durham and London

2017

© 2017 Duke University Press
All rights reserved
Printed in the United States of
America on acid-free paper ∞
Designed by Amy Ruth Buchanan
Typeset in Arno Pro by Westchester
Publishing Services

Library of Congress Cataloging-in-Publication Data
Names: Brodhead, Richard H., [date] author.
Title: Speaking of Duke : leading the Twenty-first-century
university / Richard H. Brodhead.
Description: Durham : Duke University Press, 2017. |
Includes bibliographical references and index.
Identifiers:
LCCN 2016046668 (print) | LCCN 2016049559 (ebook)
ISBN 9780822368847 (hardcover : alk. paper)
ISBN 9780822372721 (e-book)
Subjects: LCSH: Education, Higher—Aims and
objectives. | Universities and colleges—Administration. |
Duke University—Presidents.
Classification: LCC LB2324 .B77 2017 (print) |
LCC LB2324 (ebook) | DDC 378.756/563—dc23
LC record available at https://lccn.loc.gov/2016046668

"Remarks on Being Named President of Duke
University," was previously published in *The Good of
This Place* (New Haven: Yale University Press, 2004).

"On the Fate and Fortunes of Public Goods,"
was previously published in *Humanities*,
the Magazine of the National Endowment for the
Humanities 36, no. 6 (2015).

Cover art: The von der Heyden Pavilion at Perkins
Library, Duke University. Photo by Les Todd/
Duke Photography.

CONTENTS

....

From 2004 to 2017 I had the honor to serve as president of Duke. It would be hard to name a more interesting job. First, there is no overstating the miscellany of a university president's work. In no other post could you have the responsibility to recruit a dean of engineering, a chaplain, a football coach, and a leader for a massive health care system, while being ready to talk with any student who walks through the door.

To increase the interest, it's the special nature of universities that they focus the deepest hopes and most perplexing challenges of our culture. In many ways, the first years of the twenty-first century were a bright time for higher education, especially in private institutions. Financially there was some margin for investment (never enough), so these years allowed for renovation, innovation, and experiment. But as they advanced in some directions, universities found themselves facing new forms of difficulty in these years, Duke along with every other.

Unlike the previous great period of expansion for universities in the 1950s and 1960s, in recent decades prosperity has been much more unequally distributed, such that even when gifts from generous donors have run high, access and affordability have grown more challenging. After the Great Downturn of 2008, the cost issue was compounded with another challenge. Suddenly even well-educated people were asking, Is it really worth it, this mysterious thing colleges provide? As rarely before, universities needed to defend the most elemental assumptions of the education we offer—but it would not do to just stay in place. While preserving the best of tradition, universities have needed to re-create their programs for new times, having the courage to change while resisting facile nostrums of reform.

All the while, there were other challenges on the horizon: how to accommodate the increasingly global world our students will live and work in, to name just one. Meanwhile old questions took challenging new forms. Having opened their doors to excluded groups many years ago, universities now wrestle with the question of how to achieve the deeper integration—the full measure of inclusion for all and the optimal enrichment of each *by* all—that more diverse campus communities could deliver.

These are questions university presidents wake up to every day. The point is, there is no picking and choosing among them. Approaches to such issues need to be endlessly recalculated in changing campus situations, with dozens of audiences to listen to and coax along and without forgetting our basic mission: advancing knowledge and unleashing human potential.

If you are the president of Duke, the job has a further interest. It's different being president of Duke because Duke is just a very different kind of place. Having come here as an outsider and having looked every institutional fact in the face for thirteen years, I still find Duke's mythology to be substantially true. The youngest of America's top universities, Duke still has some of the spirit of a start-up. Compared to other leading universities, Duke's culture is deeply communal, broadly collaborative, and quite receptive to innovation.

At a school with that temperament, you would not escape a single one of the hard facts of higher education at this time. But you would have some prospect of working together, answering questions in new ways, striving to create the version of education that will yield the fullest benefit for individuals and our society today.

This book is a chronicle of my work as president of Duke—not in the sense that it lays out all the tasks I was enmeshed in but in that it registers my attempts to work through the challenges and opportunities higher education confronted during my years in office. The book is a series of talks. Each originated as an actual person speaking to some particular set of people gathered for some particular occasion. As such, the pieces mean to underscore the fact that, however complex and cumbersome universities may appear, at their core they are places of personal interaction and personal exchange. I call the book *Speaking of Duke* because, as I have come to understand, speaking is not an ornamental or incidental part of the president's work. Day by day, a president will be involved in a greatly varied mix of activities, but the job that is the president's before any other is the job of voicing the ambitions of the university, enlisting others to share those ambitions, and proposing new ways those ambitions can be fulfilled.

The talks come in a variety of genres. The convocation addresses were addressed to freshmen as they arrived at college, uncertain how to make use of this strange new world. The baccalaureate addresses were delivered to students as they prepared to graduate, uncertain about their new life and how a Duke education would assist them. At Duke the president gives an address to the faculty academic council every year on major issues before the university. I include samples of this genre, speaking on financial aid, international strategy, race, athletics, urban revival in Durham, and a host of other topics.

Increasingly as my Duke career went on and especially after I chaired the American Academy of Arts and Sciences Commission on the Humanities and Social Sciences, I spoke to national audiences on liberal arts education and the too easily ignored value of my own specialty, the humanities. Several of those pieces are included here. Two talks were given at institutions very different from Duke where I had the honor to be the commencement speaker: Fisk University, one of the country's oldest historically black universities, and Miami Dade College, arguably the most diverse and democratic institution of higher education in the United States.

A sad but important work of the president is commemorating people who created the university through the devoted exercise of their gifts. Three pieces here honor three Duke giants: John Hope Franklin, Reynolds Price, and Mary D. B. T. Semans.

I first thought to arrange these pieces by genre, but I came to believe it more revealing to order them as they appear here, gathered by the year in which they were delivered. In effect the book is a chronicle, registering highlights (and occasional lowlights) of successive years, while allowing the reader to see how issues entered the consciousness of the university and played out over time—as the 2008 financial crisis reverberates across genres here for a period of several years.

I am the speaker in these pieces, but they are not about me. The story is of an ambitious university navigating its way forward through difficult currents in ever-changing weather. I hope, however, that a few things will be clear about the author: how grateful I remain for the privilege of serving

Duke, how engaging I found the challenges of this job from first to last, and what confidence I have that Duke will continue to flourish long after I have passed the baton.

Finally a few words of thanks. A university is the collaborative labor of thousands of faculty, students, alumni, and staff. I offer thanks for the inspiration and good company of all who shared my adventure at Duke. They are far too many to name, but my gratitude is no less for remaining tacit.

There are a few people I must single out for special mention. My closest daily associates in the Office of the President were Lisa Jordan, my executive assistant; Richard Riddell, my chief of staff; and Carolyn Gerber, my special assistant. Their invisible hands helped with every good thing that happened during my term of office. I thank them for their loyalty and support.

A group of extraordinarily talented administrators were my partners in leadership over many years. Many of Duke's most promising initiatives had begun when I arrived; most bore the mark of Provost Peter Lange. Peter continued as provost for ten years of my presidency, serving with an unremitting energy and creativity to which all Duke is in debt. In my final three years, Sally Kornbluth brought a different temperament but the same high quality of intellect and leadership to the role of provost. Utterly unruffleable, always able to see a way out of even the most daunting problem, Sally taught me a phrase that had never been in my vocabulary before: "It'll be fine." Thanks to her, it usually was.

Victor Dzau agreed to leave Harvard and take the plunge as chancellor of health affairs at Duke shortly after I agreed to take the plunge from Yale. He was a brilliant and imaginative leader to the half of Duke that lies in the Health System, and he remains a good friend. When Victor left Duke to head the Institute of Medicine, it was my good fortune to recruit an outstanding successor, Gene Washington, whose warm humanity and acute strategic sense will lead Duke Health forward long into the future.

Tallman Trask, who has served as executive vice president for more than twenty years, saw me through my entire presidency, handling every issue of university finance and construction (among many others) with a mix of integrity and ingenuity that remains a wonder. The Duke we know would not exist without the intelligence of Tallman Trask.

Invisible in their effect on campus but absolutely critical to Duke's success have been the men and women who served as university trustees. No university has been more fortunate in its board. Totally devoted to Duke and deeply appreciative of faculty and student talent, the trustees I served with have supplied this university with wisdom, judgment, all manner of expertise, and many forms of support. I could not have asked for better partners or friends. I will name my five board chairs as my way of thanking all my trustee colleagues: Pete Nicholas, Bob Steel, Dan Blue, Rick Wagoner, and David Rubenstein.

My last mention is of a person I met in a university in our early twenties who, to my endless good fortune, has been my partner and companion in everything my adult life has contained. This is my wife, Cindy Brodhead. We took on this job as a joint commitment, and she has more than done her part. Duke has no more ardent fan.

I became who I am thanks to my experiences as a student, and, such is my luck, my education has never stopped. I have embraced every part of the president's vast portfolio, but the heart of my work has been serving the primal mystery by which minds are awakened and discover their powers. In that expansive sense of the word, I dedicate this book to the students of Duke University.

Durham, North Carolina
September 4, 2016

Remarks on Being Named
President of Duke University

Perkins Library, December 12, 2003

I thank you all for this exceptionally warm welcome. When you know me you won't often find me at a loss for words, but you'll pardon me if I'm a little overwhelmed. This is one of the great moments of my life.

Let me tell you a true story. I had been brought down to Durham, in thick disguise, for a final stealth interview last Friday, and since there was a blizzard going on where I come from, my trip home was complex. I could only fly as far as Washington, and in my circuitous journey from that point forward, I had a long cab ride. The cabbie, an Afghan immigrant, was very affable and interesting, and we fell to talking. After a while, he said, "If you don't mind my asking, what do you do?" "I'm a college professor," I told him, in my usual discreet and unrevealing way. Without losing a beat he replied, "Oh! It's the dream of my life that my daughters will go to Duke."

Hearing this was like getting an electric shock. This man, a total stranger and random specimen of humanity, could have had no idea where I was coming from or what I had on my mind. But Duke was in *his* mind, though he had absolutely no connection to it, and on his mind as what? A name for something excellent, a name for something to aspire to, a name for a place that would open the door to knowledge and all the life opportunities that education can provide. I hope that man's daughters do come here. But you know what? By the time I was in that cab, it had also become my dream to attach myself to this university and all its meanings and promise. Lucky me! It came to pass. I've been admitted to Duke, and I'm coming.

This has been a big decision for me, as big as any in my life. Let me say a word about how I came to it. I was not restless. I was not looking for a job. I've had a wonderful life at a great institution. I may be America's least disaffected employee. Yale has been a great place to teach, my first and most abiding passion; also a great place to do my scholarly work and pursue my intellectual life; and my current job has given me a thousand challenges and opportunities for what I care for most: strengthening the work of education. When I was first contacted by your committee, however, my curiosity was piqued. Duke is one of the handful of top universities in the world, after all, and if I went anywhere, it would only be to somewhere like that. So I entered into discussions, and under your committee's skillful tutelage, I came to have a clearer and clearer sense of this place. You already know it, but let me try to tell you what this stranger and outsider saw.

First, Duke is a university with the feel and human scale of a small school but the intellectual resources of a big school, with a college anchoring a full array of outstanding professional schools. Second, and this is rarer than you may recognize, Duke is a university whose different schools and centers and departments not only coexist but actually interact, and even like to interact. I've been to a lot of universities in my day, but I've never been to one where there was such a powerful sense of interschool and interdisciplinary collaboration and of the special dynamism such interactions can breed.

Third, and I felt this very powerfully, Duke is a young school that has managed to raise itself into the top ranks in a fairly short time but that manifestly continues to rise and to want to rise. When I took my stealth tour, I loved your campus, which is so beautiful in a traditional way, but what I really loved was the coexistence of tradition and heady forward progress: all those cranes towering over the Gothic buildings, saying that the building phase at Duke is something of the present and future, not just the past. I was particularly floored by those great modern research facilities hidden just behind the West Campus quad. They show that this is a school capable of having major aspirations and seeing them through—plus, at Duke all that scientific and medical research activity is right next door, where undergraduates can feel its energy and get in on its excitement, not miles away in a separate kingdom.

In the same vein, I found Duke a school with a strong sense of priorities for future improvement, priorities to my mind quite brilliantly articulated that are proof of your faculty and administration's ability to think and work together on important challenges. I've also felt no defensiveness here about improvement, no desire to treat the status quo as the pinnacle of progress. So it's a school that has come a long way, wants to go further, and is unusually well positioned to succeed in doing so.

But then, over against all this dynamism and drive, or accompanying it with no sense of contradiction, I also learned that Duke is just an overwhelmingly friendly place, a place full of people who are both very smart and very nice, a place where people appreciate each other, are relaxed around each other, care about and enjoy each other, and have a healthy sense of the good things of life. In addition to the sense of community on campus, it's also a place that takes seriously its role in the community— the community of Durham, the Research Triangle, and North Carolina more generally. If it's true that we live in a knowledge economy, then universities have special things to contribute to the surrounding world and a special obligation to make those contributions. In Duke I saw a school that wants to be a good citizen in the strong sense of that word, and I believe in that.

Put it all together—what you are and what you want to be—and I must say, it made an impression. A growing impression: I moved, over the course of the last weeks, from being intrigued to deeply interested to quite excited by what I saw here, and I had a stronger and stronger sense of the work to be done here and the fun there might be in doing it. And then came the day when, as Huck Finn said, I had to choose, forever, betwixt two things, and I knowed it: my wonderful life in a known world or the adventure of Duke. Well, you know my choice. I'm a person of strong attachments and powerful devotions who has a lot of energy and wants nothing more than to use that energy on behalf of the deep goals of universities: education, the creation and transmission of knowledge, and the training of the young for constructive lives in the world. It has been my pride to do that work at Yale. Today I transfer my loyalty to this place: from here forward, it will be my honor to do it at Duke. The switch should not be hard. Everything I own is blue, and I am used to four-letter names.

Let me say a few words of thanks. The first is to the search committee and its extraordinary chair, Bob Steel. During the time when I scarcely knew Duke, these folks embodied Duke for me, and they could not have shown it in a more appealing light. They were by turns smart, serious, committed, and fun. What struck me the most was how much they loved Duke and appreciated and admired each other. I could like a place like that, I thought—and here I am. Second, in addition to being wonderfully helpful to me as I tried to get a sense of Duke, Nan Keohane has been a most remarkable president. This is bad for me in one way but good in another. On the one hand, she sets terribly high standards for her successor, and I'm sure I will live to regret the many days when people say "When Nan was here" or "If only Nan were here." Thanks, Nan. But far more than that, Nan has helped shape a university where the faculty trusts the administration (and even likes the president) and feels that we are all working toward common goals. I am lucky to inherit that achievement. This time I mean it: Thanks, Nan. Third, and here I will not say by any means all that's in my heart, I thank my family—my mother and father, who nourished my education in every way, and my wife and son, who give me strength and joy every step of the way. I'm a person who has had many blessings. My new life at Duke is among the chief of them. But my family is at the heart of them.

Last, to every member of the Duke community, let me say thank you in advance for the work we will do together. People speak of educational leaders, but the main truth about universities is that absolutely nothing happens in them through the strength of one. I bring high hopes to this job, but whatever I accomplish will be accomplished through our common labor and with your constant help. Together, you have made this a great school. Together, let's keep it great and make it better yet. I pledge you my full commitment to Duke and to what we will make Duke through our work together.

Authoring a Community

Duke Chapel, August 19, 2004

Parents and friends of the Class of 2008, since Duke Chapel has just enough room for the winners of the 2004 admissions sweepstakes, I must greet you at a distance in the simulcast mode. But though my greeting is virtual, I welcome you to this happy event and your new bond with Duke. After this ceremony I will be outside to meet you in person, but truth to tell, your location this hour makes a kind of sense. One of the kindest humans I ever met said this to parents on the opening day of college: "You've done so much for your sons and daughters, supported them in so many ways, now there's one more thing you must do for them. Go home." You know what he meant. Your goal when your children were younger was to help them grow into splendid independent people who could carry on on their own. Well, the day has come to make the test, and your hour in Page Auditorium could be thought of as a trial separation. Will your daughter wake herself up in time for class without you there to help? If you don't call every ten minutes, will your son eat regularly and go to bed at a sensible hour? I trust the answer is yes, but the honest answer is, we shall now see! In fact your children will thrive here, but for them to get the good of their new life, you need to back off. Parents, I join you in this day's sorrow but still more in its excitement and pride.

Well, I got rid of them! Now for you, my Dukies! As I'm sure you have already felt, you and I have everything in common. I too spent last year deciding where to go to college; I too weighed alternatives while others were weighing alternatives to me; I too was lucky enough to have the choice of Duke; I too was clever enough to take it. And since the orientation for presidents starts a bit earlier than yours, I've already scouted the territory and can report on what's ahead. Your faithful scout brings you this news: you'll love it here. Duke is very beautiful, very stimulating, very challenging, but very friendly and fun. It may take a week or two to settle in, but you have this on high presidential authority: you stand on the verge of a great new life.

When I asked myself what I could say to you on this occasion, I could only think to begin with this overwhelming fact of newness. This is, for you, like the earliest days of creation. Everything stands before you in its primal freshness and strangeness; you have not yet marred a single hour or messed up in a single way. As I reflected further, my mind gravitated to a feature of this convocation that's completely new to my experience and that helped symbolize the larger fact of newness: the chance you will have, after this ceremony, to sign the Duke Community Standard.

I won't comment here on the content of the Standard, which is printed in your program and straightforward enough. (If you plan to have trouble being honest and behaving honorably while you're at Duke, please raise your hand now so the ushers can eject you.) What I found myself puzzling at was the idea of a public signing. My response to this had a certain complexity. On the one hand, I said to myself, What's the point of requiring a visible, physical affixing of the name? These are minimal moral expectations and, to my mind, just as binding whether you sign them or not. (Plus if the legalistic among you should someday say "But I never signed them," we will reply, "Oh yes you did!" You agreed to these conditions when you signed your acceptance of Duke.)

But as I continued my reflections, I came to think that there was something interesting, possibly even something quite wonderful, about the idea of this ceremony. If the physical act of signing doesn't make these norms more obligatory, it does give your embrace of them the quality of a deliberate, conscious, voluntary act. Further, it enacts the thought that you become a member of this community by embracing certain values—an idea I much admire.

From there I found myself thinking of the larger historical and philosophical resonances of a ceremony of this sort. As you'll have the chance to learn, early modern philosophy is full of the thought that human societies are not something established by nature or divine law but something humans themselves make through some primal founding act. Thomas Hobbes, who did the thinking for his great *Leviathan* (1651) during the English Civil War, posits that in the state of nature, no man was enough stronger than any other to be able to protect himself to an absolute extent. The state of nature was a state of endless competition and self-assertion in which men were independent and, for that reason, radically and incurably insecure. According to Hobbes, civil society began when, in face of this intolerable condition, men formed a contract: covenanted with each other to each give up a measure of freedom in order to create a collectivity, the commonwealth, that could supply the security no individual could win on his own.

There are many variants on this theory of the social contract, and as you may know, contemporaries of these thinkers put such theories into practice in real historical events. In the first document printed in English in America, an oath devised by the Puritan leader John Winthrop, men and women were asked to make a community, literally to call one into existence, by affirming their acceptance of certain values and obligations. One hundred thirty years after the Freeman's Oath, the United States came into being through conscious founding acts of public profession and agreement: the signing of the Declaration of Independence and the ratification of the Constitution.

From here my train of thought led back to you. For what all this served to remind me is that each of you, this day, has the signer's power, the power to author a community through your agreements. The reality of your life at Duke has as yet no determinate character or shape. It's you who will create that reality, through the habits you lay down. What will be the nature of that way of life? That's not resolved yet. It is you who will settle it, through the choices that you make. I could imagine some relatively thoughtless choices that would result in a relatively uninteresting (though still perfectly pleasant) Duke experience; I could also imagine a far more fulfilling version that you could build from the same set of opportunities. But in the hubbub and stress of arrival you may be scarcely aware that you have such choices, let alone recognize their fateful nature.

In this state, this morning's signing ceremony could have a special value. My bright idea is that this signing could be your chance to envision and affirm all the good intentions you could live by at Duke: all the intentions that, individually and collectively embraced, would construct the best commonwealth for your new life.

I have the microphone, so I get to propose some terms for your compact. For starters: Four or five years back, Duke adopted a set of curricular requirements (recently simplified) that mandate that you take courses in certain competences, areas of knowledge, modes of inquiry—you know the rest. How are you going to deal with this somewhat complicated beast? One choice would be to approach these as a set of troublesome requirements handed down by some obscure and ill-natured bureaucrat to no end except to complicate your life, which you could nevertheless manage to outwit without too serious discomfort, checking off all the boxes, by appealing to the great "they say"—the news you heard fifth-hand that Course X is a painless way to fulfill Requirement Y.

Even loading your matrix in this relatively low-minded way (yes, I have heard of curricular bingo) would yield some educational profit. But do you know what? There would be another way to cover the same ground that would yield more pleasure and more profit. You could construe those same requirements as your own intellectual goals, guides to mental muscle groups an educated person would want to develop, knowledges and competences that would help you build a capable, powerful mind. (If you really can't think what good being competent at writing or a foreign language or quantitative skills could ever do you, you'd better come see me.) Having turned bureaucratic hurdles into instruments of aspiration, you would then set out to find the classes that would give you the most interesting and engaging way to advance toward these goals—making your academic life an act of curiosity and exploration, not a mere exercise in compliance.

Since curiosity is a prime educational value, I'd ask you to have some curiosity too about those around you. Since Duke looks for students with the intellect and character to make a contribution to the world, and since such people are found in every human setting, you'll have classmates from every state and global region, every ethnic origin, every income level, every religion, every political persuasion. Let me take this occasion to say to each of you, wherever you come from and whatever you believe: This is your place. You are all equally welcome to Duke and equally entitled to all its benefits.

But you, far more than I, will be determining what kind of community grows up among you in practice, and since it's still the very first day—since you're literally still deciding whose music will be played and who gets which bed—nothing has been fixed yet about the world you'll build. More correctly, everything is being settled by your first acts, by the forms of interaction you initiate—and it's still in your power to reflect and choose. Though we all hate prejudice, we are all deeply skilled in the mental sorting devices by which humans parse a world of strangers and identify, on the basis of superficial external signs, whether they are "my kind" or not. With the guidance of this social positioning system, you don't even need to talk to a person—don't need to engage in conscious labor of any sort—to know that he's too northern, she's too southern; one person is too jocky, the next too wimpy; one acts as if he owns the place (the jerk!), the other is way too retiring. And this inventory has just begun.

If you take seriously the notion that you are making the commonwealth you'll inhabit, then you have your choice here, and it matters. Proceeding on autopilot, you could locate the universe of those "like" you on such initial measures and silently erase the rest of your classmates; or, a little more adventurously, you could open yourself to other types and take a deeper measure of what you might share. Which do you suppose you will learn more in: a world of mutually repelling comfort zones or a world of free, spirited interaction across all real or imagined social lines?

Might there be friction in this sort of interaction? We would be absurd to doubt it, but even there you have a choice. Will you take those who annoy you and cast them out as hopeless, irremediable Losers? Or might you find a way candidly to identify differences, learn to see them from different sides, and work out a way to accommodate the rights and needs of all? In the larger world we see both courses at work, and you know which comes to a better ending, but it's not settled yet which will prevail on your version of Planet Duke. It will be settled by your own conduct: by the way you handle a new life's strains.

But being respectful and open wouldn't be the highest you could aim. One of the problems of modern pluralism is that to the extent that heterogeneous populations have embraced the idea of getting along together, an amazing feat given the world's history of prejudice and strife, a new reality has sometimes emerged. Where the lion lies down with the lamb to the tune of "It's a Small World After All," peace and pleasantness can be purchased at an unspoken price, namely the suggestion that no one should feel or assert anything very passionately lest someone else should find it offensive.

We have to hope that the world of equal rights and mutual respect will not be a world of self-neutralized convictions and watered-down consensus. Imperfect though it may still be, the new world the civil rights movement created would not have come into existence without hot convictions and sharp elbows. But it requires work to get this balance right. Something I would love to see Duke pioneer—and for this to happen it will have to be our common creation—is a culture of positive intellectual difference, or what the poet Blake called mental strife. American universities have taken far more trouble to host athletic contests than most sorts of intellectual contention. But since powerful differences shape the force field of our lives, the sides had better learn something about each other and, dare one hope it, learn something from each other.

In this election year, there are questions more interesting than which will be a red and which a blue state, questions it's hard to be certain of the answer to unless a partisan position short-circuits the inquiry. What rights should we give up as the price of collective security (Hobbes's questions have not gone away), and at what point does security ask too high a price at the level of individual freedom? To what extent is it better to go it alone in international affairs, and to what extent will any international effort fail without some larger consensus behind it? To what extent is the globalized economy a system for draining away jobs that should stay at home, and to what extent do its dynamisms increase economic vitality in all regions, even at the cost of local dislocation? How can radical inequalities of health be kept from tracking other forms of inequality in America and the world, and how is the better care that is now scientifically available to be paid for and made economically available?

If you think these are trivially easy questions, then you need some education. Coming to college was a good start, but then you have a choice: whether to evade such challenges as best you can or learn to engage them with knowledge, subtlety, and creativity. To do the latter, you'll need to be surrounded by people trying to answer hard questions and tune in to what they say. But you need to be more than a good audience: you'll need yourselves to become skilled arguers. By skilled arguer I do not mean a person who can achieve a technical knockout in the early rounds by goosing up the level of rhetorical force. I mean a person who can put forward what she understands with all the intelligence and sincerity she can muster while still staying open to the truth that lies on the other side, and who, while not eager to give (or quick to take) offense, is willing to engage in that struggle with contrary minds that produces deeper understanding for all.

The man whose statue stands in front of this chapel sent this message to the assembled student body when the old Duke library was opened: "Tell them every man to think for himself." I'd have you add this to the pact you make here today: an agreement that you would actively think here rather than lounging in passive acceptances, that you would protect the space in which others are also free to think, and that you would so engage and contend with each other within that space as to stretch and deepen one another's minds. Is this enough to sign your name to? Of course not, but you can write the remaining terms, and I count on you to do so. And lest you forget the pact we made this day, download these words in your iPod and let me croon them to you each night as you go to sleep. Men and women of the Class of 2008, my first four-year class at Duke, you will love this place—but you'll love it more if you help make it the place that you believe it should be.

The Virtues and Limits of Specialization

Duke Chapel, August 19, 2004

This morning I had the pleasure of making my first address to an incoming class of Duke undergraduates. This afternoon I return to greet students equally central to this university's mission: the new entrants to Duke's graduate and professional schools. When you were freshmen, and I'm sure that day seems almost inconceivably remote from the maturity you have attained to now, you were probably looking to four years of college as the end of school—but in a troubling recidivism, here you are back again. In truth you've come here for the next chapter of your education, training, and personal growth, and I hope it will be a splendid one. On behalf of Duke University, I welcome you most warmly.

Though this is, as the program notes, the 167th year of Duke's institutional life, Duke did not always have the schools you've enrolled in. What was founded 167 years ago was a one-room elementary school called Brown's Schoolhouse. But as I have come to know the history, what I have found striking is that this first creation had the gene of self-advancement built into it from the start. Unlike the hundred other backwoods academies created at about the same time, the school that became Duke always had a special drive to extend itself toward the highest known levels of education and, by offering training in the higher learning, to put advanced knowledge to a larger social use.

While this school was still in its infancy, its leaders got wind of the ideas of the common school movement emanating from states like Massachusetts, ideas since codified in this country's public school system— a familiar feature in our time but a radical novelty in the 1830s. Inspired by this notion, these educators in the hinterlands of one of the South's then-poorest states remade their little institution into a normal school, a place for preparing trained teachers: one of the common school movement's principal innovations. Having barely survived the devastations of the American Civil War and Reconstruction, this school had the presumptuousness to hire as its leader a trainee from the brave new world of graduate education, an outsider with the newfangled degree called the Ph.D. This person brought Trinity College ambition for the activities that marked the new advanced university of the 1880s: intercollegiate varsity athletics and systematically organized graduate and professional study. (Not everyone knows that these two American staples were contemporaneous developments.)

President John Franklin Crowell succeeded in introducing football to Trinity College and moving the school to the more metropolitan Durham, but he did not realize the rest of his dream. It would not be long, however, before that ambition would reassert itself. As the relocated undergraduate school grew in strength, another of my predecessors, William Preston Few, proposed a vision of a college with a full array of graduate and professional schools constellated around it, and a great industrialist-philanthropist from the school's principal family of backers, James Buchanan Duke, put up the money to make the vision real. In the late 1920s and early 1930s a gothic campus was thrown up in thick woods; bright young faculty were raided from the Johns Hopkins Medical School and elsewhere; and the Duke we know was born.

The founders of this university had two dreams in mind. One was to make this a place of outstanding intellectual eminence, "a place of real leadership," as Mr. Duke called it. But in Duke's idea such leadership also involved harnessing the power of higher learning for the larger social good. The schools you are about to enter were formed to the end of training men and women who, by virtue of their special knowledge and depth of reflection, would be equipped to staff and lead the world's great institutions—its hospitals, churches, corporations, universities, courts—and so to meet the world's great needs: the need for intellectual understanding, the need for bodily care and healing and for spiritual inspiration, the need for justice, the need for economic productivity, and the need to understand and care for the natural world. We are proud of what you will go on to accomplish in the careers you came here to prepare for. When you succeed, we will boast that you owe it all to your time at Duke. If I could ask one thing to you as you start out, it would be to set your own sights sufficiently high.

This new phase of your education is governed in a fundamental way by the rule of specialization. Your very enrollment was organized through the idea of the division of labor and knowledge. You were admitted to the graduate program in philosophy or economics or neuroscience—and will now begin the study of law or medicine or engineering. But there was a time when the highest intellectual and social creativity did not obey the law of specialization quite so strictly. James Gleick's recent biography of Isaac Newton reminds us that Newton was not just the great physicist of mass and motion but was also a great student of optics, a great astronomer, and a great mathematician, and in addition a master of scriptural arcana and cabalistic lore pertaining to biblical prophecy, and, as well, the man who figured out how to standardize and stabilize the national currency of England. With nothing like Newton's formal education (he founded a university but never attended one), Ben Franklin made famous contributions as a printer, scientist, inventor, statesman, diplomat, and deviser of the first national communications system, the Post Office.

If we do not find such astonishing ranges in the careers of our time, it is not principally because humans in our day have shrunk in power. It is because, in one of the decisive historical developments of the past century or so, the place of major discovery has become the place of specialized expertise. Within the memory of living people, medical research has brought us closer to the secrets of life and health than would ever have been imaginable a short time before. The action and possible regulation of hormones was not understood until the 1920s; the discovery of antibiotics is little older than I am; this is only the fiftieth anniversary of the unraveling of DNA. But none of these discoveries was made by a generalist, nor, realistically, could they have been. In our day, if colleagues work on a single organism or gene or protein year after year, subjecting smaller and smaller objects to the play of more and more complicated techniques of inquiry, it is not because they have limited curiosity. It is because they are convinced that only this sort of tightly focused inquiry will be able to puzzle out the clues through which larger mysteries will one day be understood.

Given this linkage of deepened expertise with tightened focus—and every field has had its own version of this development—there is no way to access the most powerful forms of contemporary knowledge except by passing through the narrow gate. Omnicompetence may be a legitimate object of nostalgia but is likely to look like amateurism or worse when we meet it in practice. When people start talking to me about my area of expertise on the basis of some general knowledge of that and other fields, I am usually struck not by the larger wisdom or deeper truth of what they say but by its superficiality or banality, and when I want someone to advise the university on a complicated issue of intellectual property rights or the comparative merits of rival health care models, I'm unlikely to call on a jack of twenty other trades.

You're about to enter a space of intense, demanding concentration. You have chosen to do so in the knowledge that this is the route by which expertise is struggled toward and won. I wish you the joy of your discipline, and the growth in understanding and power for which this discipline is the precondition. But let me add my hope that you will not let this focus narrow you beyond the point where narrowing is needed and productive.

For though it is true that many advances have had specialization as their enabling condition, the greatest contributions have come, arguably, from those who have retained a sense of the larger field of humanly interesting things even as they have narrowed their sights for strategic purposes. I was struck by the suggestion by Tom Cech, who won the Nobel Prize for his work on RNA before becoming the head of the Howard Hughes Medical Institute, that outstanding research careers in the sciences correlate with liberal arts study in college—with an initial education that is broadly based and promotes multiple trainings, as a supplement to later specialization. China and Singapore, countries with a vigorous sense of the role educational development plays in sustaining economic development, have become increasingly interested in a liberal arts alternative to their system of tight early specialization, in the thought that this rival model may nourish a superior versatility and creativity. Further, we are all increasingly recognizing that many of the most interesting problems are radically interdisciplinary at their core. If so, the women and men equipped to attack them most constructively will not be those who have learned to work them in one dimension but those who have been trained to grasp the interaction of many sides of the puzzle and bring to bear multiple sets of analytic skills.

You had the genius to come to the American university (in my expert judgment) that sponsors the most vibrant culture of cross-disciplinary exploration. The care of those at the end of life is obviously a biomedical issue, and so the object of biomedical research; but it is no less a question of the management and delivery of care, and so part of the province of nursing; but it also involves a problem no medical school will ever cure: the spiritual crisis posed by death. Elsewhere you might study one or another of these aspects in isolation from the others. At Duke, thanks to a joint program of the schools of medicine, nursing, and divinity, you might instead learn to see these dimensions as co-constituents of a single existential problem. Similarly it would be rare enough elsewhere, but it's quite natural at Duke, for health care to be studied at once as a medical issue, a matter of biological discoveries and therapies, and an issue of management economics in a joint program between the Medical School and Fuqua. At a time when the boundaries between the mechanical and the organic are being eroded in a way new in human history, Duke not only sponsors biomedical engineering but is literally building its research space between those of medicine and engineering. In our world every environmental issue has both a scientific and a social cause and will require both a scientific and a social cure. Typical of Duke that when these issues are studied at the Nicholas School, the resources are at hand to grasp the science of environmental problems together with the legal, economic, and policy dimensions of possible solutions.

Whatever you came to study, this place offers the resources to help you to that sharpened seeing that comes through a tight disciplinary focus and the means to rejoin fields of vision that academic study can put artificially asunder. But to get the full benefit, you have to reach out from your home base, and to remember to want to reach out.

I have been speaking as if only programmatic links forge bridges across disciplinary chasms. In truth you have another asset even nearer to hand.

I am referring to your graduate and professional school contemporaries, people like you in intelligence who have chosen to direct that intelligence down a different path. My own graduate school experience was good in many ways but extremely lonely at first, and when I made friends (and I made wonderful ones; one is now my wife), they were almost exclusively people in my field. Easy to understand why. In a world organized by school and department, they were the people nearest at hand, and when I was spending twelve hours a day studying a single subject, they were the people I could most readily discuss it with.

But transposing the intellectual boundaries of the disciplines onto one's social life can be extremely impoverishing, since it shuts out a larger community of friends and shuts you in from what they could teach you of other fields. Here again, the special character of Duke can be of help. Of the major research universities I have been associated with, this is the one where the graduate and professional students are most emphatically welcome to participate in the life of the university outside their local borough. Duke is also, in my experience, simply an overwhelmingly friendly place. So as you enter this school, you should have the courage to join its community in the fullest sense. Make friends outside your academic island, as many as you can from across as many borders as you can. This will give you more than a happy life, though I do not underestimate the value of that. Every friend you win from outside your specialization could be your bridge to knowledge you have shut yourself off from.

If you can bear it, I have one final word of advice. You are very smart and successful people. You would not have been admitted to the schools you are about to enter if you had not compiled compelling academic records. You have also shone in those specialized feats that are America's intellectual equivalents for the Olympic games: the MCATs, the LSATs, and similar tests of strength. I salute you for your achievement, but all that success and discipline can also have a downside, making you highly attuned to demands made on you from without.

Doing what you think your new schools officially expect of you will almost certainly assure a considerable success, both in your time here and in your later career. But this is not the road to the highest success. There is a lesser and a larger way to practice every profession. The difference does not lie in embracing or resisting the discipline of the profession: that is necessary for both. The difference comes from the degree to which you remember to think, deep down, what your studies are really about, what deep question they were meant to answer, and the degree to which you remember to ask what your knowledge is good for, what service it could render to human life in your time. The Duke culture of community service that will put so many of you to work in neighborhood legal clinics, medical clinics, small-business consultancies, and the rest will give you a splendid occasion to practice your new knowledge while still in school and to think how this knowledge can be translated into a social good.

Hanging around in pulpits seems to have activated the preacher in me! And I confess, it's great fun to have you for my congregation. But the first truth about sermons is that they must be of bearable length, so I will hasten to my close. Graduate and professional students of Duke, we want you to get a great education, not a good one. But it's going to take some work from you to make this happen, and I do not mean only work of the homework sort. Approach this place with broad ambitions and high aspirations and you will get its greatest reward. Isn't that what you had in mind? If so, please signify by saying amen. I welcome you to Duke.

More Day to Dawn

Duke Chapel, September 18, 2004

Distinguished guests, colleagues, students, friends, I thank you for joining me on this great day. Never having been inaugurated before, I didn't
know exactly what I was in for, but a stray remark gave me a clue. As you
may know, I had a deep attachment to my former school, having spent
my whole adult life there, and when the news broke that I was leaving,
not everyone took it well. A student I knew put her dismay this way:
"See, it was like Dean Brodhead was married to Yale—and now we learn
that he's leaving us for someone younger and more athletic." To this I
could only reply, Well, these things happen! And by the logic of her analogy, today we solemnize my new union. Let's do it right. Do I, Richard,
take you, Duke, to be my chosen life? I do. Forsaking all others, will I do
everything in my power to further the aims of this university? I will.
As we pursue these goals, will I work to promote the welfare of every
member of the Duke community—every faculty member, student, li-
brarian, lab and office assistant, food server, maintenance worker, chaplain, coach—every single person whose labor and devotion make this
place thrive? Yes I will. I'm grateful for your welcome and will do my part
with energy, dedication, and joy.

When I reflect on what I'm coming into, the scene around us supplies
a major part of my idea. Venerable and time-worn though they seem, this
gothic village and chapel rivaling many European cathedrals in beauty
were not always here. Less than eighty years ago, the place where we

stand was thick, unbroken woods. The site became the campus of one of the world's great universities through a great act of making and imagination, and properly seen, every one of these buildings is a physical signature of that act. When I first walked this space, the raw force of this primal act of construction put me in mind of Faulkner's Thomas Sutpen in *Absalom, Absalom!*, wresting his baronial estate from the uncleared forests and swamps of northern Mississippi, "dragging house and formal gardens out of the soundless Nothing and clapping them down like cards upon a table, the Be Sutpen's Hundred like the oldtime Be light." But this analogy, I've learned, is both right and wrong. Right, because building this place did involve the insistence into being of something that at first existed only in the mind; wrong, because that creation was not the work of one time or one man.

The school we know as Duke was founded in the late 1830s in Randolph County, one hour to the west (Cindy and I made a pilgrimage to the site as one of our first acts as new settlers), in the hinterland of what was one of the South's least developed states. But no place is so poor that its people can't care about education, and no group is so ever deprived that it can't take steps to acquire this good. Urged by these motives, Methodist and Quaker families built a one-room school in what is now Trinity, North Carolina. Unlike the hundreds of other backwoods academies founded at the same time, however, this school had a gene of self-advancement that acted on it in powerful ways. Within its first few years, it had transformed itself first into a normal school, a center for the production of trained teachers, then into a somewhat rudimentary liberal arts college, Trinity College. Though the Civil War left it almost decimated, it continued to dream of what it could be. After Reconstruction, at a time when it was not always able to make the payroll, this school hired as president a product of the new-model graduate education just being elaborated in the American North who brought Trinity the dream of becoming a full-fledged university. President John Franklin Crowell did not see these ambitions fulfilled, though in preparation he did succeed in relocating the college to the more metropolitan Durham. But a generation later, this ambition was powerfully reignited. In the early 1920s, in a document I have hung on my office wall, President William Preston Few sketched out a vision of an undergraduate college with a full array of graduate and professional schools constellated around it. He then pitched it to James Buchanan Duke, the industrialist-philanthropist from Trinity's principal family of backers. Three years later Duke agreed to fund this expansion; a short while later the land was cleared and the building began; and a surprisingly small number of years later, Duke University opened its doors.

My history is severely abridged, but you will get the point: this place has always had the character of a rising school. Duke could have leveled off in any number of inertial orbits, but it never did. Instead, from generation to generation, it has been driven by the desire to be more than it has thus far succeeded in becoming, to push toward the limit of what a great school could be. Another striking trait, Duke's extraordinary institutional plasticity, derives from this first. Much as it might admire what it had already become, Duke is a school that has been continually willing to remake itself in sometimes fairly drastic ways to the end of becoming better.

President Few and Mr. Duke produced a high point in this history, but the story did not end there. Each of my predecessors—and I am honored to have three of them here today, Douglas Knight, Keith Brodie, and Nan Keohane—has presided over a raising of the sights. I come to this university in the conviction that, in Thoreau's words, there is more day to dawn. I take this office with the idea that, together, we will write the next chapter in this school's rise.

In the last few decades, Duke has become a center for the sorts of research and teaching that characterize the greatest universities in this nation and the world. But I have been finding that Duke has a distinct character (within the company of great universities), one that marks its doings with a certain Duke difference. One thing that amazes and delights me every day I spend here (I recognize that when we have been married a little longer we may take each other's charms a little more for granted) is the way this school permits, even encourages, the crossing of intellectual boundaries. Duke has the same divisions by school and department as everywhere else, but at Duke these administrative conveniences have not hardened into the walls and barriers they form elsewhere. Faculty here are in conversation with people in a wide array of other fields, combining and recombining their expertise in compelling new compounds and conjunctions.

The other thing I'm struck by virtually every day is that the balance between theory and practice has been struck in a somewhat different way at Duke. In the modern state of things, no school can be expected to produce much new understanding that does not give free rein to highly specialized research. But at this school, such study does not enclose itself within the intramural exchange among specialists that characterizes much modern academic life. At Duke it forms the research end of an arc that extends from inquiry through discovery to translation into practice, a continuum that links the most abstruse research with practical improvements to actual lives.

I remember the day last winter when I first visited the Duke Clinical Research Institute. (It's fun to be the president. You get to go everywhere.) I had already spent considerable time in the medical and nursing schools and taken the measure of their strength across the spectrum from basic science to patient care. But until that visit I did not grasp what it meant to say that Duke leads the world in testing medical discoveries for their value for human care. On the day I visited, DCRI was at work on two studies with vast implications for bookend phases of life: a major study (since published and widely noted) on the treatment of teenage depression and a study of an intervention that might prevent bone breakage in the elderly in nursing homes. DCRI has now launched a study of heart disease, the largest cause of death and disability in the world, that will involve fifteen hundred hospitals in thirty countries.

This facility does more than contribute to improved health care in Durham and around the world, important though that is. It supplies the bridging device that puts research-generated knowledge in effective contact with practice and service—and once I started to notice, I found myself surrounded by such bridges. It seemed typical of Duke that when I visited the Divinity School, I would learn of a collaborative program between the schools of divinity, medicine, and nursing on care at the end of life—typical that schools should cooperate so deeply and effectively across disciplinary boundaries, and typical that this collaboration should be grounded in an address to the multiple faces of a fundamental human need. When the forest was cleared to build this site, there was small thought for the meaning of the environment or the harm humans do themselves through their actions on the natural world. As we grasp the gravity of these issues, the Nicholas School of the Environment and Earth Sciences gives a powerful means to address them. But what's so "Duke" about the rapidly expanding Nicholas School is how it is building the interface between scientific research and its application at the level of social cure—a marriage of pure and applied science strengthened by collaborations with colleagues in law, economics, engineering, medicine, and the Sanford Institute of Public Policy.

Further features of Duke began to make new sense to me once I detected this pattern. The culture of public service is immensely strong across this campus. Last winter when I had lunch with students in the Law School and the Fuqua School of Business, what they wanted to talk about was their volunteer work in clinics giving legal advice to local nonprofits and advice to small business owners. A recent day in my new office began with a current medical student and a recent econ major who have mounted an ambitious health and fitness program for city kids under the sponsorship of Mike Krzyzewski, Coach K. What I've come to understand is that at Duke, public service is not some ornamental activity extraneous to the real business of the place. The culture of service is strong here because it grows directly from the mission of the school—this school having been founded, in Mr. Duke's words, to serve "the needs of mankind along physical, mental, and spiritual lines."

So too I rejoice in the Duke-Durham Neighborhood Partnership that Mayor Bill Bell and President Keohane did so much to further, and I pledge to carry this partnership to new heights. But this partnership works, on Duke's end, not because the administration pushes it but because it is rooted in the genius of this place. Duke has something more valuable than money to give to the community we share: namely, the expert knowledge faculty and students bring to bear in the schools and health and legal aid clinics in this town. What we get in return, beside the satisfaction of citizenship, is the education that flows back to theory from practice: the learning that arises when theoretical intelligence is tested in the arena of real human needs.

I was lured here by the spectacle of a school that has established itself in the top rank of research universities and professional schools but that habitually connects the pursuit of knowledge with the search for the social good. It's my guess that our society is going to require universities to have a character more like this in the future. If the public is to continue to fund inquiries largely unintelligible to the common understanding, and the progress of knowledge in our time would grind nearly to a halt if this support were lost, universities are going to need to become far less self-enclosed and self-absorbed, to take more pains to demonstrate the value of advanced research for men's and women's lives. As I assume the presidency of a school with this inspiring character, my role will be to build on its special strengths. This isn't the place for a litany of detailed plans, but I might touch on a few aspects of the tasks ahead.

Duke has many initiatives under way, and I was attracted here by Duke's ability to identify and advance toward key strategic goals. Starting these ambitious projects took one kind of work, but as we near these destinations we need to engage in another, namely remembering what we were trying to accomplish and making sure we reach that goal. The newly opened Center for Interdisciplinary Engineering, Medicine, and Applied Sciences is a glorious interdisciplinary research facility, and the competitor in me is eager for all representatives of other universities to go see it. (P.S.: Eat your heart out.) But the goal of CIEMAS wasn't to build another laboratory but to enable the ascent to the higher level of creativity in technology and biomedical engineering—key tools for our time—that such a facility could facilitate. With this, as with all our projects, we need to be careful to remember the ends we built toward and not mistake the means for the end. That would bring us somewhere, but not to the place we seek.

More generally, as Duke completes a phase of building surpassed only by that of the 1920s and 1930s, we reach the time for building of another sort, a building of intellectual capital commensurate with a splendid physical plant. Every great university is great by virtue of its faculty, and an aspiring university will always be adding to its company of great minds. The kind of scholar-teacher the best future university will be built from is only partly identified by the standard markers of academic achievement. We need to look for people who enliven inquiry in their field but retain a sense of a larger picture, the larger questions their specially trained powers could help engage, people too who will keep asking new questions and engaging colleagues in flexible and opportunistic combinations to help them toward an answer. These scholars will be real teachers too: people whose love of their subject compels them to share that love with students and to nourish their independent mental growth.

There's no knowing what apparently arcane study will prove to be of burning relevance some future day. (Think of the changing role experts on Islam have taken on in American universities after 9/11.) So I would continue to build intellectual strength in every field, not in obviously "applied" ones alone. That said, it does seem that a school of Duke's character has special opportunities to lead in certain crucial areas, one of which is global health. Duke medical researchers are already active from Tanzania to Singapore to Honduras and back to the Carolinas and are working on virtually every health challenge a growingly populous, growingly interdependent world will face. As a by-product of its profoundly interdisciplinary character, this school also spawns every day the sort of partnerships that might solve multisided problems in this domain: problems at the interface of medicine and engineering—imaging, cell and tissue engineering, the design of new medical devices; problems at the interface of medicine and law, like intellectual property rights in breakthrough discoveries; problems at the interface of medicine and the social sciences—the management and economics of health care, the cultural factors that keep people from making full use of available care; and problems at the interface of medicine and ethics. In my dream, Duke would be the place where people from around the world come to learn and contribute to a growing understanding of our shared health future, and no student would leave without a deeper understanding of this dimension of our common lot. As we build the best facilities and programs, we must keep in mind the students they are meant to serve, and ensure that the university fully delivers on the promise of education. The graduate and professional students at my new home seem not just very smart but wonderfully positive in outlook, and it's my impression that this school does better than many others in mentoring and in including advanced students in the full life of the place. (Yes, I did visit your campground last Saturday. Where else do they do these things?) Nonetheless, the specialization and discipline exacted by advanced study can be powerfully isolating, and we must work to realize the full community we might achieve among these students—a community of friends but also an intellectual community among disciplines and disparate points of view.

Graduate and professional students have chosen their calling. But college is a place of discovery and becoming, a place where students find their interests, their powers, and their mature selves. This fall Duke freshmen read Tracy Kidder's biography of Paul Farmer, the humanitarian doctor in rural Haiti and leader in the fight to secure the benefits of medical research for the world's poor. Paul Farmer went to Duke, but it might be truer to say that he became Paul Farmer by going to Duke: this is where he found the calling we know him by, through an unplanned convergence of experiences in class and out. I'd like every undergraduate to run the risk of such self-discovery and self-enlargement by enrolling at Duke. Toward that end, we need to find more and more ways to include Duke students in the excitement of direct academic inquiry and to make the whole of college life a maximally stimulating, growth-inducing experience. Building projects in key undergraduate spaces—the rebuilding of Central Campus and the area around the Bryan Center—will take place on my watch. We will get these right if we remember that the point is not to build buildings, but by means of building to support the richest forms of communal life.

Going to such a college is one of the most valuable privileges our society affords. For that reason, as we strengthen this already strong place, another part of our work must be to assure that this university stays wide open to every young person with the requisite talent and commitment. It was not so long ago that schools and universities (the best not least) played a role in reinforcing received social hierarchies, assuring that to those who had, much was given, while denying others the best means to advancement, a first-class education. The namesakes of this school were far more enlightened than many of their time, but Duke remained racially segregated until the 1960s, and the first African American undergraduates and medical students at Duke (I've met members of both groups) are people my exact age. (I myself attended a college that excluded women until 1969.) Through the work of men and women, many of them still alive, the high places of American education have been reconstructed from sites of exclusion and inequality into scenes of access and opportunity, but it's not time to stop that labor now. We must make the whole of Duke, every school and every department and every office, a place of open opportunity—and we need to make this a place not just of numerical demographic inclusiveness but of real mutual engagement, a community in which each of us will educate and be educated by every other.

Nowadays the danger is that colleges and universities will exclude not in the crude old-fashioned way, by category of social identity, but more invisibly, by cost. The figure for tuition, room, and board for an undergraduate at Duke approaches $40,000 a year. Mention of this figure provokes a predictable spasm of outrage from the American public, but for all the polemics that may soon be mounted on the issue, the problem of private college cost is not trivially easy. In the last generation and indeed in the last decade America's selective colleges have offered a more and more super-enriched experience to students, and every component—state-of-the-art labs, the most up-to-date information technology, instruction in more and more foreign languages, the widest array of extracurricular activities—comes at considerable expense. But the problem can't be solved by simple-minded cutting. Rich or poor, the students a school like Duke wants would never be attracted to a no-frills university or the academic equivalent of a generic drug.

Just for that reason, however, universities must do everything they can to mitigate the problem of cost for those who can't pay the full fare, and to advertise the availability of aid to those who might miss such opportunities out of ignorance. This university admits undergraduates without regard to need and spends in excess of $40 million a year meeting their financial need, and on my watch it will continue to do so. But the comparative youth that gives Duke enviable vigor does have a downside, namely that we lack the endowment older schools have accrued through time to meet this fundamental need. Recruiting the support to assure that this school never closes its doors to a worthy applicant will be a project especially close to my heart.

I could go on—I could rip an hour, as Herman Melville once wrote—but lest you perish of rhetorical overload, I will conclude. My colleague A. Bartlett Giamatti, who became president of Yale at thirty-nine and died at the age of fifty-one and whose professorship I had the honor of holding, introduced me to this line from Rabbi Tarfon from the *Pirkei Avot*: "You are not required to complete the work; but neither are you free to desist from it." Amateur that I am, I will interpret. What is the work? It can only be the great work given us as humans: making a better world wherever we happen to find ourselves with whatever tools we have to hand. Why are we not required to complete the work? Because we never could: if that work could be completed, others would have done it already and we would be spared the struggle. But why, if we cannot complete it, can we also not be allowed to give it up? Because that would be cowardly and would leave an imperfect world in even more desperate shape than it needs to be.

My predecessors at Duke did not complete the work, and neither will I. But like them, I will embrace the work that awaits me here. This is the work of a great university: the struggle to expand the domain of knowledge, the struggle to share that knowledge through education, and the struggle to put that knowledge to profound human use. On this, the day of our union, I know that whatever I will do will be accomplished with your partnership and help. Others have given us this great place. Let's see what we can build together.

....

Literature as Life

Cambridge, Massachusetts, October 9, 2004

The American Academy of Arts and Sciences elects members in five categories, embracing the full arc of scholarly achievement. At the annual induction for new members, a speaker is chosen to speak on behalf of each category. I was asked to speak for the humanities and the arts when I was inducted in 2004.

It's an honor to speak for Class Four of new members of the Academy. As students of rapids know, Class Four events are massively energetic and thrilling but typically not life-endangering. That fits the humanities and the arts, and no doubt explains why we were assigned this number. I won't speak here as a professional humanist, still less as an administrator of the modern home of the humanities, the university. Instead I'll say a word about the founding need for this form of human practice, and with your permission I'll make it personal.

I knew poetry from the days of nursery rhymes, but the first time I "got" it was in my fourteenth year. I remember the moment fairly vividly. I was in high school not thirty miles from here and at the low-water mark of self-esteem. Each day, changing classes, my fellows would parade past, every one of them an image of some adequacy I lacked: this one cooler, that one more handsome, this one more popular, that one more athletic. Doing my homework one day, I started into a Shakespeare sonnet where I was met by these lines:

When in disgrace with Fortune and men's eyes,
I all alone beweep my outcast state,
And trouble deaf heaven with my bootless cries,
And look upon myself and curse my fate,
Wishing me like to one more rich in hope,
Featured like him, like him with friends possessed,
Desiring that man's art, or that man's scope,
With what I most enjoy contented least . . .

(Shakespeare, Sonnet 29)

That's me! I could have cried. How did he guess?

This was my first recognition of the power of someone else's creation to give voice to my experience, an experience self-imprisoned and un-self-knowing until a stranger's words brought it to expression. But soon thereafter, I learned another primitive power of art. That same spring I read the first poem I ever really loved (I must have been going through a sort of literary puberty), Wordsworth's "Tintern Abbey," which flooded me with nostalgia for the more intense experience lost with my youth. It was some years before I realized that I had not in fact lost my youth at the time when its demise seemed so drenched in pathos. When I recognized this fact, I learned that this poem had not so much voiced my experience as induced a new experience, given me access to a state of feeling that I knew through the poem that I did not yet know from life.

Some time later I learned a further variant in which, art having given me a foretaste of certain forms of experience—let's call them virtual experiences, experiences imaginatively induced and entertained—I came to know them in reality. My sense was never of the gap between life and art. Rather, I had the sense of learning at last what art's images had been referring to, with art still providing words for what I now came to know. I knew King Lear's famous line over the dead Cordelia many years before I ever stood over the body of a loved one of my own. When I did, I felt I grasped at last what Lear (or Shakespeare) meant, but Lear's line gave me a way to name the tormenting, gratuitous, inexplicable proximity of some things (for no good reason) living to others (for no good reason) dead: "Why should a dog, a horse, a rat have life/And thou no life at all?" I had long been struck by Whitman's empathic identifications with the sufferings of common men in *Leaves of Grass*—not just the runaway slave but, less predictably, a fireman pinned in the rubble of a collapsed building:

> I am the mashed fireman with breastbone broken . . . tumbling walls
>   buried me
> . . . . . in their debris,
> Heat and smoke I inspired . . .
> I heard the yelling shouts of my comrades,
> I heard the distant clicks of their picks and shovels . . .

September 11 supplied a real referent for what had heretofore been an imaginary experience. But in the wake of 9/11, while the rubble was still being sifted and the eventual toll of life not yet known, I felt I could enter into a plight made real by history through the medium of these 150-year old words.

Strange beasts, we humans, who need not just to live but also to understand our lives; stranger yet that we should know ourselves not directly but through borrowed understandings, through images composed by others' hands. The officially designated divisions of the humanities will have their ups and downs, but as long as these needs stay in play, the core activity of the humanities will not go away. As Academy member Henry James once wrote, "Till the world is an unpeopled void there will be an image in the mirror."

On Education and Empowerment

May 13–14, 2005, Duke Chapel

Men and women of the Class of 2005, the end is near. If this were a basketball game and you were the opposition, we would have reached the point when rude Duke fans would chant "START THE BUS." If I were not your best friend and well-wisher, I might even stretch forth my hand, waggle my fingers, and launch a cry of "SEE YA!" Before we get serious, I just want to say that I take it amiss that you should be leaving so soon. That's not very nice! I just got here, and already you are planning to take off. If, upon fuller consideration, you decide that you'd rather stick around, do let me know. It may not be too late: your diplomas are not yet signed.

Class of 2005, I have been thinking of you these last weeks as you finished your final papers, climbed the chapel tower, attended endless barbecues, and began your farewells. I have been thinking about what you are going on to, and how your time here will serve you when you get there. Since my field is American literature, this naturally led me to a classic work of American autobiography, *The Education of Henry Adams*, published posthumously in 1917 but written one hundred years ago this year. The grandson of President John Quincy Adams and great-grandson of President John Adams, Henry Adams was marked by birth for high success. But then, as he tells it, something happened: the world changed. Born in the shadow of the Boston statehouse in 1838, Adams came to consciousness in a nineteenth-century world still strongly linked to the eighteenth and seventeenth centuries, the world of the American Revolution and the Pilgrim fathers. But born together with him were technological developments that, though the scope of their effects was not at first apparent, would rupture the continuity of history and produce a different, modern world: the railroad lines new in his childhood; the new transatlantic steamships that would replace sailing ships and cut the length of ocean travel; and the new telecom system of the 1840s, the telegraph, the world's first source of instant messages.

In early life, Adams received the premier schooling his world had on offer. But by his later reckoning, this education perfectly failed to grasp the new world of collapsed distances and national and global connections where his lot would be cast. In consequence, the aging Adams wearily laments, the education he received was exactly not the education he needed, leaving him "condemned to failure more or less complete in the life awaiting him."

For all its intelligence, this book makes gloomy reading, and seeing you in its light could induce the question whether, fifty years from now, you might not have a similar tale to tell. When were you born: 1983? 1984? When did you come here: 2001? Then it would be easy to compose your biography as a story of rupturing historical transformations. Two or three weeks after you got here, an event occurred after which (we were quickly assured) nothing would ever be the same: 9/11, and our fall from innocence to experience of the fact of global insecurity. One message of Tom Friedman's new book *The World Is Flat* is that the post-9/11 fixation on terror and the Middle East may have obscured a far more fundamental historical change: the contemporary creation of the linked world where any point on the globe can be reached instantaneously from any other via fiber-optic cable, and where any job can be broken into component parts and distributed to any site, however remote.

Add to this the hundreds of millions in once-backward countries who will soon be joining this new global order through education and Internet connection, and it would be easy to generate an almost apocalyptic case of heebie-jeebies about this weekend's proud event. For as we acclaim your success in college, might it not be that you too have learned what worked in the recent past, not what will be needed in the quickly arriving future? In that case (I now switch on Adams's sepulchral tones), what will become of you, poor children of the twentieth century, when you wake up to find yourselves required to play the game of the twenty-first? I pause for effect.

But though it's not hard to conjure up a vision of your pending anachronism and future ineptitude, there's something a little unimaginative about this gloomy account. Is the world changing more rapidly than ever? I'd be a fool to deny it. But the world has always been changing, and the notion that things were relatively stable until just now has always proved an ahistorical illusion. If we project you forward twenty, thirty, or forty years, it's certain that you will be playing on a field that has been reconstituted not once but many times, in ways no one now is gifted to see. That's just a given, not necessarily either a tragedy or an opportunity. As for that, time will tell.

In any case, it's an even greater error to think that anyone's formal education could possess lasting adequacy for the life of their times. There are childhood vaccines that give permanent immunity, and James Bond is always equipped at the start with just the set of magical tools or toys needed to face that film's preposterous predicaments, but neither of these is a very good model for education. Your Duke days could never teach you how to cope with every challenge the future will throw at you—if that's what you think you got here, you are in for a big surprise. But it could give something far more valuable: it could lay the foundations for deep habits of character and mind that will keep developing as you engage your world, such that when you face new circumstances, a growingly capable you will be there to meet them.

It's my great hope that your Duke years have confirmed in you an unbreakable habit of curiosity. In your classes you've learned habits of high performance, of doing what is expected of you and doing it well, and these will certainly take you far. But I'm trusting that your schoolwork also occasionally triggered something deeper and finer, a sheer will to understand, that pressed you on past the point of the passing grade: kept you noticing relevant facts, drawing out their implications, testing your theories against available evidence, and revising them when they proved inadequate. If that power has been born and strengthened in you, then as you leave the artificial world of schoolwork, you'll possess the real source of education: the linked habits of attention, mental integration, articulation, and imagination that will help you keep taking in what emerges around you, deciphering its meanings and challenges and opportunities as it evolves.

Together with curiosity, I'm betting that you are carrying forth another relevant life skill, though you may scarcely have been conscious that you have been perfecting it. There's an air I've noticed among Dukies—not a swagger exactly, but an air of confidence, of cheerful, natural self-engagement. In its evolved form, this too can be a profoundly enabling resource. Place Henry Adams in your mind next to some of his nineteenth-century contemporaries—put him next to W. E. B. Du Bois, who studied at the same university as Adams but became his generation's most effective addresser of the problem of race; put him next to Jane Addams, who had the same partly disabling upper-class upbringing but found a path to constructive action by embracing the new facts of her time (Addams pioneered in bringing education to new American immigrant communities); even put Henry Adams next to a world-beating entrepreneur like James B. Duke, who exploited the global linkages and shrunken distances of his time to create a string of world markets. Pick any such pair and my point is made. Before the same historical situation, one person sits puzzled and disabled by all the impossibility that surrounds him, while another, not necessarily smarter in an intellectual sense, finds a way to engage that situation, to bring his or her distinctive powers to bear, and so to create possibilities that were not apparent until this force of character was added to the equation. As between the passive-depressive and the active-constructive, I know which kind of life I want for you, and I am not pessimistic. When I have seen you engaging yourselves in campus debates, in sports, or in any of the hundred organized activities you have created, I've seen this elemental courage in early but authentic forms.

Your chances in any foreseeable future would be grim indeed if you didn't bring intelligence and personal creativity to the bargain. With those added, who can say what you can't do? Every future looked bleak until some person found a way to make something of it. But for your maximum success, I look for you to take something more from Duke than curiosity and courage, valuable though they are. When I look at Dukies, I'm continually struck by the spirit of other-directedness in your campus friendships and involvements in the Durham community. As the college world dissolves, it matters that this has become a part of who you now are. Our world still favors the rhetoric of individual achievement, but we've long known that men and women can achieve results by working together that no one of them could have reached on her own. You'll live to see forms of collaboration that can't be imagined now. I trust that you will play a constructive part in these interactions, possibly even pioneer them as new means for human problem solving. Further, whatever the future world holds, it's a shrewd guess that the sum of human need will not diminish, and that the growing prosperity enjoyed by some will continue to be shadowed by the profoundly unequal opportunities available to others. In this world, it is going to matter whether you aim for a narrow personal success or one that creates a larger human benefit.

I'll end by telling you a secret. You are very old. Compared to the you who arrived here four years ago, you have put away childish things (well, some of them) and become strikingly more mature, not an aged child but a plausible adult. But as everyone even a little older can tell you, you're just reaching the interesting part of your life. Should you be melancholy as your college life dies around you? It's natural—but the day will come when you have as little thought of clinging to college days as you do now of returning to sixth grade. Why is this? Because you will have grown beyond them, because the path of personal development that brought you from there to here will carry you forward to a more realized life. Will you meet hard things in the future, things the you of today is ill equipped to handle? I'm betting you will; as they say, that's life. But you'll be adequate to what life brings if you pursue the career this place trained you for: the career of education, a life of continual growth.

Women and men of the Duke Class of 2005, I see you moving off into the future full of shining promise, promise you will fulfill if you nurture the best things you take from here. Do that and I will speak a line from an American author of a different stripe. Emerson said to the young Walt Whitman what I say to you this day: "I greet you at the beginning of a great career." Go well.

On Founding as a Continuous Labor

Duke Chapel, September 29, 2005

This is a forward-looking university, a place with little sense of past at its back, but we spend one hour each year viewing the present in light of the past—on Founders' Day, which we celebrate today. One of the pleasures of Duke is that its founding is close enough that we still have living connections. I note with pleasure the presence of Mary Semans, a powerful force for good in this city and state, the granddaughter of our benefactor, Benjamin N. Duke; also Robin Chandler Duke, wife of B. N. Duke's grandson Angier Biddle Duke.

In addition to these personal links, Duke's founding is sufficiently close that we can reach back in memory with minimal strain. When I moved here a year ago and faced the task of decorating my office, I sought help from the University Archives, which were founded by another of today's honorees, Bill King. With the help of current director Tim Pyatt, I've surrounded myself with scenes of Duke's founding, such that every day is Founder's Day in the President's Office. On one side of the room I have a photo of a big locomotive belching steam as it plows its way through a massive construction site. That site is now the West Campus, which had a train track down the middle to bring Duke stone from a nearby quarry. On another wall I have the letter in which William Preston Few outlined a vision of Trinity College transformed into a great and comprehensive university, which might bear a certain person's family name if he would please send a certain number of millions. Next to it I've framed James B. Duke's curt and peremptory telegram: "Send me the plans."

I love these pictures. They give a daily reminder that a school that seems so permanent as we walk through it was in fact constructed, brought into being through human work. And the correspondence of President Few and James B. Duke tells me that this creation was a two-sided process, not the work of one hand. Few's dreams would have come to nothing had he not found Duke, and, through him, the means to turn that vision into reality. But Buck Duke would have had nothing to found if Few had not envisioned what this school could become.

These documents tell me that universities are created through a joint labor of envisioning and enabling, and that does not happen at one time alone. Paradoxically the school that was founded as Duke in the mid-1920s had been founded more than eighty years earlier in rural Randolph County and had already been reconceptualized and rebuilt at least once before. John Franklin Crowell, hired to lead Trinity College in 1887 while still in his twenties, came with the notion that an emerging modernity required something profoundly different in the way of college preparation. In face of the industrialization, urbanization, and internationalization of markets that were new facts of that time, Crowell believed that colleges should prepare students to understand and act on the new social forces. He proposed a new curriculum no longer anchored in classical languages and unapplied mathematics, a new postgraduate program for advanced training, and a coordinated college for women; and he insisted that for students to learn the lessons of new times, the school would need to be physically relocated, moved from the hinterland to a place where the forces of modernity were palpably and dynamically at work.

Without Crowell's reenvisioning, Trinity would have remained a backwoods academy and lucky to survive. But like President Few, Crowell's planning succeeded only because he found partners and supporters for his vision—above all Washington Duke, who offered to endow the school if Trinity would move to Durham. Together Crowell, Wash Duke, and his fellow backers built a new school in a new place, and this long-running collaboration continues in our time.

For we are not yet done founding this university. Virtually every week we are dedicating a new center or building and opening new opportunities for inquiry, exploration, and education. Each is the product of the conjunction of vision, ambition, and support I have been describing. Nicholas is the name of a Boston family and an Institute for Environmental Policy Solutions launched one week ago at Duke. When it opens three days from now, Nasher will be the name for both a great family from Texas and a great new museum, a home for—and a powerful spur to—creativity in the visual arts and all arts. One week later, we will dedicate the new Goodson Chapel in the new Westbrook Hall, breathtakingly beautiful new spaces for spiritual life that honor a distinguished trustee emeritus and a generous friend of the Duke Divinity School. In early November, Rubenstein will become the name for both a loyal alumnus and the building that doubles the activity space of the Sanford Institute of Public Policy. A week after that, "Bostock" and "von der Heyden"—people, to some of us—will begin to designate buildings to Duke students, new library spaces where knowledge can be retrieved and recombined in new ways.

This university has been lucky in its partners and has been co-created *with* its partners. In celebrating founding, we celebrate a shared work that is still going on.

As they continue to be created through time, one great mystery of universities is how they manage to retain their distinctive characters. The great research universities of this country have embraced many of the same goals and built many of the same facilities: libraries, labs, museums, and the rest. But this hasn't made them interchangeable or indistinguishable. So how does it happen that the things we build perpetuate the identity "Duke," while the ones someone else builds perpetuate the different identity tied to their different name?

This isn't a question that can be answered in fifteen minutes, but the answer has something to do with the history of a school's founding. In reading the autobiography of John Franklin Crowell, I've been struck that Crowell wanted to create a different kind of college: one that would build on traditional strengths but direct study toward contemporary problems and opportunities. (Crowell was hired to the Trinity presidency partly on the basis of an essay he had written on the child labor issue.) In the indenture for the Duke Endowment, James B. Duke wrote of *his* wish to support a form of education "conducted along sane and practical lines." (He goes on to specify that he means "sane and practical, as opposed to dogmatic and theoretical"; at first hearing you might have thought he meant sane and practical as opposed to insane and impractical, or kooky and clueless.)

I don't totally believe in the deterministic power of founders—institutions are created by everyone who serves them and uses them—but universities do bear the stamp of their origins in a continuing way. One of the things I've found most distinctive about Duke is the real-world orientation Crowell and J. B. Duke long ago prescribed: the way academic inquiry is naturally brought to bear on real-world problems, and intelligence used to create solutions to pressing human needs. Last year, at my first Founders' Day, I gave a medal to Sam Katz and learned that I had, as one of my new colleagues, the man who had made the key breakthrough in creating a measles vaccine—a highly specialized research accomplishment yielding a profound and immediate human good. At dinner it was suggested to me that we could just as well have honored his wife, Professor of Pediatrics Catherine Wilfert, who pioneered in interrupting AIDS transmission from infected mothers to their babies. This summer another Dukie, Barton Haynes, was selected to lead the $350 million international research effort to unblock obstacles to the creation of an AIDS vaccine. And it seems to be my fate to come across such yoking of knowledge, application, and service pretty much wherever I turn. If I have dinner with faculty from the Divinity School, for instance Greg and Susan Jones, they will just have returned from ten days in Rwanda, where they have been working on peace and reconciliation projects. If I meet a professor of psychology, for instance Wendy Wood, she will turn out to study how habits derive psychic support from the context set by other habits, such that if one wants to disrupt one habit, it's easier if the supporting context can be disrupted. (I had a sense of this—pardon me, shade of James B. Duke!—from giving up smoking many years ago.) In a typical Duke way, Wendy Wood and her colleagues have taken this potentially purely academic work and applied it, brought it to bear on the problem of drug addiction and the search for effective interventions.

In a way I have come to find quite inspiring, Duke has taught me to think of the university as a problem-solving place, a place where intellectual inquiry can be mounted with subtlety and power without shutting itself into an isolated space of abstract expertise; a place where intelligence is energized by the challenges of real-world problems and exercises its powers in devising their solutions. And since students help set the character of a school quite as much as faculty do, I'm not surprised to find the same institutional mark on their brows. Today we will honor a student of the Duke Class of 1982, Paul Farmer, a living bridge between advanced medical research and the poor deprived of care in the developing world. If a current student stops me outside my office, chances are I will learn, as I did from Sonny Byrd, that he spent last summer working in a burn clinic in South Africa. Or I'll find out, as I recently learned of Marcia Eisenstein, that she has devised a college advising system for kids in Durham high schools who would otherwise lack access to such advice.

I rejoice in this institution's mixing of learning and service, and I will do everything I can to support a blend so characteristic of the genius of this place. But the question is sometimes asked, What about you? I am not a doctor, or a nurse, or an environmental scientist, or an engineer, nor expert in management, finance, law, policy, or any useful art. I am a humanist, a student of literature and cultural history, the very antithesis, some might feel, of the sane and practical. So where do people like me fit in?

But that question is not as hard as it appears. My conception of useful learning was never a concept of narrow utilitarianism, and Duke's never was either. After all, even in fields whose discoveries have obvious real-world benefits, those benefits aren't reached by being "practical" in some humdrum sense. Hunt Willard, director of Duke's Institute for Genome Sciences and Policy, has reminded me that scientific breakthroughs come in bursts of creativity and invention, crazy guesses that can then be validated as truth. As for the notion that the more qualitative disciplines perform no real-world service, that would be true only if we had a seriously impoverished concept of human need. Together with many others—the need for cures, devices to administer cures, a world governed by effective policies, and so on—humans have a no less fundamental need for self-understanding. This is another need a university can aim to meet.

To get my point, think of the main public event of recent history: the aftermath of Hurricane Katrina. Such devastation has not been visited on the United States in the lifetime of anyone in this room. We had thought such things happened only at a distance—long ago, as in the San Francisco earthquake, or far away, as in the Indian Ocean tsunami—but it turns out we too are susceptible to the force of natural catastrophe, even here and now. But in the scope of its devastation, this hurricane showed this university to me in a powerful new light. I'm not referring to the humanitarian efforts Duke people made for the victims of the storm, impressive though those are. I'm speaking of the way highly rarefied academic expertise turned out to be relevant to this disaster. In very short order, Duke doctors and nurses had staffed emergency hospitals on the Gulf Coast. Duke Marine Lab faculty like Orrin Pilkey were explaining to the public how the reengineering of the lower Mississippi had removed natural protections that could have been buffers against the storm. A Duke engineer, Karl Linden, alerted us that by pumping out floodwaters without testing for industrial and other toxins, we might be creating a new, man-made disaster in the act of cleaning up a natural one. When the National Institute of Environmental Health Sciences wanted someone to help comprehensively locate toxins and health exposures in the storm-affected area, they guessed—and they were right—that Duke's Marie Lynn Miranda, an environmentalist specializing in the spatial analysis and visual display of health data, would be the person to do the job.

It's impressive to see arcane-sounding domains of knowledge reveal their critical importance in this way. But other disciplines showed that they could be useful too on this occasion. In this land where so many things are amazing because so many people are ignorant of history, it was helpful to be reminded that this was not the first American disaster aggravated by the low elevations of major settlements. Duke's Henry Petroski reminded us that Galveston was rebuilt on man-made higher ground after the great hurricane a century ago, and that Chicago too had the ground beneath it artificially raised.

And if poetry never rebuilt a city, it could help us find words and so bring to expression an otherwise brute experience of loss. I know something about the ephemerality of permanent-seeming things because I have read these words in Yeats: "Everything that man esteems/Endures a moment or a day." The New Orleans disaster also resonated with and found description in words from St. Paul: "We have no continuing city here." It also made me think of Vergil's *Aeneid*, the great poem about refugees and displaced persons and a specifically civic form of disaster, the special victimization entailed in the destruction of a city. Remember the amazing words spoken at the moment of the fall of Troy? "Fuimus Troes," we *were* Trojans: we used to tell people who we are by telling them the name of our city, but that city has now been killed, so we can only speak that identity in the past tense.

I was particularly mindful of *The Aeneid* because that work has such a strong sense of the meaning of defensive structures like walls or levees: the way human community is secured by them and the particular horror that arises when they are breached. Wherever the refugee Trojans go in *The Aeneid*, the first thing they want to do is rebuild their violated walls. When they visit someone else's city, they are mortally pained by the sight that others already have the rebuilt defenses they still lack: "How fortunate these are/ Whose city walls are rising here and now!" In empathy, we could say for our still-displaced fellows from New Orleans what Aeneas says for the Trojan exiles: "O God . . . grant a home/And walls to weary men, grant us posterity/And an abiding city." Aeneas too bore the burden of having to be a founder—he had to found Rome because his city was no more. "For years/They wandered as their destiny drove them on/From one sea to the next: so hard and huge/A task it was to found the Roman people."

This Founders' Day, we celebrate the fact that Duke University was founded, and we remember that it is still capable of being built, through the labor of living men and women, toward greater visions of what a university can be. This university was founded to put intelligence to human use, not in a narrow sense but in a way that draws on all our capacities and speaks to all our needs. I presume this is what James B. Duke meant when he expressed his wish "to make provision . . . for mankind along physical, mental and spiritual lines." That large work is still our work. Let's have the strength to do our part.

....

Note: Quotations from *The Aeneid* are from the translation of Robert Fitzgerald, published in 1980. John Franklin Crowell's *Personal Recollections of Trinity College* was published in 1930.

....

Financial Aid,
the Problem-centric University

October 20, 2005

Honored colleagues, although I am not the newcomer I was at this time last year, I still am not confident that I fully grasp the genre of the president's annual address to the faculty. My first instinct has been to envision it as a kind of State of the Union address, and that has touched off a variety of distracting images: the thought that I should enter the room to the strains of "Ruffles and Flourishes," or perhaps a contrapuntal arrangement of "Ruffles and Flourishes" and "Dear Old Duke"; the idea that I should have my own Dick Cheney and Dennis Hastert sitting behind me (Peter Lange and Paul Haagen), ready to leap to their feet and lead the applause every time I bring a thought to a full stop. And I certainly can say to you, in keeping with this generic conception: My fellow Dukies, the state of this university is strong. It's my guess that the right use of this occasion is to share my thinking about some major issues facing the university as we go forward. I'll focus on two this afternoon.

As you'll have learned, one of my priorities is to significantly strengthen support for financial aid at Duke. To share an increasingly open secret, later this fall we'll be launching an initiative to raise major endowment funds for this purpose, and the magnificent challenge gift of $75 million recently announced from The Duke Endowment will start this effort off with a bang. I am not imagining that this initiative is particularly controversial, but it's worth reminding ourselves why it is important.

I pretend to no personal originality when I say there are three main reasons for the university commitment to financial aid. The first is a matter of justice. As the great source of inward enrichment and the great enabler of worldly success, education is arguably the premier privilege our world has to offer. Those of us of a certain age can remember a time when this privilege was available in America on profoundly unequal terms; when quality education was open to some with relative ease but closed to others—closed to women at certain schools, closed to African Americans in many places—on grounds extraneous to ability or intelligence. During my adult lifetime, those injustices have been remedied in substantial measure. But it would be a poor sequel for less visible economic discriminations to be allowed to stay in place when gender and racial ones have been abolished.

It's not an idle anxiety. As figures like *New York Times* columnist David Brooks and Mellon Foundation president William Bowen have increasingly reminded us, in modern America, qualification for college admission has come to have a very high correlation with family income, such that in selecting for merit as it is currently conceptualized, and without any conscious economic intention, America's premier universities tend to recruit classes substantially tipped toward upper income sectors. (As an aside, I should note that those currently underrepresented in such universities include not only the very poor but those from incomes ranging well up into the range of the middle class. One consequence is that if affirmative action were introduced in college admissions for those from the lowest income quintile, as President Bowen has proposed, not only would those from middle-income bands fail to benefit; their places would be even further squeezed by the plus factor being added for the poorest applicants.) Universities alone can't affect or right every cause contributing to the unequal preparation of the young. But just for that reason, we have a special obligation to do what we can. The university's commitment to assume the share of costs that a family cannot afford to pay is our chief way of assuring that we select and recruit students on the grounds of ability, dedication, and promise alone, not of family circumstance.

But our society has a profound self-interest in seeing that the talented young have access to quality education even apart from the question of justice. We tend to take for granted the dynamism that makes our economy and culture throw off so many benefits of wealth and quality of life, but there's no reason to believe these things are self-sustaining. They are driven by human intelligence and creativity, and for their renewal, these resources need cultivation and investment. Making sure that those gifted with these traits get the education that will allow them to give the greatest return on their talents is the best way to provide for this social good, and it's a safe bet that the talent we will someday want to draw on is not confined to a single social origin or income band. Financial aid is the investment we make to produce the trained talent our future world will require, and when we think of graduate and professional schools, this means the talent that will keep our own fields strong and strongly advancing.

Let me quickly note that even in the absence of these considerations, there would still be an overwhelmingly powerful argument for wanting to decouple admissions decisions from family income, this time an educational reason. If my long life in school has taught me anything, it's that everything is more interesting when people come to issues from different places. Real education begins when something breaks in on our self-satisfied and apparently sufficient understanding, making us realize that what we call our "thoughts" are only inertial, residual mental placeholders and that if we want to come anywhere near the truth, we will need to begin to *think*. It's hard to produce this disruption when people come from the same background and share the same accustomed understandings, but it's hard to stop it when different initial positions come into regular collision. When we provide the funds that enable students to come to Duke from other income groups, other regions, other countries, we create a better experience not just for them but for every student.

I'm aware that financial aid may seem to be a student issue and so a strange subject for a faculty address. If I dwell on the subject here, it's in the conviction that this is all of our issue and must be a priority for us all. If one of you were so churlish as to ask, "What is the faculty interest in financial aid funding?," my answer would be, first, that the interests I have been urging in justice, in education, in investment in talent pertain to all members of our society, faculty certainly included. But faculty have further interests in this cause as well.

If teaching and mentoring were alien to our deeper careers and functions—if, as at some schools, students were thought of principally as a distraction, an irritating intrusion on one's real work—then it would scarcely matter who one's school admitted: the less interested, the less demanding, and so the better for me! But if students are thought of as partners in inquiry, people whose independent vitality and intelligence can help advance the work of discovery, then it matters whether one's school attracts students capable of the highest form of engagement and creativity. That, at bottom, is what aid is about. Students on financial aid are not the only interesting students in a university, but I'm wagering that the best faculty would find little to stimulate or hold them in a school where all the students could afford to pay their own way.

Then further, while Duke already has enlightened aid policies and already funds undergraduate, graduate, and professional student aid in hefty sums, at Duke, far, far less of our aid budget comes from restricted endowments than is the case at our strongest rivals. What this means is that Duke meets its aid commitments out of the same pool of funds that support most everything else here, including academic programs. And what *this* means is that, in lean years or hard times, Duke's need to fund student aid will be in competition with its need to fund the programs that would make top students and faculty want to come here in the first place. I want to keep Duke accessible to talented students in all foreseeable futures, *and* I want to prevent any future collision between two fundamental imperatives: our obligation to social openness and our obligation to academic excellence. If we can raise permanent support for financial aid, we'll have done something crucial for this university's future health.

Let me turn to my other theme, which I'll introduce this way. Since arriving here, I've needed both to learn Duke and to learn how to describe or project the idea of Duke; if you've heard me speak, you have listened to me struggling to articulate my emerging understanding of the strengths and aspirations of this place. There are two things that I've continued to find striking since the day of my arrival: first, the high level of interdisciplinary and interschool collaboration at Duke, and second, Duke's real-world orientation, the way academic inquiry is naturally brought to bear on real-world problems.

I run into these paired Duke strengths virtually every time I turn around. One of the numerous high points of this fall term was the launch of the Nicholas Institute of Environmental Policy Solutions. *That's so Duke*, I had to say: an attempt to bring the most advanced scientific research into closer touch with the world of policy choices and to translate the implications of academic inquiry in such a way that politicians, corporate leaders, and the media can win a better sense of the meanings and consequences of different environmental choices. (It was at the NIEPS launch that I learned that when FEMA faced the need to chart the location of environmental hazards in the wake of Hurricane Katrina, they called on one of us: Nicholas School Professor Marie Lynn Miranda, who was able to redeploy her expertise in spatial analysis and digital display of environmental health risks from her usual subject, children's health in Durham, to the crisis on the Gulf Coast.)

Another recent day, I had lunch with Anthony So, a faculty member in the Sanford Institute who is an expert in both the medical and the social and economic aspects of health care delivery in third-world settings and who, like others of you, served on the planning committee for Duke's global health initiative. It took minutes to learn that he was coauthoring papers on intellectual property issues (a major source of obstruction in this field) with Arti Rai and Jerome Reichman of the Duke Law School, Tracy Lewis of Duke's Fuqua School of Business, and Bob Cook-Deegan of the Institute for Genome Sciences and Policy. *That's so Duke*, I could have repeated: *so Duke* because it exemplifies a kind of cross-field collaboration that's rare elsewhere but relatively common here, and *so Duke* because it was a shared devotion to training academic intelligence on real-world problems that gave these partnerships common ground. Interdisciplinarity does not thrive here because people are friendlier but because faculty tend to be less oriented to a map of the disciplines than to living human issues—environmental degradation and health and health disparities are prime examples—their knowledge might help to understand. When we're oriented toward the academy's map of the disciplines, the disciplines are naturally divided. When we're oriented toward challenges of this order, they are naturally united, since no discipline holds all the pieces of the puzzle to be solved.

Allow me one more example since my enthusiasm is unbounded. In rapid succession within the past two weeks I attended the fiftieth-anniversary celebration of the Duke Center for the Study of Aging and the dedication of the new Divinity School building that houses the Institute on Care at the End of Life. You already know my refrain: *That's so Duke!* What's a better example of a real-world problem than aging, a physical and existential crisis under any circumstances and a growing social challenge as the ever-more-aged aging fill an ever-growing share of the population? Once a problem was the focus, it was natural for communities to form across the bounds of disciplines and schools. At the Study of Aging celebration, I met people studying the genetics and molecular processes of aging, the sociology of aging, the psychology of aging, and the nursing problems aging poses. Care at the End of Life bridges the schools of medicine, divinity, and nursing to address a crisis at once of body, soul, and family support.

Faculty configured in such ways find their complement in a kind of student I've come to find fairly typical of Duke: an academically well-trained person who is keenly alert to challenges and opportunities in the larger world and instinctively puts his or her intelligence to the service of solving real-world challenges in independent and ingenious ways. Last week a senior in the Pratt School, Tyler Brown, was killed by a drunk driver in California. I mention him partly to mourn his loss, a tragic waste of youth and talent, but partly to exemplify the human type I want to celebrate. As a volunteer in Engineers without Borders, Tyler Brown went to Sumatra in the wake of the 2004 tsunami and, freely and imaginatively adapting things he was taught in classes, helped design new aerators to help restore the shrimp fishery in a storm-damaged area. You've got to love it: a kid who takes in what's taught him, combines it with innate energies of creativity, joy in action, and passion for service, and redelivers it to the world in a form no teacher could ever have envisioned. Closer to home, I learned that the city avoided the expense of a high-priced consultant to analyze how an area of Durham could be redeveloped to broader social benefit because a Fuqua student, Jill Homan, used what she had learned of economic analysis and entrepreneurial imagination to do the study, and at a level the consultant would have been at pains to match. George McLendon taught me this cute trick: Discovering the Use of Knowledge is Education. DUKE.

As I said in my Founders' Day address, Duke has taught me to think of the university as a problem-solving place, a place where intellectual inquiry can be mounted with subtlety and power without shutting itself into an isolated space of abstract expertise. I've further come to think that it matters for a university to have such a character, and that, going forward, Duke could enjoy a growing advantage from its special nature.

In the current political climate, mistrust of universities is compounded with growing restrictions on all forms of discretionary funding. In this circumstance, it's hard to see how research universities will continue to succeed in either defending the autonomy of our enterprise or maintaining the funding of research projects unless the university itself makes a more persuasive show of what it's good for, what value it returns on society's continuing investment. In such a climate, a school of Duke's character will be able to give a far better account of itself than many. I'm betting that over the next generation, schools designed for problem solving will command growing allegiance from scholars, students, and the public alike.

In the light of this prospect, I want to make three points. First, I want to make clear that I am not praising a narrow utilitarianism or looking to enforce a Tyranny of the Applied. To deliver the social good I have been describing, academic inquiry can't be held to the criterion of quick returns in practical results. We need to support inquiry with no clear payoff for one reason: because there's no saying what things we may, one day, desperately need to understand. Our colleague Ebrahim Moosa is expert in the past and present history of the madrassas in the Islamic world. This was an arcane subject until we learned that jihadist terrorists were being educated in some madrassas, on which day we became glad that somebody knew a little bit about them. As fear of an avian flu pandemic begins to spread, we may find a new relevance in the work of our colleague Elizabeth (Lil) Fenn on the role of the smallpox epidemic in the American Revolution, a use she could scarcely have anticipated when she was writing the book. In any case, deep intellectual contributions to real-world problems often come not from shots efficiently targeted but from a larger, less focused action of curiosity. Our new colleague Peter Agre won the Nobel Prize for Chemistry for discovering the mechanism by which the cell regulates the intake of water. Since this process goes awry in many well-known diseases, this discovery may have an impact of almost incalculable proportions. But I've been told that before he reached the discovery, Agre was thought to be wandering down fruitless byways. To be useful eventually can require patience, stamina, and the courage not to seem useful day by day.

In projecting the university's future, therefore, we can't insist too narrowly on the logic of the useful. But appropriately applied, Duke's way of linking the work of inquiry to the social good is a differential advantage for this university; and if that's so, we should not fail to recognize this asset and develop it in thoughtful ways. As you know, a new strategic planning exercise is under way at Duke. If translation is something we're naturally good at and that will be increasingly important for universities to do, then this needs to be a guiding concept in the new strategic plan, the light in which we read the values of different potential priorities. Ideas are being explored in the schools of medicine and engineering on how to assist basic and clinical researchers in advancing their discoveries along the way to practical application without subjecting them to the logic exclusively of near-term commercial prospects. Even at this early stage, this local project has the advantage of advancing the larger institutional value of the translation of knowledge into social good. Later this term the Academic Council will be discussing the future course of the Sanford Institute. If what I've said is right, the real question to ask is not whether Sanford should be called an institute or a school, but in what form it can best serve its function as a promoter of translation: a point of exchange between intellectual inquiry and policy application in fields like international order, third-world development, family and child policy, and media studies.

Finally, I'd suggest that if we're right to be enamored of the strengths I've been lauding, then we ought to allow them to put pressure on other parts of our institutional practice. In most great universities and to a considerable extent in this one, what counts as faculty accomplishment is conceived in purely intellectual ways and measured by intradisciplinary metrics (acclaim from the subfield, publication in the leading journal of the subfield—you know the drill). But if there's value in bringing intellectual work to bear on extra-academic problems, that value will not always be registered by the traditional gauges, and a university committed to supporting and pioneering this somewhat different model of excellence will need to be more imaginative (I do not mean loose) in finding ways for the requisite virtues to be established.

Something similar might be said about the shape of academic programs. I've said that Duke has a special ability to turn out students strong in entrepreneurial innovation, will to service, and the use of intelligence for problem solving in the world, but a person looking at the undergraduate program of study might wonder how exactly we produce this result, given the insistence on a fairly traditional concept of majors. In a truly strategic exercise we might dare to ask: Is it possible that the received map of the majors—the projection into the undergraduate curriculum of the map of the disciplines formalized at the time of the birth of the research university circa 1890—is it possible that that map could be disrupted and redrawn to bring the organizing forms of education closer to the virtues we want it to promote?

A half hour of inspiring mission statements and bold proposals, and not one standing ovation orchestrated by Messers. Lange and Haagen! I confess, it's pretty deflating. For I have been talking about the state of the university and the things that will keep it strong. For me these come down to two questions. First, as the lawyers say, *Cui bono*: For whom the good? Who derives the benefit of the university? And second, what is the university good for? If we make this a place where the freest and bravest exercise of curiosity can regularly lead to discoveries large with consequence for the betterment of human life, and where any deeply thoughtful, deeply creative person can join in the fun irrespective of their parents' income, we'll be able to look at our work with satisfaction. I offer these thoughts for your questions, critiques, and eventually, I trust, for your support. They should not seem too alien: I learned most of them from faculty like you.

I thank you for your work in the service of our great aims.

Duke and the Changing Landscape: A Planning Prologue

Duke University has profited from a succession of strategic planning exercises that draw faculty from across the range of schools to help chart the academic future. For the 2006 plan, an effort led by Provost Peter Lange and Vice Provost John Simon, I wrote this preface, which aims to set the proposed initiatives within a vision of the changing function of universities—to explain, in short, what makes them strategic.

Five years ago, in February 2001, Duke University issued a strategic plan entitled *Building on Excellence*. Five years later this university can look back with satisfaction—and even inspiration—at what it accomplished with that plan's direction. Candidly assessing Duke's current state in face of the array of challenges all universities would encounter, that document proposed a set of overarching goals to govern this school's institutional choices. At the same time that it set these ambitions, Duke also embraced the discipline of designating significant resource streams that would be available only for strategic projects.

Thanks to this combination of ends and means, Duke University as a whole and each of its component parts have become significantly stronger over the past five years. New buildings have created the spaces for pioneering research activities; having embraced the goal of strengthening science and engineering, for instance, Duke opened the Fitzpatrick Center in 2005, and the French Family Science Center is now nearing completion. The difference these splendid facilities make for recruiting top faculty and students is already apparent. New programmatic strengths have arisen together with new buildings. Guided by the commitment to extend our global reach and influence, Duke has become a leader in internationalization, exceeding all American universities in federal support for international area studies and engaging unusually large numbers of students in study abroad. Under the influence of *Building on Excellence,* our core infrastructure has been radically strengthened as well. Duke has changed from a follower to a leader in the use of information technology, and the university's central academic resource, its library, is being renovated with dramatic results. Since the Bostock Library opened in October 2005, library use has increased by an astonishing 40 percent.

One less obvious achievement needs noting as well. *Building on Excellence* was a university plan in the sense that its goals were not particular to any individual school but relevant to them all. In addition to their own local strategic priorities, Duke's various undergraduate, graduate, and professional schools were asked to embrace these shared values and decide how to pursue them to advantage on their own terms. In consequence of this approach, as each unit has become individually stronger, Duke's component parts have knit themselves together far more closely over the past five years by working toward common goals. The sense of common purpose and the habits of university-wide collaboration created through *Building on Excellence* are among the most remarkable of its accomplishments.

In many universities, strategic planning is an unromantic prospect, a bureaucratic exercise doomed to produce recommendations that will gather dust while the status quo moves forward more or less unobstructed. At Duke strategic planning is exciting to undertake because it actually makes a difference: it produces visible transformation in the university's capacities and direction. Having realized many of the ambitions hatched in the last planning period, the time arrives for Duke University to plan the next phase of its evolution. So the question arises: If we really are capable of making a difference, what are the most valuable differences we could seek to make?

Upon arriving at this point, it might seem that the next move is to begin drawing up a wish list of things Duke would like to have and do. But the university will need to make choices among our desires, and to make the choices that will do the most good, we need to think about what fundamentally matters. The last planning document defined the ambition "to be among the small number of institutions that define what is best in American higher education." That is still the right level for our aspiration, but what is a university at its best? A great university is a great gathering of intelligence: a place where issues of deep human consequence are addressed with profundity and creativity and where every question interesting to ask is being answered in interesting ways. At such a place students are not just beneficiaries of but also central players in this process of exploration. The poet Yeats said that education is not the filling of the bucket but the lighting of a fire. In the logic of this figure, a great university is a scene of constant combustion, a place where energies of intelligence and creativity are being continually released through the encounter of lively minds.

If this is so, the most strategic moves a university can make will be the ones that most further the goals of stimulating inquiry and enlivening education. But in our time, those processes are clearly not static. They are changing in response to a variety of new challenges and forces, and the university that will best serve these ends going forward is one that will best anticipate and accommodate these changes starting now.

To be more particular, universities as we know them are organized around a model of knowledge production and knowledge transmission that was consolidated in the nineteenth and perfected in the twentieth century. This model is based on the logic of specialization, the development of powerfully disciplined expertise within tightly bounded areas of inquiry. The logic of specialization gave us not just the great intellectual breakthroughs of the last century but the academic landscape as we know it: the familiar map of academic departments, specialized graduate programs and professional schools, the undergraduate major in a single discipline, and the like. We are clearly not at the end of the day of specialization. To arrive at the point where we can join in the creation of new knowledge, we still have to travel deep into the territory of specialized expertise. But we have come to a time when the limits of this system have become more apparent and the need for new forms of knowledge increasingly clear.

In our world, information circulates instantaneously without restrictions of time or space, and virtually every point on the planet has been incorporated into the global networks new technologies have enabled. As economic activity, health menaces, and security threats become increasingly global in their causes and consequences, education more than ever needs to have an international horizon. But this is not the deepest educational challenge posed by a more interactive world. Through this accelerated and ever more inclusive process of exchange, understanding itself is continually metamorphosing, so that no single body of learning is likely to supply the enduringly adequate base for a whole career, as was imagined in the not so distant past.

In this new order the complexity of problems will be increasingly apparent. We already begin to understand, for instance, that every health issue has a pathological, a genetic, and an environmental dimension, not to mention a psychological, a sociological, a legal, and a spiritual one as well, and that health care is a problem at once medical, cultural, economic, and policy-dependent in solution. In a world where challenges take this form, an educated person will need to be able to pull together and integrate disparate bodies of knowledge, and to do so not by some fixed formula teachable in advance but improvisationally, opportunistically, in response to changing arrays of facts and resources.

To develop the skills of problem solving in many-sided and rapidly changing situations, the abstract mental exercises that have formed the staple of education as we have known it will need to be supplemented with the chance to encounter problems in their unabstracted, real-world forms, where the plurality of their dimensions and the specificity of their challenges can be fully grasped. Further, although mental independence and solitary reflection will be as important as ever, many issues will require the sharing or pooling of understanding, the bringing together of bodies of knowledge that no one person could possess alone. Working in teams will be as characteristic of the integrative regime of knowledge as working alone was of the regime of specialization, and learning how to supplement our understanding with that of others with different mental horizons will be increasingly essential.

Seen in this light, many relatively new features that have become familiar in the modern university can be understood not as the separate, add-on developments they first appear but as manifestations of new ways of using and training the mind. Interdisciplinary programs can be seen not as suburbs springing up mysteriously around the standard curriculum but as new-model learning based on the merging, not separation, of intellectual fields. The culture of diversity in universities, the promotion of inclusiveness, cooperation, and respect across boundaries of gender, ethnicity, race, religion, and national culture, originated as (and is still meaningful as) a quest for social justice. But if this value will be more, not less, important in the future, it is because it also promotes the collaboration across horizons that will be the precondition for mental breakthroughs in time to come. There is probably no single greater change in selective American universities in the last thirty years than the explosion of organized extracurricular activities. Some analysts have suggested that this extracurricular mania arises from the will to perfect in youth the overworked, hyperscheduled life habits that will prevail in successful middle age. But this phenomenon makes a different sense if we recognize that the extracurriculum has become a prime site for the teaching and learning of the new curriculum, the curriculum of improvisational, team-based, problem-solving education.

When students make a film or plan a concert or bring engineering know-how to disaster scenes in foreign countries, they are redeploying skills they had acquired separately and for other occasions to create something none of them could have made alone.

If we are in a transition between one model of knowledge formation and another, then we have to keep this fact centrally in mind as we plan for the university's future. Duke needs to be strong in every traditional way, but Duke will not realize its potential simply by building to a traditional model of the university. For the good of faculty and students alike, we need to build new versions of those activities based on integration, collaboration, and reconnecting knowledge to real-world problems as we support the enduringly essential aspects of specialization-based research, teaching, and learning. Duke has special advantages in meeting this challenge—not least its relatively weak addiction to the status quo. But the measures we choose for the future cannot just be good things we can do and build. Our plans will be strategic in proportion as they help us accommodate this deep change in the university's fundamental mission.

Thanks to the work inspired by the previous strategic plan, Duke enters this planning period in a significantly stronger position than it had five years ago. As noted, the distinctiveness of Duke's institutional character also gives it many benefits in facing a challenge all of higher education will share. Duke has long attracted faculty whose interests range across narrow disciplinary boundaries. As a result interdisciplinarity is a healthy feature of much existing intellectual life, not an imported exotic to be forced unwillingly on hostile departments or narrow minds. The walls between departments and schools are also notably weaker at Duke than at most leading research universities, and collaborations already happen freely and spontaneously across significant intellectual distances. It is a further part of Duke's institutional culture that while pure research is pursued with great intensity and subtlety, the pursuit of knowledge tends not to stay shut in on itself. It is natural to many Duke faculty to seek to bring their knowledge to bear on real-world problems, and the institution facilitates the passage from inquiry and discovery to translation and real-world service in a number of formal ways. The Sanford Institute of Public Policy facilitates the interchange between pure research and policy application in fields like the welfare of children, global security studies, and international development. The Institute for Genome Sciences and Policy systematically connects genomic research to the devising and testing of new therapies. The Nicholas Institute for Environmental Policy Solutions supplies a point of exchange between academic science and environmental policymaking in government, business, and nongovernmental sectors.

The presence of such features means that Duke does not need to make a hard turn to prepare for a new organization of knowledge. Our current situation equips us with highly relevant strengths; indeed, the balancing or blending of specialization with the countervirtues of integration, collaboration, and application is already deeply rooted in our institutional character. Armed with these advantages, it is time to ask in a more comprehensive way how Duke can meet a changing landscape of knowledge and education. The current report looks across the whole university, from the sciences to the arts, and across the whole range of the university's activities, from faculty hiring through facilities planning to curriculum design and student life, in the light of that challenge. Working with the best in current practice, we seek to identify a family of concerted moves Duke could make to assure that faculty can seize the most important new opportunities in research and teaching and that students can emerge well prepared for the world of their time.

Like *Building on Excellence*, this is a university plan to be pursued in conjunction with the planning each school has undertaken to meet its particular circumstances and needs. The plan is itself an example of the virtues it recommends, a collaborative labor profiting from input from deans, administrators, faculty, and students from every school. Duke University commits itself to this plan in hopes that, under its guidance, we will gain as much ground in the next five years as we have in the five years past. We look forward to making a difference within the university so that Duke faculty, students, and alumni can be fully equipped to make a difference to the world.

Commencement Address at
Fisk University

May 7, 2007

Madam President, trustees, faculty, friends, I thank you for including me in this great event. Exultant graduates, I congratulate you on your proud achievement, and I rejoice with all who supported you on the road to this great day. You had a dream for your life, a dream of training your powers through first-class education. Thanks to your commitment and hard work, that dream has come true. Now it's time to dream your next dream, the dream of the service you can offer to the world with the knowledge you've acquired at Fisk. I wish you future success as splendid as today's.

I too am receiving a Fisk degree today—did you know? I'm happy about that. Now you may think it's a little unfair that I get to collect the same reward as you without doing the work. How did he get to stick his face in the photo crossing the finish line when he didn't even run the race, you might rudely ask? I have two replies. First, I really did study at Fisk. I spent many a day in your library editing the unpublished journals of Charles Waddell Chesnutt, the principal African American author of the post–Civil War generation. (And by the way, how he would have loved the chance to study at a place like Fisk.) And second, even if I didn't earn a diploma at Fisk, no one here is prouder to join the procession of those who have passed through this ceremony before. This is the same graduation that W. E. B. Du Bois went through in 1888, on his way to his career as a scholar, editor, and leader in the war for civil rights. We stand where John Hope Franklin stood in 1935, on his way to becoming the twentieth century's greatest African American historian. We stand where Hazel O'Leary stood in 1959 before going on to become the secretary of energy, the first woman and the first African American to hold that post. We stand where Nikki Giovanni stood in 1967 before becoming one of the principal poets of her generation.

And now it's your turn.

I've been thinking of you and your future. This train of thought led me to the Fisk graduate I know best: John Hope Franklin, my friend and colleague at Duke. Dr. Franklin has won every award a historian and American citizen could win, including the Presidential Medal of Freedom and the Kluge Prize, the Nobel Prize equivalent for work in the humanities and social sciences. At ninety-two he remains as sharp and forceful as any person I know; he gave the commencement address at Duke last May, and it was as inspiring as any I have ever heard.

What was it like when he stood where you stand, age twenty, in 1935?

The name of that year conjures up a dark and menacing time. When John Hope Franklin graduated from Fisk, the United States had been in the grips of severe economic depression for six years with no end in sight. Domestically, official segregation was at its most brutal and pervasive: a young man from a nearby Nashville neighborhood was carried off and lynched during John Hope's junior year. Internationally, the Nazi Party had already come to power in Germany, and the menace of international fascism was already on the horizon for those who had eyes to see.

Turn to 2007, and what a difference! We live in a period of sustained worldwide economic growth unrivaled in human history. Thanks in part to graduates of this university, we live in a country that has dismantled official barriers to opportunity and freed human potential to make its mark. Human well-being has made other notable advances: thanks to modern medical research, conditions are treated as routine that used to cause death, blindness, or disability. Most unimaginable of all, the whole world is now magically accessible on the easiest of terms. If you were not busy listening to me, you could be downloading news from around the world or broadcasting pictures of this ceremony to friends in any land— without leaving your seat.

But as you know, our time isn't quite as simple as these facts make it sound. These changes have made an undeniable difference, and life is immeasurably the better for them. But these improvements turn out to be compatible with persistent challenges, even to create new ones. Worldwide prosperity has lifted billions out of poverty in recent years, but it has not eradicated the most basic forms of human need, and income disparities have grown steeper instead of disappearing. The doors of opportunity have been opened to a significant extent at the legal and institutional level, but other and more elemental forms of inequality continue to give children an unequal start in life: unequal access to a healthy environment, unequal access to family literacy, unequal access to quality schooling, and so on. New cures have been discovered, but not everyone has equal benefit from these discoveries. Meanwhile the consumer habits and leisure lifestyle generated by our new prosperity have created new forms of ill health, diseases of plenty that now have epidemic force.

Plus we're all connected, except that we're mysteriously disconnected too. Paradoxically, the world where we can all call and text each other all day long has also hosted new forms of separation and division, including renewed school segregation and new hardening of partisan political bounds. We have more and more in common in some domains—we buy the same brands, hear the same news, know the same tunes. But this superficial sharing has turned out to be compatible with an erosion of a deep foundational common sense, a shared sense of what we owe each other and can expect of other as members of one community.

Our country has got out of the business of asking us to make collective sacrifices, not because we're selfish but because we've failed to refresh our sense of the values that lie beyond self-interest. We can't have new taxes, not because we're too poor in money but because we have grown poor at articulating the idea of a public good, a shared benefit that would be worth a shared cost. We follow the news of the criminal justice system, but it doesn't make us reflect on what it would actually mean to be just. We tune in each day to learn the latest outrage some celebrity or public figure has committed, but raging against insensitive others isn't the same as building the grounds for broad and deep mutual respect.

So if the battle lines aren't as clear today as they were in the past, this is a time with its own abundant challenges. Among others, we need to rebuild the idea of the common wealth or the public good. This will be the work of many hands: it will take work from public officials but also from teachers, business leaders, ministers, doctors and health care administrators, developers and planners, and many more. I certainly hope you're up to doing your share. We'll be in a mess if everyone leaves this work to others. But how are you going to get from here to there?

If the answer is unclear, don't feel bad. None of your predecessors marched out of the doors of Fisk straight on to their distinguished careers. They were young people with some hopes and much uncertainty who took their chances and followed their hunches until life gave them their opening. John Hope Franklin came to Fisk planning to become a lawyer, until his studies seduced him onto another path. Following an interest that steadily grew in power, he trained as an academic historian and wrote seminal works in the field. When the great school desegregation case *Brown v. Board of Education* came along, Franklin made the contribution that only a historian could make, recovering the relevant constitutional history for the crucial Supreme Court brief. He was able to contribute to one of the most decisive public events of the last century not because he planned to but because he developed his distinctive strengths and moved when he saw his chance.

Hazel O'Leary was secretary of energy at a time when energy issues became ever more crucial to the economy, the environment, and international war and peace. But I bet she did not spend her Fisk afternoons daydreaming about a future cabinet post. For all I know, she never studied energy at all. She trained as a lawyer, found her way through a set of unfolding opportunities in law, government, and business, and so built the powers that would eventually equip her for a high public role.

Fisk students of the Class of 2007, so far so good. You had the talent, you had the ambition, you did the work, and today you win the prize. I congratulate you, but what you've done to date is just the promise that the rest of your life will fulfill. It won't be clear to you every day where you're going, and there will be days when you'll wonder if you're going anywhere at all. But you'll get there if you keep a few thoughts in front of you. Follow your passions and keep working to build your strengths, and remember that those gifts weren't given you for your personal success only, but to serve and enrich the life of your time.

Now it's your turn to write the future.

Have the courage to do it well.

....

The Ethic of Engagement

Duke Chapel, August 22, 2007

Class of 2011, what a happy morning: you're together at last. As recently as March, you were total strangers randomly distributed across this country and the world, with nothing in common but great promise. On the day we accepted you and you had the good sense to choose Duke, these strangers became a potential community, since you would one day converge on the same destination. This summer you have done little else but meet and greet in cyberspace, so you arrive not strangers but virtual friends. But now comes the real thing, the assembly of a critical mass of highly combustible talent, the Duke freshman class, seventeen hundred strong, ready to befriend each other and spark each other to an explosion of personal growth. This is a hushed and awesome space, but if you were suddenly unable to contain your joy, I bet Duke Chapel would tolerate a joyful noise. Men and women of 2011, my warmest welcome to Duke.

As for the parents and families currently banished to remote viewing areas, I know this is a day of strangely mixed emotions. Today your child enters one of the world's great universities. It doesn't get better than that. And today that ungrateful wretch abandons you and leaves home to start another life. I feel your pain, but I want to warn you, things will get worse. A mother reported that toward the end of our rather extended Christmas vacation, as the time approached for her freshman son to return to Duke, he casually remarked, oblivious to the damage to her feelings, "I've really enjoyed being with the family, but I'm about ready to go back home."

Well, that's the point. It may not seem so for a day or two or a week or two, but for every student sitting before me, that's what Duke is about to become: your home, the place where you belong, the place where others know you and care about you, the place that nourishes your growth of self.

Like other schools, we talk about these first few days in the language of orientation. As you know, orientation is a compass word—Orient means the East, from *oriri*, to rise; the word suggests that you'll be lost in space, disoriented, until you learn the coordinates for charting your way. You'll learn many things this week, but my job could be to name the cardinal points of Duke's compass, the values you'll need to observe to navigate this new world. As with the compass, there are four.

First, Duke is a place for excellence. Whether it's on our famous athletic teams or our no less famous research activities, this place becomes Duke to the extent that people recognize the difference between the best and the very good and are willing to work the extra measure to achieve the best.

Second, Duke is a place of community. Duke is different from some places where people are driven to outstanding achievement in that at Duke, it's not about doing better than someone else. This is an amazingly friendly place, a place where people of extraordinarily various backgrounds learn to accomplish things together they couldn't achieve on their own. It's a place where people take trouble to challenge each other, to support each other, to respect each other, and to enjoy each other. You will find it so. Help keep it so!

Third, every thing we do at Duke is done for the sake of education. By education we mean something far beyond formal course enrollment or transcript building. We mean the continual deepening of your grasp of the world and strengthening of your capacities to act intelligently in that world. Please don't settle for a lesser goal. If you have a smaller aim, you'll get a Duke degree, but you won't get a Duke education.

Excellence pursued as a community toward the end of ongoing education—that's a fair description of Duke's project. But my fourth value is as important as any other, since without it there's no reaching the other three. With my current fondness for the letter E, I'll call it engagement. To give the flavor of what I mean, let me tell a true story.

I have office hours most weeks in the President's Office, and students somewhat randomly come by—in the best version, not for any official reason but just to chat. Last winter two undergraduates, perfect strangers to me, came by within an hour of each other. The first, a freshman—by chance it was a woman, though I've had many such chats with men—was somewhat disappointed after her first term at Duke. Had she found interesting classes? Yes, her academics had been just as she hoped. Had she found friends? Yes, and good ones. But she had not found enough to do here, wasn't attracted to some of the pastimes other students favored, and in general was feeling a little down.

We had a thoughtful conversation and I was sympathetic, even though some part of me knew that every student in the history of the world had passed through moods like this. (I certainly did.) She knew it too. At the end of our chat, she brightened and told me she had upper-class friends who told her they had passed through such phases, but things had worked out for them, and she expected they would for her as well.

This was still fresh in my mind when a second student came in, a sophomore, by chance a young man, though I have had many such conversations with Duke women. In two seconds we were off and running. Me: What led you into engineering? He, after giving an interesting reply: Did I like the novels of Cormac McCarthy? Me: Yes, though *Blood Meridian* was hard to take. He: And had I read *The Road*? Yes, I just had—an extraordinary piece of writing and envisioning that we discussed in some detail. He: By the way, did I know about the Duke Conversations program—a program by which groups of students get to invite interesting people to campus and sit down with them for small-group discussion? (In fact I did know about this program, since I helped create it.) He'd found that an especially interesting and enjoyable part of his life and supplied some details. Oh and by the way, what did I think about the charter school movement? Me: Why do you ask? He: Oh, I took a course in the Forging Social Ideals FOCUS program and did a project on charter schools and got very interested in them, and why different people support and oppose them, and what's going on with schools in Durham, etc. etc. It's now widely recognized how crucial the quality of elementary education is to America's competitive future, and whether such education can be delivered through reformed versions of existing schools or only through alternative models is a key topic for debate. We went at it for a while, and then our time was up.

Now I'm not pretending that I knew either of these characters thoroughly at the end of twenty minutes, and on a different day I might have caught each of them in a very different state. But by complete chance, their visits put before me two very different versions of a Duke experience— one defined by a sense of waiting for things that seemed missing, the other full to bursting with interests and involvements. It matters which you end up with. One of these lives sounded like a lot more fun to live, and not by coincidence one sounded like it had a lot more education going on in it. So let's stop and try to understand where the difference arose.

To me, the most striking fact is that it was not a function of external circumstance. These two students were attending the same university and had all the same realities and opportunities surrounding them. If one was getting a lot more from this place, including a lot more satisfaction, it's because that person was engaging it much more vigorously: subjecting Duke to a higher level of internal activism, adding their own enterprise, curiosity, and creativity to the mix. Duke Conversations? This is still a growing program, but under its auspices Duke students have had a chance to sit down (among others) with liberal and conservative national political advisers, inventors and critics of the new media, and, closer to home, Duke faculty members from across the university, for intimate conversation. I promise you, you could learn something from people of these sorts! But it took initiative to connect with this program; as they say of the lottery, you can't win if you don't play.

Similarly with the charter school business. A Duke sophomore was able to sit with me and talk intelligently about one of the complex and consequential issues of current American society (this is not a rare experience for me) partly because he had taken a course—but far more because, instead of just doing the homework and collecting the grade, he'd invested the work of the course with his personal curiosity, used the class to help him know more about something he wanted to understand, and carried his active inquiry on long after the course was completed. (I can't pass up the chance to mention that this male engineering student had this experience in a class taught by a professor of women's studies.) As for Cormac McCarthy, even in the days of iPods and YouTube, educated people still can and do read books, and not just books someone else assigned them. Let your curiosity do the driving and you'll always have somewhere interesting to go.

My point is this: You've come to a place extraordinarily rich in opportunities. But like certain famous energy sources, Duke's offerings will remain inert until something is added to start the reaction. The missing ingredient is your personal engagement: your taking the initiative to seek and seize opportunities and to charge them with your energies of mind. I'm not asking that you just keep busy. Being tightly scheduled is not the same thing as being engaged. And I'm not asking that you model your life on anyone else's: the proof that you're engaged will be that your Duke career will have its own distinctive plot, driven by your gifts, your passions, your concerns. But if you don't make it your business to activate this place with your interests, then a lot of Duke will just be nice scenery—which is great, but you could be more than a tourist.

Your class will be the first to have full access to something highly relevant to what I'm describing: the program called (did you guess it?) Duke-Engage. We want to challenge you (and will assist you) to find ways to complement your academic study with involvement in real-world problem solving, in settings reaching from Durham to around the world. I could see future versions of you in the Duke students who used their public policy training this summer to help complete a crucial study for the government of New Orleans, where officials singled them out for their vital role helping the city qualify for $300 million in federal disaster funding. I could see you in the premed student—a noted member of our women's basketball team—whose blog I've followed while she worked in the highlands of Guatemala introducing small stoves into areas that previously cooked on minimally ventilated indoor fires, causing high levels of respiratory disease. We see this program as a triple winner. First, it helps Duke students get out into the world and learn the problems and prospects of national and global cultures firsthand. Second, students often become more deeply invested in their academic work when they see how things learned here can be brought to bear on lived human challenges. And third, such opportunities help Duke students learn their power to make a difference and to put their knowledge in service to society.

DukeEngage will make a great complement to the education we give on campus. But being engaged means more than signing up for a program with the word in the title. Nor is this the only way to fulfill my charge. I'm inviting you to see every chance that comes to you every day as something you could meet either in a more active or in a more detached fashion; this includes your dealings with each other. Colleges have no greater joy than the endlessly fresh, utterly unforeseen ways that groups of students come together to do things just because they seem like they would be good or fun to do—play sports, make films, plan concerts or comedy shows, join neighborhood service programs. This group creativity is a source of exuberant delight, but it's also more than that. The literature of global competitiveness suggests that the people who will have most success in the future won't be those who have mastered fixed skills but those deeply practiced in a flexible, enterprising, self-activating creativity and in pulling teams together across boundaries to improvise ways to solve problems or capture opportunities. When I see all the student-driven activity on this campus, I see people mastering these crucial skills. So if you hang back, if you don't mix it up with all the miscellaneous human talent that now surrounds you, then you're going to lose both short and long term: your present life will be less interesting and your future powers will stay undeveloped.

When I ask you to engage with each other, I'm talking about pooling your creativity, but also enlarging each other's understanding. I met an incoming freshman this summer from Cary, North Carolina, a rapidly growing suburb half an hour from here, who told me her roommate was coming from Bulgaria, which is farther away. Each of you will now be in close contact with people from as far away from wherever you've called home as Cary is from Bulgaria, in geographical or cultural or religious or other forms of distance. (In this country, there are parts of the political spectrum that are at least this far apart in terms of their ability to grasp the thinking on the other side of the divide.) We want you to come together to create a common Duke culture that you will all be at home in, and I don't doubt you will. But it would be a loss if drawing together kept you from learning from one another's differences. You'll be way better prepared when you leave Duke if you know how to appreciate the different thinking of many more branches of the human family than you know today, and the people sitting around you could give you the means. But this won't happen unless you reach out, open yourselves to each other, and struggle to grasp the human lesson that every other person here embodies.

Class of 2011, I have another idea how to alarm your families. Why don't you call them some day and say, "Mom! Dad! Congratulate me!

I'm engaged!" Depending on how you mean this, the news could be quite welcome. You could be saying that you had mastered the first lesson of Duke, the one that opens the door to all the others. A great experience awaits you, but more than you have probably imagined, the value of that experience is yours to determine. Invest this place with the full measure of your curiosity, intelligence, creativity, and human warmth and the returns will be, as they say, priceless. We want you not just to attend Duke but to own it. Last spring we admitted you. Now it's time to come take possession.

Lessons of Lacrosse

Duke Law School, September 29, 2007

The Duke lacrosse case was by far the most difficult chapter during my thirteen years as president. In recent years stories alleging sexual abuse by high-profile athletic teams have provoked crises at many universities in this country. The Duke case was made more incendiary by the racial dimension and, in particular, by the district attorney's active role proclaiming the guilt of the players. In September 2007, after the players had been exonerated and the district attorney's role unmasked, the Duke Law School hosted a conference titled "The Court of Public Opinion: The Practice and Ethics of Trying Cases in the Media," at which I made these remarks.

This conference is not just about the Duke lacrosse case. It is about a kind of event that has taken on a central place in American culture: the legal case that creates a national community of attention, the case the public consumes every "fact" of with an endless appetite for more. Cases like these typically combine scandal, celebrity, and highly combustible social issues, race and sex perhaps chief among them. And having become one of America's principal forms of shared public life, these cases highlight crucial problems of our culture—problems of achieving justice in a media-saturated society, problems of fundamental fairness to individuals, and problems in the way the American public is informed and misinformed about the world we live in.

The Duke community lived through a classic example of such a case. When a case like this is over, it's tempting to think that the facts so clearly established at the end of the day must have been equally clear throughout the process. This was not the case. When the accusations were made, our students said emphatically that they were innocent. On the other hand, the district attorney made a series of public statements expressing absolute confidence that a crime had occurred and that the students were guilty of criminal charges. These starkly opposite versions of the truth created deep uncertainty about what had happened.

Added to this, the local and national media began weeks of highly sensational coverage, creating an air of instant, uncritical certainty that fed on itself in a remarkable way, with each day providing new "revelations" that became known around the world, confirming and reconfirming public assurance that an outrage had occurred.

Given the uncertainty at the heart of the case and given the tides of passionate prejudgment the DA's comments and media accounts touched off, I staked out a position on behalf of the university that contained three principles. First, the type of crime that had been alleged had no place in our community. Second, the presumption of innocence is fundamental to our legal system, and our students were entitled to that presumption. And third, this whole matter had to be entrusted to the criminal justice system for its resolution.

As president, I had responsibility for the statements the university made and the actions the university took in a virtually unprecedented situation, and I take responsibility for them now. But I didn't come here to retell the story or explain the logic of our acts. We are now in the aftermath of this extraordinary case, and the aftermath, we have to hope, is a time for learning. Having spent my life in the cause of teaching and learning, I am not at all unwilling to learn lessons of my own. I am happy for this chance to share some of those lessons.

First and foremost, I regret our failure to reach out to the lacrosse players and their families in this time of extraordinary peril. Given the complexities of the case, getting this communication right would never have been easy. But the fact is that we did not get it right, causing the families to feel abandoned when they most needed support. This was a mistake. I take responsibility for it, and I apologize.

Second, some of those who were quick to speak as if the charges were true were on this campus, and some faculty made statements that were ill-judged and divisive. They had the right to express their views. But the public as well as the accused students and their families could have thought that those were expressions of the university as a whole. They were not, and we could have done more to underscore that.

Third, I understand that by deferring to the criminal justice system to the extent we did and not repeating the need for the presumption of innocence equally vigorously at all the key moments, we may have helped create the impression that we did not care about our students. This was not the case, and I regret it as well.

Fourth, this episode has taught me a hard lesson about the criminal justice system and what it means to rely on it. Given the media circus and the public reactions it fed, I thought it essential to insist that the matter be resolved within the legal system, not in the court of public opinion. As far as it went, this was right. But what this case reminds us is that our justice system—the best in the world—is only as good as the men and women who administer it. In this case, it was an officer of this system itself who presented false allegations as true, suppressed contrary evidence, and subverted the process he was sworn to uphold.

Relying on the criminal justice system in this case proved to have serious limits. But for the university to strive to set the system to rights—for instance, by attacking the district attorney—presented problems as well. For one thing, none of us can lightly speak as if the system itself is tainted because some of our own have been accused of a crime. I was also concerned that if Duke spoke out in an overly aggressive fashion, it would be perceived that a well-connected institution was improperly attempting to influence the judicial process, which could have caused the case to miscarry in a variety of ways. Finally, there was no legal recourse against the district attorney, for me or anyone else. Under North Carolina laws, no one had authority to take an active case from a DA absent the DA's own request, as finally happened in January.

Even with all that, Duke needed to be clear that it demanded fair treatment for its students. I took that for granted. If any doubted it, then I should have been more explicit, especially as evidence mounted that the prosecutor was not acting in accordance with the standards of his profession.

The larger problem for society is how to create and maintain the optimal balance between the independence of the legal system and protection of individuals from false prosecution. If this state should ever again have a rogue prosecutor on the loose with no more remedies than were available last time around, the failure to have learned the lesson of the Duke lacrosse case would be intolerable. I do not want to create some instant legislative "solution" that opens the door for new injustices tomorrow. I recognize that it is not easy to get the checks and balances right when two such important interests are at stake. But it's essential for all relevant parties to work to create these mechanisms, and I trust the current conference will contribute to this cause.

Closer to home, this case highlights challenges universities face when students are tied to serious criminal charges. This challenge has many aspects: how the university advises a student in these circumstances, how the university regulates the presence on campus of students charged with serious crimes, how the university interacts with parents, and many more. My colleagues in the Duke administration are going over all our procedures to see what we can learn from our experience. But these are complex questions, and they aren't ones Duke can or should hope to solve on its own. To work through these difficulties and see that their lessons are learned not only here but around the country, we will be hosting a national conference of educators, lawyers, and student affairs leaders to discuss best practices in this important field.

I'll end with the deepest lesson this case taught me. When I think back through the whole complex history of this episode, the scariest thing, to me, is that actual human lives were at the mercy of so much instant moral certainty, before the facts had been established. If there's one lesson the world should take from the Duke lacrosse case, it's the danger of prejudgment and our need to defend against it at every turn. Given the power of this impulse and the forces that play to it in our culture, achieving this goal will not be easy. But it's a fight where we all need to do our part.

Much of me hopes the Duke lacrosse case will be forgotten someday. But if it is remembered, let's hope it is remembered the right way: as a call to caution in a world where certainty and judgment come far too quickly.

Frolics and Detours

Duke Chapel, May 9 and 10, 2008

Members of the Class of 2008, I have a bond with you that I will have with no other class. As several of you have remarked, you and I started Duke together four years back. I remember my long summer of anticipation. I remember the promising messages I started getting in this, the first summer of Facebook. ("DeMarcus wants to be your friend. Do you want to be DeMarcus's friend?") I remember the cool iPods we readied to make you the nation's most technologically savvy students. Then I remember meeting the first handful of you to arrive, the savages of Project WILD, and wondering if man can really live by cheese and trail mix alone. Then one blazing August day you were all here, East Campus was crawling with you, and I was given a hug by a FAC car unloader who imprinted his whole body in perspiration on my suit—my primal scene of Duke welcome. Then I got to greet you from this pulpit and tell your parents to go home.

And then? Then it all flew by in a whirl. Doesn't today's ceremony underline the point? It's as if every hour you spent here had been annihilated, collapsing you back into the very scene where things started, except this time, instead of welcoming you, Duke is pressing the button marked "Eject." And me? Only apparently your classmate, I am staying right where I am. See ya! Thanks for the memories. Have a nice life.

But the uncanny likeness of this event to your freshman convocation reminds me that another big part of my life before you came was thinking how to make you realize the meaning of what lay ahead of you. I spent a ridiculous amount of time that summer brooding on my first address to a new Duke class. I wanted you to feel the force of two points. First, your entry into college marked one of the rare examples life would ever offer you of an absolutely fresh start. "This is like the earliest days of creation," I said. "You have not yet marred a single hour or messed up in a single way." I also wanted to insist that Duke wasn't some fixed or finished thing you had come to "fit into." You would be making this place by the way you engaged it: more than you might realize, the Duke you inhabited would be a function of choices you made. So as you entered a new world, I urged you to mold it in the image of your own best hopes.

Now that you're done, I'll admit that not everything in education comes through choice. This winter I met a Duke grad from Atlanta who introduced me to the legal concept called "frolic and detour." If I hire you to do a task for me and you have an accident in the performance of the task, then I am liable for the damage. But if you set off on frolics and detours of your own while supposedly doing what we contracted for, the harm you cause would be your responsibility, not mine.

Invoking this wonderfully named concept, this alum told me that in retrospect, his most valuable education at Duke had come not (in his word) transactionally, by following fixed means toward predetermined ends, but through frolics and detours, by succumbing to fresh interests around him each day. I'm sure you know what he meant. Part of what you gained from Duke came from things we required of you, and part from goals you consciously devised. But an immense further part came through the chances that introduced you to friends you never knew the likes of, questions you had never been aware of, interests you had never felt the pull of.

All of the ingredients of your Duke experience, the stimulus of a thousand miscellaneous factors interacting in unanalyzable ways, produced the growth that we celebrate today. And since openness to new stimuli will always be the door to continuing education, I hope your days of frolic and detour are not done. But what is going to become of those highly developed powers now that school days are past? I have two hopes: that you'll have the courage to keep pursuing your interests as they evolve and that you'll use your powers to make a difference in the world.

At this point I could produce a litany of problems your generation is going to need to solve. Instead I will tell a little story. This February

I went to Washington to speak with members of Congress and cabinet secretaries about funding advanced research. Research in universities has produced almost all the discoveries that have driven new fields like information technology and biotechnology, with all they have meant for economic development and quality of life. If we expect to benefit from future cycles of discovery, then we need to make the research investment now. The president made this a high priority last year when he signed the America COMPETES Act, which passed both houses of Congress with wide bipartisan support. But then a problem arose. Because of budget stringencies, funds for this measure were not actually appropriated after the bill was approved.

It was interesting trooping around Capitol Hill hammering away at this inconsistency. But after lunch I had an abrupt change of scene. I had learned that the Duke Club of Washington had completed a project in a local elementary school, and I'd agreed to take part in the dedication. So off I rode, far out into the District of Columbia, to a big old-fashioned schoolhouse recently re-created as the Amos I campus of Community Academy, a K–5 charter school within the public school system.

This school had been transformed into a vibrant and bustling learning center and was crowned, to my eyes, by the new reading room Duke alumni volunteers had created from an old supply closet. This place was great. What had been a dark and scary room was now bright, spacious, colorful, and inviting, stocked with books and strewn with beanbag chairs, with school kids sprawling in happy possession of the place. (One fifth grader informed me of his intention to come to Duke.)

When I saw this sight, I had several thoughts. First, in building the room, someone had recognized a fundamental human need. Not a single one of us would have gotten where we are had we not had access, in early life, to a space where reading and learning were warmly supported. In this room a primal base of good beginnings had been supplied for kids not overrich in opportunity or support.

Further, though the act was local, a larger issue was at stake. This is the twenty-fifth anniversary of *A Nation at Risk*, the report that gave currency to the notion that American public education has profound deficiencies and that failures in early schooling jeopardize both personal development and national competitiveness down the road. This is everyone's problem. People with elite educations can often exempt their children from highly challenged public schools, but if large portions of the public aren't equipped to live up to their potential, then we all will pay the price. But instead of whining that "the system is broken" while doing nothing to fix it, here people were working to make a change.

How did they come to be doing this project? It wasn't their job; they were not working under any obligation; they had not been specially trained in the work they were doing; they were not professional humanitarians or career school reformers. They were just a group of people who had an idea of a good thing they could do. The project involved a lawyer, Duke '93, who had been a JAG officer in the navy; an '03 alum who had been director of community involvement at the school (she was the point of contact); a Duke '75 architect, parent of a graduating senior, who helped draw up the plans; the head of a construction company that specializes in monuments (he has worked on the Lincoln and Jefferson memorials), Duke '74, who supplied the building knowhow; and others who contributed their other gifts. In short, this was a miscellaneous group doing all the different things people do in the world who came together as a self-motivated, self-mobilized team, for the good they could accomplish together.

Is a school reading room the biggest difference you could aspire to make? We could all name Dukies who have had a broader transformative effect. I think of Paul Farmer, a world leader in addressing global health care inequalities (you read about him in your assigned freshman book), who sat where you are sitting in 1982; or Melinda Gates, codirector of the world's largest philanthropic foundation and a major force in global health and public education reform, who attended her Duke baccalaureate in 1986. Maybe yours will be the name my successor will single out twenty-five years from now! Maybe you will be the one who figures out how to solve the global energy challenge, or how to assure clean water to people around the world. The fact that you don't seem the type today proves absolutely nothing about what you might go on to do. The future is a story of mysterious unfoldings. Paul Farmer was not a celebrated doctor on the day of his baccalaureate but the former social chair of his Duke fraternity.

But on any day when you don't see the possibility of big difference-making available to you, you might remember the Duke Club of Washington's reading room as an image of something that is in your power. It will always be in your power to see the public good as something we're all responsible for and can all have an effect on. (One moral of my story is that it's not only Washington that can make things happen in Washington.) It will always be in your power to have an eye out for actual differences you can make in the place where you are, as Dukies spied a possible literacy center in a disused storeroom. It will always be in your power to spend some of your "dead" or "down" time in a more constructive way: our alums' choice to give time to this project was the first condition for its eventual success. And it will always be in your power to multiply your force through collaboration: in sport and in earnest, you've shown amazing skill in functioning as a team. Through the years it will make a world of difference how you choose to use these powers, in terms of good things done or left undone.

Class of 2008, I have loved your company, and it grieves me to see you go. But I rejoice in what you are equipped to do thanks to your time at Duke. I once heard the founder of Engineers without Borders, a group with a strong Duke presence and a brilliant promoter of the making of local difference, quote a line attributed to Einstein: "The significant problems we face cannot be solved at the same level of thinking we were at when we created them." We need you to forge the understandings that will lift your time past the world you inherit. You have the intelligence for it; if Duke students don't, who does? So what you really need is the will and the recognition that it is in your power. I said something to you four years ago that I'll repeat with one variation as you go. Download these words into your iPod and let me croon them to you as you go to sleep. Men and women of the Class of 2008, you will love the world that comes after Duke, but you'll love it more if you help make it the place you believe it should be.

Advancing in a Recession

Duke Chapel, May 8–9, 2009

It's nice in here, isn't it? So dark, so intimate, so much love surrounding you, the outer world so perfectly shut out. It's just like being in the womb! But I have news for you: we are about to push you out. With the contractions of the three baccalaureate services, then the mighty heave of commencement, we are about to deliver you, a squalling newborn, to the world of responsibility and independence.

I hear what you are saying. "NO! We don't want to go! Please don't deliver us! We are very happy in the womb!" And if I then say, "But we have no academic place for you," you will reply, "Oh yes you do! Didn't the business school just create a new degree so we could postpone our departure indefinitely—the MMS degree, standing for Much More School?" And if I then say, "We still can't keep you; we have no place to house you," you will reply, "Not a problem! We're very used to living in tents!"

Class of 2009, if you regard your exit with ambivalence or even horror, I understand. Duke students are always sad to leave a place so full of beauty, fun, stimulation, and growth. The grief of parting is certainly aggravated this year; indeed, your timing is spectacularly bad. You grew up in a period of unprecedented economic expansion, with the fruit of opportunity growing fatter and more abundant around you every year. Then, just as you got the chance to seize it, the illusion of perpetual prosperity went away. In your senior year alone, $4.1 trillion of wealth was lost or destroyed in the global economy; gross domestic production shrank at an annual rate of 6 percent; the U.S. economy threw off several million jobs, with whole sectors of employment grown dubious for years to come. At that moment you chose to make your post-Duke debut. Pardon me for asking: What were you thinking?

In fact, from chatting with you, I know that many of you have found interesting prospects after Duke, and this does not surprise me. Even in a time of wrenching transformation, many career paths continue to exist. And if anyone is to land the opportunities of 2009, it will be clever and irresistible types like you.

But for a thought experiment, let's put the worst case. Let's suppose that the world will never again be as it was in early 2008. Let's suppose that the inventory of familiar opportunities will be radically reduced and the supports for traditional success permanently eroded. Commencement speeches are sometimes called "as you go forth" speeches. What to say if you are going forth to *that*?

I had reached this point in my thinking when my eye fell on an article on the front page of the *New York Times*. It featured a Dukie, a biology major from the Class of 2006, who had gone to work at a Bay Area biotech company, then been laid off. Having looked for a job without success for several months, he had an idea. He started a business in his apartment making and selling jellyfish aquariums. As he told the reporter, "I hate getting stung. But it beats looking for work." He had recently sold three tanks and was getting ready to take his business online.

My thoughts on reading this story were quite varied. I wondered what life was like for the young man's apartment mates, who now share space with strange creatures in breakable containers. As a father, I also wondered how I would explain what my child was doing for a living, a high-stakes challenge for every modern parent. In any case, what a dumb idea: how big could the market for this product be?

Then again, who can be certain this person's concept will not sweep the world? People did not always spend three times the price of a traditional cup for coffees with polysyllabic foreign names, but now we do. Human life used to be possible without social networking sites and ever-new iPhone apps, but now it's not. Those were the jellyfish aquaria of recent years—everyday facts soon enough, but on their first outings just strange new ideas.

So taking the jellyfish business as an example of a nascent enterprise, I would next ask, where did it come from? It's not like there was an existing industry or career posting that gave the student his idea. It came, as we say, out of his head. But out of what ingredients in his head, exactly? Well, probably partly from his academic training—the article says the student majored in biology. For all we know, his formal learning may have cross-bred with the popular culture you have all mastered but that we give no credit for: my research teaches that a pet jellyfish appears in a lesser Will Smith film. But even with these ingredients present, some further force was needed to activate these mental deposits and weld them into a concept. This was the force of enterprise, a drive fueled, it appears, by many factors: need and even the shadow of desperation (the student had been out of a job for months); frustration with existing options ("I hate looking for work"); the ability to envision an opportunity where none was evident; then the spark that takes the unconnected contents of the mind and fuses them into an idea of a way to seize that opportunity; then the urge to take that idea and make it succeed in practice.

As I hope you've guessed, I am not interested in jellyfish economics but in the deep human act this story gives a glimpse of. If I hadn't found this primal scene of enterprise, I had a thousand other examples. I knew a student who was very smart, very stylish, and very well organized when she was at Duke. (You knew her too—she helped organize the party in Bostock Library called "Work Hard, Play Well.") After graduation, she won a Fulbright to Sri Lanka. Combining what she was here with what she learned there, she has gone on to codesign a line of stylish apparel, organize the manufacture so as to create improved working conditions for Sri Lankan women, and market these designs on American campuses, seven at last count, including Duke. I know an alum who got a job at a cable news network but didn't love it, left it, and set off to ramble around South America. In Chile, he had the idea to start a café featuring live music, art, theater, and film; learned to run a restaurant; made a success of it; sold it; and returned to the United States, where he created an online tutorial service and, later, had a career teaching social entrepreneurship, including at the Sanford Institute.

I share these stories not to boast of what students have accomplished but to offer glimpses of a way to shape a life. My March 14, 2009, *Times* story is entitled "Weary of Looking for Work, Some Create Their Own."

This suggests less a changed career strategy than a fundamental flip of outlook: a shift from looking at the world as a set of already established places to viewing it as something you can help make through your energies of invention. Even under the best of circumstances, mere job finding was never going to be a guaranteed route to fulfillment. But in our time, approaching the world as its possible creator may have social utility as well.

Let me return to my question. If the world that seemed so permanent in your youth should be radically altered by the changes of this time, what would you do then? I would reply: Then there will be a need for a successor world to be pieced together—and this will create large openings for the enterprising self. Everything that needs doing in our world needs new thinking to drive the change. The economy may recover when consumer confidence returns, but it will only sustain its dynamism as the spirit of invention moves through its sectors. Lots of small enterprises fail, but tiny companies are large employers when taken in the aggregate, and start-ups often supply the energy of invention that big firms depend on. If the jellyfish business is a success, you know that it will be a candidate for a buyout.

But for-profits aren't the only arena for enterprise these days. Teach for America, the largest employer of our graduating class, was an enterprising student's bright idea before becoming the employer of four thousand new teachers each year. One of the most striking developments in recent years has been the shift from the idea of K–12 public education as an immutable institutional given to its recognition as a challenge requiring innovation and experiment. Two years back we gave an honorary degree to the founder of the American hospice movement, once a new idea of how to accommodate the inevitable end of life. Most of Durham's downtown revival and neighborhood revitalization projects began as the ideas of an individual or small group—wild schemes one day, life-improving realities the next.

Out beyond the zones of for- and not-for-profit, there is another work that needs doing. We need a fresh imagining of what is of value and what is worth a sacrifice. Some such idea always drives our allocations of wealth, time, effort, and concern, and on the basis of recent history, our default concepts of our "interest" have not fully met either our material or our communal needs. These things don't just fall from the sky.

Men and women help articulate systems of value through the profundity of their insight and the persuasiveness of their imaginings. Whoever puts the thoughts in circulation that help make the sum of our individual choices meet our collective needs will be the real hero of the next generation.

With so much to be done, your time of apparent constraints turns out to be a time of large opportunities. Yet my point is, it's not the nature of opportunities to just sit there waiting to be seized. Opportunities exist only to the extent that they are created; they come into being when someone visualizes an opening in the status quo and sparks an idea of how to fill it. The difference you'll go on to make isn't a function of the title you'll hold but of the stance you'll take in your emerging career: whether as a contented citizen of the actual or the visualizer and realizer of the possible.

Could you really make that difference? You have the intelligence, you have the education, but you will need things of equal or greater value. You'll need to be willing to work; I never saw much accomplished without the accompaniment of sweat. You'll need to be open to new things, not entrapped by your addiction to an accustomed life. You'll need to stay in touch with your evolving sense of what really matters. Above all you'll need courage—courage not just in the sense of ability to master fear or anxiety but in the root sense of *corage*, heart, the life spirit that drives you cheerfully to assert yourself, confidently to act on your energies and beliefs.

By the authority vested in me, I hereby invest you with all these powers! Which is easy to do, because you already have them: it's all a matter of summoning your latent capacities. Have the courage of your creativity and you won't be sad for this chapter of life to end. Your motto won't be "Please don't make me go" but "Let me out of here! Let me at it!" Time to set you free, Class of 2009. Courage! Thanks for your company. Make a great life.

John Hope Franklin

Duke Chapel, June 11, 2009

John Hope Franklin (1915–2009), the distinguished historian, major contribu-
tor to the Brown v. Board of Education *case, and author of the groundbreaking*
work From Slavery to Freedom, *had lived in Durham during segregation days*
and returned to make his home here. He spent the last quarter-century of a nearly
century-long life teaching history and law at Duke and serving as a lodestar on
questions of race and justice. These remarks were delivered at the memorial held
for him in Duke Chapel.

I was the last person on this program to have met John Hope Franklin.
I always knew his work: *From Slavery to Freedom* was already a classic
when I was in college. But I didn't meet him in person until June 2004,
when as the incoming president of Duke I had my first dinner with the
trustees of The Duke Endowment.

   John Hope was the honored speaker that night because he was stepping down. With his ninetieth birthday approaching, he thought it right
to leave before his powers started to decline. But on the showing of the
talk he gave, the idea of his declining seemed quite far-fetched. Then as
every other time we met, I was struck by that upright posture that made
him seem a physical emblem of absolute human dignity, his easy and
precise command of words, and the wonderful gleam in his eye—the
sign that though he had seen human behavior at its most deficient, the
human comedy never lost its appeal.

In short, though I first met him at age ninety, I too knew John Hope in his prime, and it's one of the good fortunes of my life that he made the path to friendship so easy. Soon we were sitting down with some regularity, sometimes at my house or a restaurant, often at his house, surrounded by all his books yet always too by some work in progress, while we ranged over a host of subjects: southern history, George Washington Williams and Charles Chesnutt, his travels to the developing world, the latest turns of contemporary politics, the anguishing turns this campus and city lived through one painful year, Hawaii, his orchids, shared colleagues and friends. What made these talks memorable was that though he could retrieve nearly a century of experience with perfect recall, such that history became a living dimension of every subject, when I sat with him, John Hope always seemed right there, fully present in the living moment of our encounter. And perfectly, utterly at home.

It fascinated me that John Hope had his home here. He wasn't from this area. He came to North Carolina in his twenties in the name of love and study, to pursue his dissertation research and courtship of Aurelia. In a world of unequal opportunity, this product of the finest graduate history program in America found work at a segregated college, St. Augustine's in Raleigh. But John Hope's gift was that he neither minimized the indignities of systemic racism nor missed the opportunities they left to realize his promise. First at St. Aug's, then at the North Carolina College for Negroes in Durham (now NCCU), where he moved in 1942, he finished his first book, then, with his wife to fund him, researched and wrote the book that helped place African American history on the American historical agenda.

John Hope's ties to Duke date from this key period of achievement. For though this university would not have hired him in the 1940s, the archives of Perkins Library were open to him, and he was welcomed by Duke historians who read papers together with black colleagues— historical scholarship, the pursuit of understanding of the past, forming a bridge across the gap of official racial separation. Even this sharing had its limits. John Hope remembered that a Duke historian who would converse with him freely in the library never invited him to his office, and once asked this young black colleague, whose brilliance was perfectly evident to him, if it was actually true that he believed in integration. The notion was astonishing—because how could John Hope continue to hold his job if segregation went away? John Hope replied, If segregation ended I should not worry, because then I could compete for a job at Duke!

John Hope left Durham for points north in 1947, but thirty-four years later he chose to move back here, and though he had now officially retired (his retirements were never that convincing), he took up a new appointment, continuing at Duke the work of his long life: as a teacher and scholar, a champion of fairness and justice, and a wise confidant and friend. I remember Cindy and my last meal with him, just before Christmas. Now he had begun to decline, but there he was, still avid, still game, eager to assess the first black president's transition, eager to compare notes about India, where we had just been—and when it appeared that we were done, eager to stay on for dessert. (He ordered crème brûlée.) Why? Because he was still hungry? Yes, but not for the food. He was hungry for more contact, more talk, more mental processing of the world, more life.

That's my last picture, but it's not the right place to end. The great thing about universities is that they are places where the talented young take the measure of their world and the lives they might give to the world. So my final image of John Hope will be not of his still-vibrant nineties but of him as a student at Fisk, a youth starting out, discovering the workings of American racism, meeting the person he would build a life with, and finding his calling to history and to social action through the scholarly career.

On any given day, at any college or university in this country, some young man or woman could make such a discovery of their promise—and when they do, the world should prepare to change. That's the hope John Hope Franklin gives.

....

The University and the Financial Downturn

February 10, 2010

I'll begin by offering my greetings to the assembled faculty and my thanks to Craig Henriquez and the Executive Committee of the Academic Council for making the annual faculty meeting a special occasion. This is a chance to celebrate our community and honor those who have done our common work supremely well. It's also an occasion to take the long view of our situation and think how to prepare ourselves for the road ahead.

I'll introduce this subject with two thoughts. First, universities are among the most durable institutions the world has ever seen. They have survived wars, revolutions, economic booms and busts, and many cycles of cultural transformation. Clark Kerr once pointed out that of the eighty-five institutions in continuous existence since 1520 under the same name in the same place performing the same function, seventy are universities. But paradoxically, higher education in the form we know is not an ancient but a comparatively recent creation, an artifact of the post–World War II years.

Let me remind you of some facts. The number of students who went beyond high school in the United States was around 250,000 in 1900 and only 350,000 in 1910 but already 1.5 million by 1940, over 4 million by 1960, and over 12 million by 1980—a number that grew somewhat less rapidly to 15.7 million in 2000 and is around 18 million today. In other words, within the lifetime of living men and women, higher education changed from a relatively rare experience open to the privileged or those headed for a few learned professions to the more broadly distributed opportunity and career prerequisite that it forms today.

Similarly, it's only since the 1940s that the federal government has become a major investor in university research, stimulating the growth of the research facilities, roles, and relationships we take for granted now. Federally funded research and development at American universities and colleges totaled perhaps $5 million in 1940. In the postwar and Cold War years it expanded rapidly, to $405 million in 1960 and $4 billion in 1980. It reached $17 billion in 2000 and $31 billion in the year just past.

A third set of figures shows that another form of support is of even more recent origin, at least on its modern scale. I refer to philanthropic giving and its compounding through institutional investment. Giving to all American colleges and universities totaled around $330 million in 1940 and $800 million in 1960, but over $4 billion in 1980, and then— watch how the number takes off—$23 billion in the year 2000, and $31 billion in 2008. As market growth and shrewd investment amplified the accumulated funds, endowments and endowment spending grew in similarly unprecedented ways. The total endowments for the top 120 institutions of higher education came to $7 billion in 1960 and around $20 billion in 1980. It reached $193 billion in 2000, after the economic explosion of the 1990s, then soared to $400 billion in 2008 in the run-up that followed the dot-com bust.

As this short course in higher ed finances highlights, a confluence of fairly recent developments has created both the daily reality and the social role of universities as we know them. These developments made universities the source of a highly trained workforce, with major economic results. Lawrence Katz and Claudia Goldin refer to the twentieth century as the "human capital century" in recognition that that time's economic expansions derived not from industrial production but from new industries fueled by a better educated public. Concomitantly, the second change converted the university into a key engine of research discovery, with all that has meant for economic dynamism and quality of life.

The third development created deepened support and a base for expansion for every phase of the university's teaching and research. Total giving to Duke was $20 million in 1972, the first year for which there are institutional records, and $27 million in 1980, but $303 million in 2000 and $380 million in 2008. Duke's endowment, worth around $60 million in 1960 and only $110 million in 1980, reached $3.2 billion by the year 2000 and $6.1 billion in 2008. You know what this growth has created: endowments for professorships and financial aid, the building of technology infrastructure and the rebuilding of the library, new lab space for engineering and the natural sciences, and new buildings for every school, plus the enrichment of every aspect of campus experience, from new academic and extracurricular programs to the campus-wide revitalization of the arts. We are meeting in the Nasher Museum, a prime example of the enrichment brought to universities by modern wealth creation and modern philanthropy.

In sum, the university we know is derived far more than we usually recognize from the peculiar economic history of recent decades. In the last eighteen months we have been reminded that historical returns do not guarantee future performance, just as the fine print warned. So where are we now? Past the worst of the economic downturn, but facing mixed and uncertain prospects: with GDP growth at 5.7 percent last quarter and financial markets apparently rebounding (Duke's endowment earned an 8.5 percent return for the year 2009), but with credit still obstructed, many deep in debt, and unemployment stuck at high levels. (Lawrence Summers has termed the current state "an economic recovery and a human recession.") The market for schools like us has never been stronger (Duke saw a 33 percent increase in undergraduate applications in the past two years), but the steady income growth we got used to in recent years is unlikely to return anytime soon. Giving to Duke and other universities, well down in 2009, begins to revive, but no one can confidently predict the rate of recovery. The government upped research funding in the stimulus bill and the federal budget submitted last week, but no one knows what the massive overhang of government debt will mean for the long term.

Put them all together and these facts raise the question that faces us now: If modern universities are in part products of a historically contingent prosperity, what will it mean if that growth proves unsustainable or, at best, uncertain?

We can see the possibilities, and some are scary. They are far less daunting at a well-off private university like Duke than at some public institutions. I was in California last week and heard the anguish of UC colleagues over massive budget cuts, 30 percent–plus tuition hikes, and the indignity of faculty furloughs. In the twentieth century California built the most extraordinary public university system ever created, with its blend of outstanding research campuses and mass educational opportunity. We are about to learn how compatible those will prove with massive shortfalls in public support.

In truth, we do not yet know what this time will prove to mean for the history of knowledge and of opportunity creation. Much is at stake on the question whether, in days of scarce resources, this country will correctly weigh the value investment in higher education will return in economic development and the development of human potential—and the cost of investments shortsightedly withheld. But without minimizing our dependence on factors outside our control, I would note that we are not absolutely dependent on such factors. Even in slow-growth days a university's ability to perform its mission is partly in its own hands, through the choices it makes and the way it deploys its resources.

Last February I explained how Duke would approach its economic challenge. First, we are not free to ignore the reality of reduced funding from key sources, particularly the endowment. Through a careful university-wide exercise we are walking our way back to a sustainable budget, and we are well along with this task. Last year there was no salary increase for Duke faculty and staff earning $50,000 or more, a collective sacrifice that averted $18 million in added annual costs and protected around two hundred jobs. This year we remain optimistic that we will have funds to allocate to compensation, but since we need to shoulder rising costs for the excellent benefits Duke employees enjoy, any pay increase will continue to be modest. To speak of cuts in expenditure, over 450 jobs have been eliminated through voluntary retirement programs and the tight control of vacancies and overtime. Efficiencies in campus-wide operations—things like changing our thermostats, a coordinated system for purchasing computers, and the conversion of the phone system to voice-over IP—will lead to many further millions in savings. Taken together, steps already enacted or identified have cut more than $50 million from Duke's budget and, if luck holds and prudence continues, averted the need for sizable system-wide layoffs.

So to repeat: First, we are committed to managing to a sustainable income. As a second principle, Duke elected to effect these reductions gradually, over three years rather than through abrupt cuts. Third, Duke enlisted broad participation in the decision-making process. In our system, schools and major units have the responsibility to live within their means, but within that constraint are free to decide what choices make best local sense. In consequence, while no part of Duke has escaped a measure of pain, we have avoided across-the-board cuts and one-size-fits-all solutions.

Fourth and most crucially, even as we reduce, we are determined to preserve Duke's forward movement. We will continue to support the many activities we engage in, but at the margin we are also making choices, investing resources in strategic priorities.

First on this list is students. You have heard me argue that making Duke education accessible to the most outstanding students is not a value among others but the prerequisite for everything else we do. Selfishly and in the short term, we have an interest in attracting the students who will engage Duke most fully and stimulate us to the highest degree. Less selfishly and longer term, universities perform their social mission through the students they produce: by drawing high talent, expanding its horizons and deepening its understandings, and sending it forth to do all the things for which our world needs intelligent, constructive force. Since high talent is found in all social origins, the university has an obligation to make this experience open to all who are suitably qualified, not just the well-to-do. For these reasons, we must ensure that this time of economic downturn—a time when the needs of many families have increased—will see no downturn in educational opportunity at Duke. As we tighten our belts elsewhere, we are committed to meeting our undergraduates' full need for financial aid. Our successfully completed Financial Aid Initiative raised $300 million for permanent support of aid in every school.

The other essential ingredient of the university is the faculty. The profundity and creativity of faculty intelligence is what makes great teaching and research discovery happen; to remain vital, the faculty needs to be both supported and renewed. Hiring new colleagues brings the university fresh energy and new thinking that stimulates us all. If new faculty were not to be hired for some period, the university would miss whole cohorts of talent and lose an ongoing invigoration.

For these reasons, when the administration proposed and the trustees approved a plan for managing the downturn last winter, resources were explicitly committed for continued faculty hiring. Within the constraints of the day, this is the time to build faculty excellence, not freeze it. Having met the additions to our ranks at my reception for new faculty last fall, I can testify to the opportunity we are currently seizing. I'd add that within the plan, funds were also explicitly committed to diversity efforts in faculty hiring. Drawing talent from all sources is as important for building a great faculty as for the student body. Equal opportunity is not a luxury to be afforded in bull markets alone.

Third, Duke is committed to making continuing strategic investments in academic programs. This is not the first downturn I have seen hit the academy. The most damaging consequence I have observed came as budget cuts gave rise to a sullen protectionism: the wish, while reluctantly acceding to inevitable reductions, to lock in every surviving resource in its current form. The sentiment is understandable, but the cumulative results can be quite stultifying, since they freeze in place one moment's status quo. The school that fares best in hard times will be the one that strikes the best balance between supporting established fields and retaining the means for innovation.

Duke's 2001 strategic plan, *Building on Excellence*, guided a set of investments that made major differences across the campus and in this university's stature around the world. Our current strategic plan puts similarly important choices before us now. The plan identifies three areas that are increasingly critical to what our society needs universities to deliver. Duke is a leader in all three, and we are committed to build on these strengths. The first is interdisciplinary: developing fields of discovery arising at intersections of familiar disciplines and building education that equips students to grasp the multiple dimensions of complex problems. The second is international: opening points of contact with top talent around the world and giving faculty and students deepened understanding of the global dimensions of every issue. The third is engagement with contemporary challenges. We are committed to connecting the intellectual work that can only be done in universities with the work of real-world problem solving, in areas from health care and environmental change to energy and education, and to developing new educational models that put real-world engagement in a reciprocally enriching relation to academic study—an emerging hallmark of Duke education.

I could list the recently launched programs that advance these goals, but with your permission I'll tell a story instead—and since I have so many, perhaps you will allow me two. The president gets to invite himself everywhere in the university to see what's going on. Let me share the experience of two visits from the past month. In early January, I went to see the work our colleagues are doing in one of our seven new interdisciplinary institutes, the Duke Institute for Brain Sciences. It was extraordinarily exciting. In the course of three hours, I heard from faculty at the forefront in answering questions like What is the biochemical process by which the mind constructs a representation of the world? What is the biological basis of the fact that some people become addicted to the same substance that others can use (as we say) "socially"? Can we establish a biological basis for the fact that some of us make risk-laden decisions one way, and some another—and if so, what would that teach about the framing of policy choices? Then I went to a lab where a colleague and his graduate students imaged how the neurons in a bird's brain changed when the bird heard a song it would subsequently imitate: the process at the root of all teaching and learning. I ended the day watching a brain displayed via dissection to the first-year medical class.

Now here was a place where fundamental discoveries were being freshly made about the most basic questions, by faculty drawn together across several schools and departments, thanks to a strategic investment by this institution. Several of the faculty had arrived this very year, thanks to the provision for strategic hiring that I just mentioned. And the intellectual community thus created ran freely across academic ranks and ages. Graduate students were active partners in the work of discovery, and undergraduates were as well: the creation of DIBS and its attendant faculty hiring has permitted the launch of the new neuroscience major, which already has fifty-nine majors, all with access to front-line research experience. I have met students who told me they came to Duke for the experiences available here in neuroscience. Now that's a great reason to pick a college—and great evidence of how the university can add life and depth even when markets are down.

The week after my visit to DIBS I went to China to complete negotiations on the new programs Duke's academic council and trustees approved in December. Kunshan, the city next to Shanghai and the city with the highest per capita income and the highest concentration of high-tech industry in China, has identified a need to build outstanding higher education in order to sustain its vision of development. Kunshan has selected Duke as their partner for this venture, dedicating a large parcel of land for our purposes and offering to build buildings to our specifications. Duke's presence in Kunshan would be led by our business school, which will teach finance and management skills in heavy demand in this region. But we anticipate that those would be quickly followed by an array of other Duke programs that address other major Chinese needs: programs in public policy, environmental policy and science, and global health, and eventually potential hybrid programs in health, management, engineering, environment, and other fields. Through this presence, we would use Duke's strengths in cross-disciplinary, problem-based research and teaching to build human capital in a country with deep need for that expertise. And as the number of Duke faculty grows who have spent time in China and gained understanding of the fastest developing society in the world, students at Duke in Durham will benefit as well. At the groundbreaking in Kunshan, it did not seem far-fetched to think that Duke is doing in the Yangtze River Delta in 2010 what it did on the West Campus in the 1920s: building the means to both deepen our education and broaden the performance of our social mission.

Earlier that same week, the members of our party got another glimpse of Duke's strategic evolution by visiting the Dandelion School, a residential school for middle-school children in an industrial suburb of Beijing. The Dandelion School is a response to the internal migration from rural areas to new economy cities that has brought 4 million people to Beijing alone in recent years, including children suffering from many forms of displacement and disconnection. The school's aim is to build them a home and the educational base for positive developments in later life.

A Duke professor of cultural anthropology, Ralph Litzinger, studies contemporary Chinese migration and has worked with the school. Through him a link was created to DukeEngage, the civic engagement program that is currently sending 350 undergraduate students a year around this country and around the world, with Duke support, to learn something of human life outside the bubble of selective American schools and careers; to learn how their classroom education equips them to help with real-world challenges; and equally valuably, to find out what more they need to learn to actually grasp their world and be effective in dealing with its challenges. With Professor Litzinger as their mentor, eight or nine DukeEngage students have interned at the Dandelion School in each recent summer, and when we went, we visited a Dukie who was spending a whole year there as a resident English instructor: Sarah Smith, a Duke sophomore, an international comparative studies major who has studied Chinese at Duke. Having witnessed her teaching, I can glowingly testify to the joy in education that she and her colleagues are creating in a place of deprivation. I'm confident that she herself will know more, and her education will mean more throughout her life, because she had this opportunity to combine academic and experiential education, at Duke and halfway around the world, in the way she did.

Now, put the case that we had decided not to create or sustain innovations like DukeEngage, or our new China ventures, or brain sciences, the Kenan Institute for Ethics, Global Health, and the other interdisciplinary institutes. Much would remain, but something essential would now be missing: the force of serious innovation, our willingness to envision new ways to perform our fundamental mission. Even in a season of tightened belts, that ongoing work is a necessity, not a luxury. So we will protect resources for such programmatic innovations even as we move to a reduced budget base.

At the end of the day, I am quite optimistic about how Duke will come through our current challenges. If my optimism needs support, I find it in the history of this place. One of its most striking lessons is that Duke did not better itself in good times alone. It did especially well in hard times by having the courage to try new things—the things it deemed essential to build a great center of learning. The backwoods schoolhouse that grew into Trinity College was founded in 1838, the year after the Panic of 1837. Trinity College moved to Durham and began its modern life in the early 1890s, almost concurrently with the Panic of 1893. Mr. Duke gave the gift to convert the college into this university during the roaring '20s, but it was in 1930, after the start of the Great Depression, that Duke opened its medical school, having decided it was essential for a great university to have one. And Terry Sanford started what became the Sanford Institute in the stagflationary 1970s—not because money was plentiful but because he had the idea that the practical policymaking domain and academic fields like economics, statistics, political science, and ethics would both be enriched through closer contact. This fall we celebrated this experiment's extraordinary success by promoting the Institute to the Sanford School of Public Policy.

Colleagues, now it's our turn to show we can make this university greater even as we meet the strictures of this time. There's no avoiding facing up to current financial facts, but we can do better than simply hunkering down. I am grateful for the maturity this faculty has shown in stepping up to our own real-world problem, and still more for your good cheer, your ambition, and your imagination. If we recognize our power to continue to make this place, I'm confident Duke's best days are still ahead.

Walk Ten Thousand Miles,
Read Ten Thousand Books

Duke Chapel, May 14 and 15, 2010

"This is so nice. Everyone is here together, and the end is near, but not too near."

That's what I told a *Chronicle* reporter at the senior class barbecue in Cameron four weeks back. Well, Class of 2010, here you are together again, but this time the end really is near. Very, very near. In fact your condition is terminal. To paraphrase the poet W. H. Auden: You thought that Duke would last forever. You were wrong.

Then what? I agree: the thought of life after Duke is utterly appalling. At the barbecue one of you put it this way: Now you will be "freshmen in the workforce of life." Starting all over again, down at the bottom again, off in the unknown again, and you may be sure there will be no bright-faced FACs to unload your car this time. Want to stick around a little longer? Too bad! We have hardened our hearts. It's time for you to go.

But not to be totally unkind, I do want to give you a graduation present, and since I wanted to find something that would be valuable for you but inexpensive to me, I have settled on a gift of wisdom. Some months back, I found the perfect thing.

As you've read, in recent months Duke has been exploring a partnership with Kunshan, the municipality just west of Shanghai. The city with the highest per capita income in China, Kunshan has been a scene of breathtakingly rapid development, but though it has attracted a lion's share of high-tech industries, Kunshan knows that it lacks something essential to sustain this development: namely, high-quality higher education. To meet this need, Kunshan has invited Duke to be its educational partner, an arrangement with major advantages for us. As Duke becomes more deeply embedded in China, we will be better able to help our students understand a culture that will be a major player in your future, and so better prepare you for the life of your times.

When I visited Kunshan this January, I was taken to a famous local attraction, a beautifully preserved ancient city with canals instead of roads, Zhouzhuang, sometimes called the Venice of China. In Zhouzhuang I visited the home of a seventeenth-century scholar who was unknown to me though apparently known to all students in China, Gu Yanwu. In his house I encountered a famous dictum that I knew I was fated to share with you. My gift to you is this saying from the scholar Gu Yanwu: Walk ten thousand miles. Read ten thousand books.

Walk ten thousand miles. Read ten thousand books. Only ten syllables, and the words could not be simpler. But like all proverbs, the simple words encode a complex message. Let's work it out. To me this saying proposes an outlook in which there is always more of something stretching out before you, ten thousand of them, which is to say, infinitely many—a number you will never be at the end of. Further, in this attitude, the self actively propels itself into this space of possibility. The verbs are active, commanding: Walk ten thousand miles; read ten thousand books.

So the proverb envisions a mind continually active in expanding the sphere of its understanding. But strikingly, in this formula understanding comes in two ways, not one. This is a command to experience things, to go beyond mere book learning, to take the infinitely expansive world of human possibility and live it firsthand. Don't just read about it. Get out there! Walk! But the saying understands that if reading is not the whole of knowledge, it is still an essential form of knowledge. Humans are the only creatures who have the ability to preserve their understanding in words, to extend their understanding to others across time and space in words, and to access understandings they have not achieved on their own by mentally processing the words of others. So in this saying, immediate and word-mediated experience are envisioned as equally necessary, mutually supplementary paths to knowledge, the subject of equally urgent commands: Walk ten thousand miles. Read ten thousand books.

This concept will not be foreign to you. Having participated in programs like DukeEngage or the Sanford School internships or the Pratt Grand Challenges, you have already lived the idea of a mutually enriching relation between academic learning and engagement with real-world problems. Gu Yanwu, you will be interested to know, was both a scholar and a soldier, having fought on the losing side in the overthrow of the Ming dynasty. His claim to fame was to articulate a version of Confucianism that brought this intellectual tradition into closer touch with economic and political realities and the facts of daily life.

Walk ten thousand miles. Read ten thousand books. I offer these words in this, your last class at Duke, because they bear on the course you are about to set. I've met people (you have too) who, on "finishing" their education, have snuggled into some comfortable niche and lived there contentedly, without the curiosity to take on new challenges, or cross over into other social horizons, or learn things that might require a readjustment of attitude. You know what people are like who never go anywhere or read anything. At first we might say they are "settled." After a while, other "s" words apply: words like *stuck*, or *stalled*, or *stagnant*, or *stultified*.

To prevent that dreadful alternative, Duke's chief wish is that you will keep moving, keep enlarging your world, keep opening yourself to new challenges and prospects, keep using all your modes of intelligence to integrate new experience into your emerging understanding. You may think I should be congratulating you on the plans you have made for next year. I do, but even the best next step will prove a dead end if you don't travel through it to options you now can barely foresee. You might think I should be exhorting you to attack great problems of your day: global health inequalities, or K–12 education, or resource destruction and climate change, or hyperpartisan politics, or creating a financial system that assures prosperity while preventing risk. If you fix these I will indeed be grateful! But you won't be a constructive contributor to a single one of these causes unless you are first a certain kind of person: a person eager to keep learning, to keep advancing from an initial to a deeper understanding.

I'm pretty optimistic that you are not leaving Duke for a swamp of mental torpor. After all, whether you like it or not, what you did here put a mark on you. In his book *Outliers*, Malcolm Gladwell proposes that everyone who was really good at anything had an unsung prior career, the ten thousand hours of inglorious practice they spent acquiring mastery of a skill. Mozart had to compose all the early works of Mozart before becoming the genius we know; the Beatles' ten thousand hours singing and playing in Hamburg enabled them to become the Beatles; Bill Gates programmed for ten thousand hours before he could become the legendary computer pioneer; Brian Zoubek, Jon Scheyer, and Lance Thomas played ten thousand hours of childhood hoops on their way to becoming NCAA national champions.

Now let's do the math. You may not have read ten thousand books at Duke, and you may not have walked quite ten thousand miles, but you did put in, say, sixty hours a week for forty weeks a year for four years, which is pretty nearly ten thousand hours. From this I infer that your Duke career was your time for laying down the foundations of mastery. What skill did you master? Exactly what I am discussing: the skill of active, mobile, many-sided intelligence. Every course you took, every problem you worked, every thought you encountered, every unfamiliar person you engaged, every serious or fun thing you put your energy into accomplishing each of these, and all of these together, were your training for the career that awaits you now, the perpetual push toward broader engagement and deepened understanding that will be your life after Duke.

You played the practice; now for the game! According to my unassailable reasoning, you can't not go on to this success. From ten thousand hours of drilling, the habits are locked in, built so powerfully into your personality that no thinking-cessation program could break the addiction.

But to be frank, this is not quite true. You have had a wildly stimulating environment surrounding you these last four years; now you have to carry on the adventure without so much exterior support. And some day, you will face the temptation to stop expanding your mental world, to become addicted to the familiar round, and to think that what you already know is the truth, the whole truth, and nothing but the truth. That may seem like a day of perfect contentment, but it may really only be a day of perfect inertia, the beginning of your life as a formerly interesting person.

On that day, it's my hope that you will feel something itching in you, some trace surviving from your time at Duke, pressing the reminder that there is always more to live and understand. Walk ten thousand miles. Read ten thousand books.

My friends, a journey of becoming brought you to Duke. At Duke you traveled the next stage of that journey. Now the journey requires that you go on to another stage. There's pain in leaving a place and life you loved, but this is a growing pain: its opposite would be not pleasure but stasis or regression. In a poignant letter penned just after he finished *Moby-Dick*, Herman Melville wrote, "Lord, when shall we be done growing?" He knew the answer. When will you be done growing? With luck, never; to live is to grow. You have filled this place with splendid life. Now it's too familiar, so you have to break out of here to win room to advance. Walk ten thousand miles. Read ten thousand books. Keep going, and keep growing. Time to go. Go well.

Budgets, International Opportunities, the Humanities

February 17, 2011

My thanks to Craig Henriquez and the Academic Council for hosting the annual faculty meeting. It gives me a chance to express my main message to Duke's faculty: my admiration and gratitude for the work you do. This winter I've been going around meeting with members of the faculty school by school. Each session has reminded me how many smart people we have here; how interesting and consequential the problems are to which you've applied your curiosity; how seriously you've thought about the needs of our students; and how imaginatively you've come together to create new programs, indeed new models of education. Add your work on searches, reviews, and other committees—your "service opportunity," as I call it—and I have to admit, you do a lot for Duke. If this school is flourishing, I know whom we have to thank.

Reviewing the topics I could speak on today, I've elected to say a word on three: our financial situation, Duke's global programs, and the way traditional fields of study expand in importance even as we open up new fields.

First the numbers. Two short years ago, in February 2009, the greatest economic meltdown since the Great Depression had been in progress for months and had still not found its bottom. We couldn't know what further perils might lie in store, but given the hit to our endowment, it was clear that we would need to move to a budget around $100 million smaller than we had been projecting. By one year back, in February 2010, markets had stabilized and begun to mend. Coupled with the internal discipline Duke mounted, in which you each played a part, this enabled us to say that we had closed more than half of the budget hole in the first year of a three-year walk-down.

One year later our situation continues to improve. For the calendar year 2010, DUMAC posted a return on our investments of better than 15.6 percent. (When Executive Vice President Tallman Trask earlier spoke of 13.2 percent, he was referring to the fiscal year that ended in June 2010.) Philanthropic contributions to Duke, which had reached a historic high of $386 million in fiscal year 2007–8, then fell to $301 million in the year of the meltdown, climbed back to $346 million in fiscal year 2009–10, an increase of 15 percent. With the market crash, many gifts for endowment fell below their initial value and so failed to throw off their anticipated income. But with rising markets, underwater endowments are breaking the surface and beginning to supply the funds their donors intended. As of December 31, 2009, $380 million in endowments were underwater, leading to foregone income on the order of $19 million. By the same date in 2010, $235 million of these endowments had recovered their original value, throwing off nearly $12 million in anticipated funds.

Meanwhile continued austerity and administrative efficiency across the university have kept us on the path to a rebased and sustainable budget, while through decanal leadership and faculty ingenuity, schools have found ways to increase income while creating valuable new programs.

Through this combination of means, we have accomplished around two-thirds of the planned reduction, and revenue growth has reduced the remaining shortfall. This is good news. But for a host of reasons, it's not yet time to loosen our restraint.

Having lived through several years of extraordinary volatility and unpleasant surprises, it would be profoundly foolish for us to believe that we can predict the future now, or that our prospects can only go up. Further, even with the rebound, we have not yet climbed back to where we started, and we continue to feel the drag from the endowment's worst-performing years. In addition, if revenues and expenses have come back to something near equilibrium, we will still need spending discipline in order to create a margin for new initiatives and expenditures—including the compensation increase we intend to make after two "raise-free" years.

Also, our revenue sources have different drivers, and some are newly imperiled even as others return to health. Federal research dollars were augmented by the financial crisis in the short term. The American Recovery and Reinvestment Act stimulus, one of the first by-products of the downturn, gave an unexpected lift to Duke, which ranked fourth in the competition for ARRA NIH funding. But as the recession eases, the new politics of the federal deficit threaten serious reductions to federal research budgets, and almost certainly an end to growth. Since innovation flowing from research universities continues to be such an important economic engine, we will fervently make the case that cutting research support is a short-term fix but a long-term folly. But given current realities, we cannot be confident that argument will win the day.

In sum, though we have weathered the worst of the storm, we are not yet back on easy street, and we need to continue to exercise virtues you may have grown tired of. Through its maturity, self-discipline, and willingness to set priorities, the Duke faculty has brought this university through a season of great challenge in a remarkably healthy state. Let's not imperil that achievement by a return of irrational exuberance. The work that needed doing wasn't fun, but we've done it well. Now is the time to see it through.

At a forum I attended two weeks back, a student asked me why we are expanding overseas activities while we are still weathering a financial crisis at home. It's a fair and an important question, and I will answer it as honestly as I can. Let me say, first, that I emphatically agree that the excellence of our core business must always be our highest priority. Second, we now understand that the successful launch of our China project will likely bring the central university some cost—this is now estimated at between $1.5 and $2 million a year for the first five years, an amount we hope will be reduced through philanthropy. But this is a fairly modest sum in a budget of more than a billion dollars, and it does not significantly trade off against the many other projects we also have in hand. (For scale you might remember that Duke has laid out nearly $5 million a year in strategic funds to launch the highly successful Global Health Institute.)

Third, and for me this is the heart of the matter, our global projects are indeed distractions if they are not of high strategic value. But if they are strategic, it's crucial that we not relinquish them in lean times. The greatest threat that downturns pose to universities is to stunt forward movement and lock in the status quo. The university that fares best will be the one that, while protecting existing activities and commitments, is alert to emerging opportunities and willing to take the steps to seize them.

It's a truism but not less true for that: globalization, the interconnection and reciprocal modification of physically remote human communities along every axis of interaction (economic, cultural, demographic, climatic), is the most salient feature of modern reality. As places devoted to understanding the world and transmitting that understanding to the rising talent of the future, universities have a fundamental stake in deepening their grasp of the globalizing world. Put negatively, universities that refuse to expand their horizons will pay the price for this failure to evolve. You know the reasons, but let me enumerate the main ones.

1. Through the communities of talent they assemble, universities catalyze breakthroughs and discoveries—and the higher the talent, the more potent the result. Since talent pools are now transnational, a university must draw the most powerful and creative minds from around the world to stay at the forefront of discovery.

2. Intellectual work is increasingly done collaboratively, in partnerships not limited by physical location. The university that fails to build connectivity to a broad array of high-end partners will be the backwater of tomorrow.

3. The expansion of quality higher education outside the U.S. and developed world is in our interest, not just that of others. Education is the unlocker of human potential: no country should wish for a monopoly on that market. Also, education trains people to work constructively on the great human challenges. In a world where all major problems have global determinants, it will not suffice to have well-trained people in a few favored sites.

4. Plus we need international connectivity to teach students well at home. One function of universities has always been to de-provincialize us, to throw the world open for appreciation and discovery when we are at the age of maximum receptivity. And for each generation of students, the relevant horizon becomes

wider. To continue to draw the best students and give them what they need, we must ensure that going to Duke means initiating a mental journey into a broader world even when they stay in classrooms here.

To my mind, an international project will be truly strategic to the extent that it hits these multiple targets in a fairly direct way. Our Singapore project showed how this might work. In a 2001 study called the Oxburgh Report, Singapore diagnosed itself as lacking a form of higher education it judged critical to its further development: the sort of research-based medical education that prepares for careers in biomedical and translational research. To cure this deficiency, the government of Singapore invited Duke to partner in creating a new school that would feature the Duke medical curriculum. The Duke–National University of Singapore Graduate Medical School, which graduates its first class this May, has met Singapore's goal of human capital formation while yielding many benefits to Duke. It has made our name visible across Asia as synonymous with top medical education, strengthening our lure for global talent. It has enabled us to hire faculty who wanted to be affiliated with Duke but had reasons for wishing to work in Southeast Asia, deepening our expertise in fields for which that is a natural research base (for instance, emerging infectious diseases). It has given us a point of connection to other research sites in South Asia, for instance in India. And it has created a space to try out new teaching formats that have proved sufficiently successful that we are beginning to "re-import" them into classes here.

China's extraordinary emergence as a global player would seem a sufficient reason to increase our connection there. The role of higher education in this process has created a place for us to plug in. A nation that plans on a scale and executes with a rapidity unthinkable in this country, China determined fifteen years ago that higher education was a rate-limiting factor on economic and social development, and set out to massively expand educational opportunities. Between 1997 and 2006, higher education enrollment increased by 350 percent, to a total of 15 million students. China has since become convinced that the quality of higher education is as much a problem as quantity was once. Accordingly, it is differentially investing to build up the high end of its higher education spectrum—and reworking not just its size but its interior intellectual structures.

Two glimpses of this process were particularly revealing to me. Last April, in conjunction with the opening of the Shanghai Expo, the Chinese government convened a gathering of—guess which celebrities and global movers and shakers? University presidents, from China and elite schools around the world. If I say such national prioritizing of higher education seems virtually un-American, I do not mean that altogether as a compliment to us. But what was more amazing was that, after sitting attentively as the presidents of Stanford, Yale, Chicago, Duke, Oxford, and others explained the foundations of our hugely successful form of education, Chinese university leaders gave their own talks on interdisciplinarity, problem-based instruction, in-class debate, and other hallmarks of Western instruction, eager to display their command of international best practices.

One of the Chinese presidents I have gotten to know, an education leader as thoughtful and articulate as any in my acquaintance, told me in a private talk that China's impressive accomplishments in fields like engineering were limited by lack of related strength in the humanities and social sciences. "Do you mean," I asked, "that you want top departments of economics and anthropology and the rest?" He replied, "What I really mean is that we are a nation with problems that will overwhelm us if we do not address them soon. We are training people in the technical ends of these problems, but to fully deal with them, we also have to think them through at the level of social impact, public policy, culture and behavior—in short, in all their dimensions at once."

If this is the right time to increase our presence in China, it is because our partners want what a school like Duke can provide: broad training to engage in complex problem solving for the larger human good. You will recall that our first programs will be taught at the junction of business management, environmental management, and health. If the Singapore example holds, by projecting such Duke programs in Kunshan, we can help meet a global education need; simultaneously make Duke globally visible as a leader in cross-disciplinary education; simultaneously create a workspace for Duke faculty inquiry in China and a base for collaboration with a range of Chinese partners; and simultaneously build a place for Duke students to work together with their parallel numbers from other countries and for Duke teachers to learn things to bring back to classrooms here.

We continue to make substantial progress working out the preliminaries for the project. We have achieved a major clarification of financial arrangements with the municipality of Kunshan. Duke experts in human resources, land use, purchasing, and related fields have traveled to Kunshan to avoid misunderstandings down the road. By Chinese law, a Chinese academic partner must cosponsor the newly founded educational entity, and we appear to have found a suitable partner in Wuhan University, a top-ten university, which has been highly respectful in our negotiations of Duke's leadership role. We have also found philanthropic support to help defray the costs of the launch. It is our hope to be able to submit the application to the Ministry of Education in mid-March 2011 for an anticipated opening in late 2012. Greg Jones and Peter Lange will keep the Academic Council informed as events unfold.

As we embark on this venture, we must frankly acknowledge that China does not share this country's attitudes toward open inquiry, freedom of expression, and free access to information. These are not trivial things for an American university. The intellectual culture we take such pride in is founded on these exact values. Not only do we need to insist on them to the fullest possible extent in building a Duke in Kunshan; the Chinese themselves must learn to accept and embrace them if they are to get the worth of their bargain. Duke education is the spirit in which it is conducted quite as much as any fixed curriculum. If our Chinese partners want to re-create a world-class form of education, they need to grapple with the spirit as well as the letter of our ways.

For all that, to believe we would enjoy exactly the same freedoms in China as we do in the United States would be to forget the first truth of globalization: we're all connected, but things aren't the same in other places as they are at home. To be a good global citizen, we need to learn how to expose others to our thinking and open ourselves to theirs, and to accommodate differences without violating fundamental beliefs. I cannot guarantee that the process will be conflict-free. We do know that we have worked well with highly responsive partners over a long period, and that if a major conflict were to develop that could not be resolved, it would be in our power to terminate the venture.

But we have to hope the project will succeed. China and the United States have become big-power competitors, but none of us can wish to see another cold war. Our main hope for averting such a scenario will be that men and women on both sides have been schooled to understand one another's issues and to accommodate competing interests, to the benefit of all. Developing *that* human capital will remain a key function of the world's great universities.

I'll close with a word on another subject. At the request of a bipartisan group of federal legislators, the American Academy of Arts and Sciences has created a commission to strengthen the role of the humanities and social sciences in American life, which I've been asked to cochair. This news makes me want to say what I hope is obvious to all: if it's important for universities to keep investing in new initiatives, it is equally important to sustain the traditional bases of liberal arts education.

These forms and newer concepts like interdisciplinarity and internationalization are not mutually exclusive alternatives. They are interdependent to the deepest degree; the example at hand perfectly illustrates the fact. If we are planning to "understand" China in anything but a facile or delusional manner, that won't happen without help from the study of Chinese language, Chinese philosophy, and Chinese government and economic structures, and the way they have both revised and perpetuated elements from earlier Chinese history. We won't understand the shape of hopes and fears in a changing China without access to Chinese literature, photography, and film, not to mention psychology. If, in our China project, we become perplexed that "universal" human rights are neither universally observed nor even universally valued, and if we then want to know where the idea of universal human rights came from and what its status is worldwide, we'll be at an utter loss if we do not have recourse to ethics, the history of religion, political philosophy, cultural anthropology, international relations, and international law. Tellingly, what China most admires in us is an education built on the broad-based, combinatory learning we call the liberal arts.

For their own importance and the contribution they make to every area of understanding, universities must promote the health of the humanities broadly conceived. The humanities have sometimes felt ignored in the priorities articulated by modern universities, and humanists have not always been as active as they might in communicating their value to those outside their zone. But there will be a cost for our whole project if these fields are not both internally vibrant and rich in connectivity.

We're lucky to have humanistic colleagues whose specialized study has enriched understandings far from their fields. Art history professor Hans Van Miegroet has built on his expertise in artistic modernity to create bridges to computer science, engineering, and image-based fields emerging in the wake of the digital revolution that we scarcely have a name for, in Duke's Visual Studies Initiative. Divinity professor Ellen Davis has excavated a forgotten environmentalism in the Hebrew Bible, showing that the covenant to be God's chosen people was a covenant also to care for the land. Through her mastery of ancient Hebrew we learn of a long prehistory of environmental values that modern, typically secular environmental movements could learn to appeal to.

This January, at the second Winter Forum, the Global Health Institute simulated a pandemic, giving undergraduates virtual experience in decision making in a situation of urgency, ethical complexity, and confusing, rapidly changing "facts." It will not surprise you that faculty in infectious diseases and health policy helped devise the exercise. But another key architect was Priscilla Wald, professor of English, expert in American literature, and a pioneering student of the role of narratives in health crises.

When the earthquake devastated Haiti one year back, Duke faculty from many fields came together to create a shared research space, the Haiti Lab, with graduate and undergraduate students included as partners. The Haiti Lab was able to draw on the expertise of global health faculty like Kathy Walmer, who with her husband, David, runs a family health clinic in Haiti, and legal rights scholars like the Law School's Guy-Uriel Charles. But the lead creators of the Haiti Lab were Laurent Dubois and Deborah Jenson, professors of history and romance studies, meaning that Duke's research and relief efforts were grounded in the understanding of Kreyol history, language, and culture; and the Franklin Humanities Institute served as host for the lab.

The Winter Forum, the Haiti Lab, and the Visual Studies Initiative are wonderful examples of humanistic knowledge extending itself into apparently distant areas to enrich the understanding of all. Like Kunshan, these initiatives were all either launched or matured in the depths of the recession.

I conclude with this: Great universities don't advance by the logic of either-or. Wallace Stevens writes in his poem "Notes toward a Supreme Fiction"

> He had to choose. But it was not a choice
> Between excluding things. It was not a choice
> Between, but of. He chose to include the things
> That in each other are included, the whole,
> The complicate, the amassing harmony.

Given finite resources, Duke too is always having to choose. But it is not a choice between excluding things. Arts and sciences, here and abroad, established programs and new initiatives, traditional disciplines and cross-disciplinary inquiry—all have their place in the work we do. So our task is appropriately to support each element and to put them in their most illuminating interrelation, to build "the whole, the complicate, the amassing harmony" our partial efforts could compose. Money is scarcer than it was, but our project has never been to have a lot of money. It is to build the liveliest, most comprehensive, and most searching place of inquiry we can possibly envision, with whatever resources we have at hand. My thanks for your work in our common task.

....

Reynolds Price

Duke Chapel, May 19, 2011

The poet, novelist, essayist, and memoirist Reynolds Price (1933–2011) embodied
the best of Duke decade after decade for thousands of people both here and afar,
starting with the students he taught in a fifty-year career as James B. Duke Profes-
sor of English. Delivered at his memorial service.

Welcome to Duke Chapel and today's celebration of Reynolds Price,
Duke's James B. Duke Professor of English, national literary treasure,
and unforgettable friend. Reynolds's brother Bill tells me that the date of
this service is the same as the day of their mother's death: life's nonsense
pierces us with strange relations! We have begun by hearing Reynolds
read from a poem by Ben Jonson at the memorial for one of his great
friends, Duke divinity professor W. D. Davies. This magic triad formed
the circuitry of Reynolds's life: a self, the word, and a friend.

Reynolds was supremely a man of the word; lover of scripture, which
he translated so powerfully; lover of literature, whether ancient or modern, since both were equally alive to him; and of course producer of his
own memorable words, written but also spoken, his conversation being
arguably his greatest masterpiece. (If he were here, you know he would
be whispering sly asides and rolling his eyes.) But to a remarkable extent,
the word was the agent of affection for Reynolds, creator and sustainer
of deep personal bonds. Love of the word brought Reynolds the friendships that form a who's who of twentieth-century literature: Spender and

Styron and Welty, John Updike and Anne Tyler and Toni Morrison, and many more. And connecting to others through the heritage of words was the heart of his other great vocation: his work as teacher.

Reynolds started as a freshman at Duke in 1951 and, after his brief truancy as a Rhodes scholar, served continuously on the faculty from 1958 to 2011. For more than half a century, Reynolds gave Duke its main embodiment of the man of letters and, above all, its figure of the great teacher—the teacher using his profound engagement with texts to awaken the capacity for profound engagement in his students. I came across a quote from Emerson that put me in mind of his special effect: "The whole secret of the teacher's force lies in the conviction that men are convertible. And they are. They want awakening. Get the soul out of bed, out of her deep habitual sleep." Through the medium of Milton and the gospels, by animating those words with his energies of insight and feeling, Reynolds woke up generations of Dukies, making students his cherished friends in the process.

I have yet to speak of Reynolds as disabled. His illness and disability meant that there were in effect two halves to the lives of Reynolds Price. Remember what he said in *A Whole New Life*? When you irrevocably lose some power taken for granted in your daily identity all life long, the only thing to do is to "find your way to . . . the next viable you," "the next incarnation of who you must be." (I think of Milton and his blindness: "So much the rather thou, celestial light/Shine inward, there plant eyes.") On the other side of the divide that made a total difference to his experience of his body, Reynolds's core self remained or became, if anything, stronger. To the end of his days, Reynolds was the lover of words and of the friends created through the sharing of words. He wrote in one poem, "Who thinks deepest loves the liveliest."

We are grateful for the friends who will share in words their love of Reynolds Price.

On the Use of New Freedoms

Duke Chapel, August 24, 2011

I read a story in the *New York Times* that put me in mind of you. The story was about an American high school student who, drawing on his summer experience in China, was able "to create a standout personal statement" in his college applications, which told of exploring ancient tombs of the Ming dynasty and "trading jokes with long-dead Ming emperors." Don't laugh: last year you too had to create the impression that you were one of the wonders of the world. And it worked! Human marvels, I welcome you to Duke.

I believe that each of you is great. But my point in telling the story is, you don't have to do that any more. You no longer need to compose a show of yourself in order to impress colleges. You are *free* of that. In fact, you are entering on a freedom the likes of which you have never experienced and will seldom experience again.

Let's take the measure of this new, free life. First, you'll be out from under parental supervision (bye bye, Mom and Dad), with no loving busybodies to wake you up or ask what time you got in. Second, your new life is amazingly unprogrammed. Unlike high school, where the algorithm filled your academic program pretty predictably from year to year, here you'll have a wilderness of choices, with a few simple rules on how to use the menu. Third, for years your life has been structured by routines whose origins were long forgotten. But you haven't formed a single Duke habit; your life here is a blank slate waiting to be composed.

Fourth, one day you'll have others to support, but as of now, you're free of dependents. Fifth and best of all, you don't need to get a full-time job. One of the beauties of going to college is that when people ask you what you do for a living, you can simply say, "I go to Duke." End of discussion. If you are already fretting about the job you'll get after you graduate four long years from now, all I can say is, some people just can't stand the taste of freedom.

I want you to stop and do justice to this profound truth. Around the world, people fight and die for freedom. But when you enter Duke, this priceless privilege is yours for the asking. Released from so many constraints, you have the chance to be the maker of your life. My plea to you is, put this great freedom to some extraordinary use.

Let me descend to some particulars. In college you will have freer access to alcohol, sex, and other what used to be called adult pleasures. I trust this is not news to you: the association of college, drinking, and sex in an alcoholic haze was already well documented in Chaucer's *Canterbury Tales*, written in the fourteenth century. As for drinking, you know the law and are obliged to obey it. But such laws have never made alcohol and the conduct it aggravates less prevalent on any American campus. Many of you have strong values on this score, and many of you will find those values tested. My message to you all is, this is a domain of freedom. Make it the object of your conscious and thoughtful choice.

It would be disappointing if, after telling us that you longed to chat with Ming emperors, the height of your college aspiration really was to live like a bit player in a college reality TV show. I say it seriously: Take responsibility for your conduct; don't do things you are not proud of. And if you say, of any practice you'd really rather not partake of, "Well, I have to, or what will They think?," I reply, "Have some courage and see where it gets you." Having escaped the tyranny of all kinds of adult supervision, it seems a poor sequel to cave in to the tyranny of some imagined Them. Here's the truth: If they were candid, they might turn out to be ambivalent too and to welcome alternatives and frank discussion.

My first rule for the use of your freedom is Build a life you can be proud of. My second, at least as important, is Make great education happen for you.

You've come along at a strange historical moment. The economy used to rebound from recessions, but no one knows where it is heading now.

In the twentieth century the spread of consumerism drove economic expansion, but now free spending has brought us to a crisis point. But how to reduce personal and national indebtedness without stifling growth? It's complicated. Meanwhile, a raised standard of living has raised energy use and unhealthy diets around the world. How to separate the growth of well-being from the health and climate disasters that come in its wake? It's complicated. We thrilled at the stories of freedom's global spread last spring, but creating a new social order has proved far more challenging than those happy headlines suggested. As I said: it's complicated. Here in the U.S. no one is certain if our vaunted political system is capable of making hard choices or solving complex social ills. It's very complicated.

With uncertainty at every side, it's easy to see how you could think your main college task was to make a beeline for some well-paid job. But there are at least two things wrong with that picture. For one, our emerging challenges are so interdependent and all-encompassing that no known job can reliably remove anyone from their reach; and second, the world will be in sorry shape if all smart young men and women withdraw into insular, prosperous cocoons. You're going to have greater success and a happier life if instead of fleeing the hard facts of your time, you try to understand them, engage them, and shape better outcomes in place of worse.

You are the very people who could make that kind of difference. That's why we admitted you. (Did you really think it was because of your standout personal statement?) But to deliver on your potential down the road, you need this place to broaden and deepen your understanding and strengthen your active powers. Which brings us back to your freedom and your use of it at Duke.

Duke is a place of amazing abundance. The resources are here to teach and fortify you in every way you can imagine. Plus I never saw a school where so many people are so responsive to student interest and initiative. But as the saying goes, you can lead a horse to water, but you can't make him drink. To turn Duke opportunities into your personal strengths, you have to want them, reach out to them, and actively incorporate them into your life. It's your choice, but it matters what you do.

It's in your power to create the dullest academic program compliant with Duke's minimum formal requirements—if you want to do that, we can scarcely stop you. But it's also in your power to make our curriculum light up with your curiosity and discovery. Out of class, you could give your brain a four-year rest; or, with the slightest effort, you could involve yourself in the flow of discussion that fills this campus every day, by which people sharpen each other's ability to think. It's in your power to create a Duke filled with people of the sort you already know and have least to learn from. Or you could take advantage of belonging to one of the most varied and talented human communities on the face of the earth and open yourselves to each other, teach each other, and find out what you can accomplish together. Wherever I go, what I find most in demand throughout the world are smart, quick minds who know how to work creatively with others across divides of expertise, discipline, and culture. At work and play, every day here is a chance to learn that critical skill—or, with some difficulty, I admit, you could leave this skill undeveloped. It makes a difference. You make the choice.

I once saw a guy in a shirt that read, "I Went to the Sorbonne and All I Got Was This Lousy Tee Shirt." It's up to you what you get from Duke. I don't doubt that you will have an extraordinary experience here; I just don't want it to fall one inch short of what it could be. Want to know how you could really make a standout personal statement? By having your own dreams for your education and using Duke to help you fulfill them. That's what you came for. That's what we're here for. Come in and join the fun.

The Fire That Never Goes Out

Nasher Museum of Art, October 21, 2011

When U.S. Representative David Price received the John Tyler Caldwell Award from the North Carolina Humanities Council, I was asked to give the Caldwell Lecture in the Humanities.

Eudora Welty's 1944 essay "Some Notes on River Country" begins with this memorable line: "A place that ever was lived in is like a fire that never goes out." Some years back, I went to see the country she describes. This is the stretch of land west of Jackson, Mississippi, and north of Natchez whose settlements are at once weirdly abandoned yet also weirdly preserved. Its chief sites are Windsor, a mansion near Port Gibson whose pomp survives only in an intact set of Corinthian columns; Grand Gulf, a thriving international cotton port until the Mississippi washed the town away; and Rodney's Landing, a river town successful enough to have built a series of exquisitely ornamented churches in the 1840s, until the river changed course and left it high and dry.

These are enchanting places, but the average visitor would draw their lesson very differently from Welty. For these are icons of desolation, images of the utter transience of this world's glory. Windsor, once a great house, survives exclusively as a ruin. Grand Gulf, once a boom town, was wiped from the face of the earth, leaving only the overgrown graves of forgotten entrepreneurs. Rodney's churches still stand, but wholly disconnected from the people who built and used them. Those people have vanished—and lest anyone miss the lesson of the extinction of the human, this town is approached through mile after mile covered exclusively with vines.

So how could she say, "A place that ever was lived in is like a fire that never goes out"? If one thing is true of these places, it's that their life did go out. And yet, and yet: Welty felt their distant force when she visited, and I experienced the connection when I went decades later. So how was this? Welty's reply is that the spark of "original ignition," having been once struck, lives on: "Sometimes it gives out glory, sometimes its little light must be sought out to be seen, small and tender as a candle flame, but as certain." But in truth, these places did not simply stay in life: they were brought back to life by the mind of a latter-day observer, reanimated by her powers of perception, sympathy, and imagination.

I am here to speak in praise of the humanities, and I begin with my Welty tale to remind us what the humanities are. The humanities aren't just the subjects listed in college course catalogs—literature, philosophy, history, music, and the other arts—though those are certainly included. The humanities are a name for the process by which all the things humans have made, said, thought, and done come back to spark the understandings of other humans across time.

Two facts make this transaction possible. The first is that humans make things, express themselves through the materials that surround them, and that these wrought things—a tool, a house, a picture or song, an expressed idea—live on when their fashioners have departed. Faulkner said that the work of art is "the artist's way of scribbling 'Kilroy was here' on the walls of the final and irrevocable oblivion through which he must someday pass." But it isn't only art objects that have this trick of persistence. The idea of representative government was envisioned, once upon a time, by people who have long since left the scene. In Faulkner's *Requiem for a Nun*, the most everyday mark made by the homeliest figures—the name a country wife carved in a window pane—announces the fact of her human being: *Listen, stranger; this was myself; this was I.*

Second, as we make things that outlive their makers, another of our innate capacities is that we go out in spirit toward the works of others. Humans have the peculiar ability—and, judging by the amount of time we spend reading, watching videos, and listening to music, arguably even a fundamental need—to exit the confines of our own experience and to take up mental residence in spaces created by others. Put these two together and you get the difference the humanities make. This gift for *going out* of ourselves and *entering into* things is what gives fresh being to creations whose origins are distant in space and time. As we "get into" it, the book or song composed by another comes to life again as our experience. As Welty trains her gaze on Windsor or Rodney, she feels the obscure life of which these are the remains.

When we live outside ourselves with sufficient intensity of feeling, we in turn have a chance to be changed. This is the way we annex understandings that have been struggled toward by others that we would never have reached on our own. This is how we get to see the world differently from the way our own mind or culture habitually presents it, and recognize that our customary outlook is not the only point of view. This is how we learn that there is more to human history than the present, and that our present is itself a moment in time. This is how we begin to understand the other customs, beliefs, and values men and women live by in other countries (or indeed within our own country) and to imagine how differences can be accommodated for a common good.

Understood this way, the humanities are not a specialized taste but the root of the most basic human and civic competencies. If we lacked these gifts, we would be condemned to the harshest of poverties: dependence on our own unaided selves. Collectively we would have little idea where we came from or where we could be going. So it matters how this impulse is fed.

I spoke of the humanities as the interplay of human making and human receiving. But a third thing is needed for the reaction to work: some mediating or connecting force, something to bring the past to the present's attention. Welty was brought to her River Country partly by her work as a photographer for the Works Progress Administration, the Depression-era agency that commissioned photographers to record the life of regions. I was brought there through the medium of Welty's essay and photographs: in a million years I would never have happened onto these places on my own.

Since this is so, when we think about the health of the humanities, we need to think of the agencies that carry the human legacy across to its new receivers and that teach the forms of attention that bring distant things to life.

I'm not a native North Carolinian (had you guessed?), but since moving here I've learned a fair bit about the lives that have been lived in this state, so I have my own thank-you list of institutions that taught me. It was in the brand-new Nasher Museum that I got to see the films H. Lee Waters made in small Piedmont towns in the 1930s and 1940s, when he would first catch everyday people in everyday activities, then circle back and allow the town to become the movie audience for their own daily selves. It was at the North Carolina History Center at Tryon Palace in New Bern that I got to see the tools of timber workers from the naval stores industry and oyster harvesters from the Sound and to hear letters in faint and fading hands voiced into compelling life.

Sorry I started it; this list is far too long to complete. The agencies involved in this broad work of education include elementary and high schools, colleges, universities, and community colleges, museums, libraries, and concert venues, and all manner of formal and informal community activities, from book clubs on up. Keeping all these strong is essential to our civic well-being. Tonight's host, the North Carolina Humanities Council, helps North Carolinians by the thousands learn the many stories that, entered into with delight and added to our store of knowledge, can make us one people, as your tagline says.

But with every gratitude to this rich array of teachers, my first North Carolina immersion came through my own research. So I hope you'll allow me to share the story of how I began going to Carolina in my mind, long before I ever imagined living here.

Charles Waddell Chesnutt was the major African American writer of the post–Civil War generation. Like many writers in his tradition, he was unread and virtually unheard of at the time of my graduate training. He began to be noticed in the 1980s, at which time I read his volume of tales *The Conjure Woman*, loved it, and began to teach it. From there it was an easy step to giving a paper on Chesnutt at a scholarly conference, in which I mentioned drafts of an early Chesnutt novel named *Rena Walden*. After the talk, a stranger in the audience, Reynolds Smith, longtime humanities editor at Duke University Press, came up to ask if I would be interested in doing an edition of this manuscript. Perhaps so, I said, and filed the thought away.

Some months later I had the idea of going to inspect this manuscript, which, like all Chesnutt's papers, had been deposited in the Special Collections of the Fisk University Library. Five minutes after arriving, it was clear that there was no such edition to be made. But since I had two days in Nashville before my return flight, I opened some other boxes in the archive and started into the journals Chesnutt kept in his late teens and twenties, between 1874 and 1882.

This was one of those uncanny moments when the past's fire reignites. Here I was, reading the penmanship of a young man who had written these words 125 years before, in a moment that must have felt as present and alive to him as my present moment was to me. I was hearing confided hopes, fears, and ambitions he had perhaps only ever shared with his diary, with no thought that they would ever be read by others.

After that, off and on for the space of a year, I kept company with Chesnutt, transcribing the journal and trying to grasp the milieu it arose from. This took me mentally to Fayetteville and what to me were a series of revelations. I knew in some abstract way that North Carolina had an unusually large free black population before emancipation: John Hope Franklin, later to be my colleague, had written a book on this subject. Well, here was such a person in his living actuality: a black man from a slave state, neither of whose parents had been slaves. From Booker T. Washington I knew of the ardent desire of blacks during Reconstruction to reclaim the education that had been denied them before. But I would not have guessed that, when free blacks, including Chesnutt's father, contributed the money to found the Howard School, the consequence was that Fayetteville had a grade school for African American children before it had one for whites. History is particular and thus full of surprises.

Charles Chesnutt was the prize pupil of this newly founded school. Astonishingly precocious, he became the head of school at the age of twenty-two, when it was designated to be one of North Carolina's first two state-supported teacher training institutions, the State Colored Normal School. (The other, white school was the education school at UNC.) Chesnutt's journal supplies access to the thoughts and feelings of a gifted young black person living with the new opportunities and old restrictions this time and place provided. Let's tune in to a moment in this vanished yet visitable past.

July 1874. "While Mister Harris was packing up to-day for his Northern trip, I came upon his journal, one which he kept several years ago, and obtaining his permission, I have read a part of it. In fact nearly all. After reading it, I have concluded to write a journal too." From this first entry, we know that diary writing was a learned behavior for Chesnutt, a tribute of imitation paid to an admired teacher, and an index to how deeply Chesnutt identified with the new world of teachers, learning, and black educational opportunity.

Summer 1875. Chesnutt hunts for summer teaching jobs in the hinterland between Charlotte and Statesville. It's clear at once how the milieu that supports his aspirations gives him a jaundiced view of other, less privileged lives: "I inquired the way to Jonesville church, and by dint of stopping and inquiring at every house, and by climbing fences and crossing cotton fields, I arrived at Jonesville. Where the 'ville' was I am not able to say, for there was but one house within nearly half a mile of the 'church.' The church itself was a very dilapidated log structure, without a window; but there was no need of one, for the cracks between the logs furnished a plentiful supply."

On this scouting visit, Chesnutt found dinner and a bed with a local family, and his journal lets us tune in to a remarkable dialogue. "After supper we had a talk concerning schools, schoolteachers and preachers. The old man said that 'you teachers and preachers are too hard on us. You want us to pay you thirty or forty dollars a month for sitting in the shade, and that is as much as we can make in 2 or 3 months.'" It took me a while to learn that, having obtained a first-class teaching license (itself a fairly new bureaucratic invention for both white and black educators), Chesnutt was entitled to earn $40 a month as a teacher at age seventeen—a stupefying sum to the agricultural laborer he is speaking with. (Chesnutt was neither the first nor the last teacher whose work was not thought to be work at all by those doing manual labor.)

Secure in the superiority of certified skills, Chesnutt looks scornfully on this lame reply. But by chiding the older man for his cheapness, Chesnutt provokes a fuller articulation of where this man is coming from. "Well, but we haven't got any chance. We all of us work on other people's, white people's, land, and sometimes get cheated out of all we make; we can't get the money." I'm not too cheap to pay, the man rejoins. I am a tenant farmer. I live in another new postemancipation status, legally freed yet economically still dependent. So my income is not under my control.

As he gains a deepened sense of the social position of the person he is speaking with, Chesnutt becomes able to fashion a far more effective retort. "Well, you certainly make something?" "Yes." "Now, I'll tell you. You say you are all renters, and get cheated out of your labor, why don't you send your children to school, and qualify them to look out for themselves, to own property, to figure and think about what they are doing, so that they may do better than you?" To paraphrase: Education isn't an expensive scam; it's an investment. The less you think you can afford it, the more you actually need it. Put your money into your kids' education and they'll know how to control their social destiny.

Through this moment in Chesnutt's diaries, we catch people in the act of arguing out the costs and values of education in rural North Carolina ten years after the Civil War, at a time when both were new realities. The argument between educators and the public that pays them is a never-ending dialogue. But it helps to be reminded that funding arguments in our day come out of a long history; that people's views on such issues are always embedded in the circumstances of their social lives; and that we argue more effectively when we become better able to enter into another's other point of view.

With the slightest encouragement, I would go on all night on my work with the Chesnutt diary. But to ensure that David Price can go home with the medal he deserves, I will draw to a close. You have heard my argument. The humanities aren't a luxury good to be enjoyed by those with high discretionary income and a long pedigree in school. They're a fundamental need of our humanity. They enrich us as persons and enable our life with others. When access to them weakens, we pay a major cost.

Now as ever, the humanities need supporters, but we need to think how best to advance the case. In my experience, humanistic advocacy tends to take one of two general forms. On the one hand, devotees repeat mantras that resonate with those who have already undergone humanistic conversion but draw blank stares from the uninitiated. ("Only the humanities raise issues of life's meaning." If you don't already know, what exactly does that mean? "The humanities promote critical thinking." Now there's an un-self-critical thought!) On the other hand, aware that this sales pitch is falling flat, we reach for arguments thought to be surefire winners with the unhumanistic public, though we know they don't do justice to the cause: The arts are great because they are essential to economic development (they are, but that's not why they're great); or If we aren't trained in foreign languages and cultures, we won't be able to decode intelligence from terrorists (ditto).

What we need, before we ask others for investments, is to challenge ourselves to say what the humanities are good for, as simply and truly as we can manage, with examples that prove the point. It's not the easiest of tasks, but it's worth our hard thinking. The life you save may be your own.

....

Mary Duke Biddle Trent Semans

Duke Chapel, January 30, 2012

Like John Hope Franklin and Reynolds Price, Mary Duke Biddle Trent Semans (1920–2012) linked Duke's present to the best of its history, in her case stretching all the way back to its founding. The granddaughter of Benjamin N. Duke and the great-granddaughter of Washington Duke, she was an irrepressible force for good in Duke, Durham, and the region, and when she died at age ninety-two, the outpouring for her was unforgettable. Delivered at her memorial service.

Duke University welcomes you to this celebration of our beloved Mary Semans. This institution and Mary were so intertwined that neither had a life apart from the other. Mary was a young member of the Duke family when Duke University was created. The East and West Campuses were built when she was still a child. She moved to Durham full time at fourteen, shortly before Duke Chapel was completed. At fifteen, she enrolled at the Woman's College. From those days to this, she loved this university, knew pretty much everything that happened here, and gave support to every act that took Duke forward.

But though she had a profound institutional impact, in Mary's case good works took a very personal form. I remember how it started with me. On a December day in 2003, a stranger to this school, I was announced as the president who would succeed Nan Keohane. After the news conference, I was taken on a kind of victory lap to meet the greats of Duke University—a celebrated cancer surgeon, a celebrated basketball coach, and more. As the tour drew to a close, my guide told me with obvious excitement that it was going to work out for me to meet one more of Duke's giants, Mary Semans, our chief link to Duke's founding family.

Now Mary's name was not so well known to me as Coach K's. From a brief account, I was expecting a grand dame or even a kind of local royalty—Mary Duke Biddle Trent Semans! All those names! And I was not totally disappointed. When I was taken in to meet her, in the words of the novelist Henry James, this lady did have the air of being someone in particular. Such a sparkle to those eyes! Such stylishness! (Don't you love the fact that the commemorative picture on the Duke website is of Mary in bright yellow with the skirt quite short? As they say in Durham: Not Afraid of Flavor.)

But if she cut a figure, haughtiness was no part of the equation. When I arrived, Cindy and our son, Dan, had already been with Mary for ten or fifteen minutes, and when I came in, they were going at it a mile a minute, moving from one shared pleasure to another, as if they had known each other for years. She had engaged them; she had taken outsiders and made them quite at home—and at the end of two minutes, she had done the same for me.

I dwell on this because if Mary's work will live on through the institutions she supported—Duke University, The Duke Endowment, the UNC School of the Arts, the civic and cultural activities she supported in Durham—her effect arose from her unique skill at personal relations, the way she imbued each individual encounter with grace, attention, and love. Did you ever receive a thank-you note from Mary? I remember dozens, each of which made me feel like I was being fully *appreciated* for the first time in my life. When Mary took Cindy and me to the fiftieth-anniversary production of *West Side Story* at the School of the Arts, she singled out each young performer for the sincerest, warmest, most discerning appreciation. I have studied up on Mary's leadership in civil rights causes in Durham. As you know, as a widowed mother of four, she was one of the first two women ever elected to the city council, on the ticket with the integrationist mayor Mutt Evans; later she became the leader, with Elna Spaulding, of the cross-racial group Women-in-Action for the Prevention of Violence and Its Causes. But these civic acts were built on personal acts of engagement and appreciation, friendships Mary built person by person across artificial social divides. Not just racial divides, but *all* divides. Who hasn't heard tales of Mary stopping to embrace people and ask about their families as she did her grocery shopping, or stopping by at a local merchant's to ask how business was? If Mary knew you, then you mattered.

When Mary Semans was honored at the Nasher Museum two years back, I found a phrase that I haven't been able to improve on: she was the embodiment of unconditional love. She saw more good in others than any of us are used to seeing in ourselves, and she made you want to *be* the person that she believed in. She made this city, this university, and this region better in actuality by the way she believed in their possibility. She couldn't help it: that's what it meant to be Mary D. B. T. Semans.

Lucky us, to be part of the world that Mary Semans loved and made.

Duke and Race

Duke University, March 22, 2012

Through the years I've used this address to take a step back from the particulars of this council's business and reflect on some larger challenge confronting the university. In recent years I have spoken on the affordability of higher education, the financial downturn and our need to keep innovating even when resources are stretched, and the rationale for Duke's growing activities abroad. While I was considering possible topics for this spring's talk, a series of events kept returning my attention to a common theme. Within the space of a few weeks, this campus experienced controversy over a piece of unpublished faculty research that appeared to disparage the choice of majors by African American undergraduates. Shortly after, I attended the inaugural meeting of the steering committee planning the fiftieth-anniversary commemoration of the enrollment of the first African American undergraduates at Duke. A few days after that, I joined the university-wide celebration named in honor of Samuel DuBois Cook, Duke's first black professor and the first African American to hold regular rank appointment in any predominantly white college or university in the American South. That same day, we learned that the Supreme Court had decided to hear a new case regarding affirmative action in admissions, an issue last joined in the *Gratz* and *Grutter* cases in 2003.

Today I'd like to address the issue these episodes all converge on. I want to speak to the issue of race and inclusion in Duke's history, our recent progress, and the nature of the work that lies ahead.

To any present member of this community, it's almost inconceivable that Duke ever could have maintained a policy of racial exclusion. The school we see around us is so manifestly and exuberantly diverse, and the interaction of talent from all backgrounds is so clearly the precondition for the stimulation we experience here every day, that it's hard to fathom that Duke ever could have *been* otherwise, let alone that it could have been *wished* otherwise. But racial discrimination was once the official practice of this school, as it was of the surrounding region and, de facto, much of this land.

Segregation insisted that African Americans be restricted to a system of unequal opportunity that barred them from social privilege and cast them as inferior. Within this system, the most prosaic daily needs were tools for manufacturing invidious difference. Whites could ride in the front of the bus; blacks were sent to the back. Whites could use the "Whites Only" restroom; blacks were consigned to the one marked "Colored." Whites could stay in the best hotels when they traveled, but blacks had to hope to find a facility that would accept them or plan complex itineraries around welcoming stops. Whites could try on clothes in Southern department stores, but blacks had to buy clothes and hope they fit.

In one sense, school was just one more scene in this endless drama of discrimination, but in another, it was the key to the whole system. By consigning black children to separate-but-equal schools that were virtually never the equal in facilities or resources, the world of official segregation strove to make African Americans inferior in reality by giving them inferior access to knowledge and the power knowledge brings. It never totally worked. But even where outstanding personal achievement triumphed despite separate-but-equal schooling, the system imposed the emotional burden of frustration, exclusion, and consciousness of imputed inferiority.

My first acquaintance with North Carolina came from editing the journal that Charles Waddell Chesnutt, the premier African American author of the postbellum generation, kept as a young man in Fayetteville. This journal gives the most comprehensive record we have of the educational resources that became available to African Americans in the wake of emancipation. Chesnutt himself made extraordinary use of these resources: promoted to head the state-funded school for training black teachers when he was only twenty-two, he had already taught himself Latin, French, and German in his spare time. But while Chesnutt's journal documents an unsurpassable love of learning, it also chronicles the pains of inequality. When Chesnutt eventually met someone who could listen to him read Latin verse aloud and confirm that he had got the pronunciation right, it was a moment of swelling pride for this self-taught prodigy but also of stinging hurt, another reminder of everything he had been denied. Chesnutt writes, "It was like discharging the matter from an old sore."

The founding family of Duke University was extraordinarily progressive for its time in the matter of race. Washington Duke assisted the black entrepreneur John Merrick in founding what became the largest black insurance company and one of the largest black-owned business enterprises in America, Durham's North Carolina Mutual Life Insurance Company. Washington Duke's son Benjamin worked with James E. Shepard to provide support for the North Carolina College for Negroes, today's N.C. Central University. Duke family members gave funds and served on the board of the black hospital created in Durham, Lincoln Hospital. When James B. Duke wrote the indenture for the Duke Endowment, he made provisions for hospital care and higher education for both whites and blacks.

But measures like these mitigated the harms of segregation without undoing its conceptual core, and in its first decades, this university was surprisingly welcoming to blacks in certain ways yet closed to them in ways that count. Whenever I walk by Perkins Library I remember that John Hope Franklin did research for his classic book *From Slavery to Freedom* in the stacks at Duke. In the 1940s he was free to research here, but of course he could not teach here. It's an astounding proof of the logic of segregation that after John Hope got his PhD in history from Harvard, with support and recognition from some of the most prominent historians in America, the only jobs he could get in North Carolina were at black colleges: first St. Augustine's in Raleigh, then the North Carolina College for Negroes in Durham. Certainly not at Duke. Had he gone to a football game in Wallace Wade in the early 1960s, he would still have faced the humiliating signs indicating a separate entrance and seating section marked "Colored."

This history of racial exclusion is the history Duke set out to reverse with the admission of the first African American undergraduates and with the hiring of the first black professor. These pioneers have testified to the friendship and support they found here, but they have also spoken of the vestiges of the residual culture of imagined racial superiority they encountered and the burden of being "the first" and a "representative" of a whole people. Next year, when we celebrate the fiftieth anniversary of their arrival at Duke, we will celebrate the dignity and courage these individuals brought to an extraordinarily challenging experience—and equally important, the new history they helped Duke begin to write.

From that day to this, this university has had a commitment to making Duke a place of access, opportunity, and mutual respect for all. This commitment was confirmed in Duke's most recent strategic plan, and I reconfirm the commitment today. In fifty years of struggling toward this goal, this university has made significant progress, which we should remember with pride. Where there's work still to do, we should acknowledge it frankly and keep at our task.

Let me say a brief word on things accomplished and things left to do.

In the years since the 1960s, Duke has come to embrace a far broader mission of inclusiveness than was first foreseen. But while it neither is nor should be our sole concern, given our location and the history of this region, Duke has a special and continuing interest in affording opportunity for African Americans. The measures on this score are heartening. Between 9 and 11 percent of Duke's entering undergraduate classes in recent years have been African American. In given years, the proportion of African American students at Duke has been rivaled only by Stanford and Columbia among all our peers, and Duke has maintained the highest ten-year average among peer schools. The Duke Medical School continues to have one of the highest representations of blacks and underrepresented minorities among all the top medical schools. Brenda Armstrong, who was herself among the first African American students at Duke, recently shared this data with the President's Council on Black Affairs.

Actively working to broaden the pool of candidates has brought comparable gains to our faculty. Regular rank faculty appointments of African Americans in all schools have risen from 44 in 1993 to 72 in 1998 to 97 in 2003 to 122 in 2008 and 140 in 2011. The Faculty Climate Survey compiled every two years gives us a way of measuring the qualitative experience of Duke faculty both in aggregate and broken down by race and gender. The results of recent years have suggested generally comparable degrees of satisfaction across racial categories. This information is followed closely by the provost and vice provost for faculty diversity and faculty development and is reported annually to the Academic Council.

Staff are critical to the strength of this community, and on this front too Duke has made significant advances. Education is not important to our students only. Ideally, every job at Duke should give the chance for a continuing education that allows employees to do their work better and groom themselves for advancement. Two programs that help employees build their own human capital are the tuition benefit and the Duke Leadership Academy. Duke used to give employees a tuition benefit to pay for Duke course offerings relevant to their careers. Early in my administration, we made a change so employees can use the benefit for relevant coursework anywhere within North Carolina. Since this change, the number of staff taking advantage of the program has risen from 320 to 742. Fully 75 percent of these are women and 34 percent are African American, compared with 8 percent in 2006. Under guidance from Vice President Kyle Cavanaugh, the Duke Leadership Academy gives leadership training to employees across the university identified as promising candidates for further levels of responsibility. In each of the three classes to date, roughly half the attendees have been women and a significant number African American.

Duke can also take pride in the contribution we have made beyond our walls—in Durham and around the world. The change in admissions policy made in the 1960s was motivated by the desire to end the manifest injustice of exclusion on grounds of race, but it has had a far broader impact. By helping talented students from every background get the education to live up to their potential, we help our society reap the full measure of their promise. I get to see Duke alumni in action across the country almost every week. Come with me and you will see Duke graduates of every background and from every school filling virtually every career with energy and intelligence. When the 2012 White House Fellows were announced last fall, an extraordinarily selective honor, two of the fifteen were Duke graduates, and both were African American: Reggie Chambers, Class of 1998, a lawyer with expertise in finance, and Kisha Green Davis, Class of 2000, a doctor with expertise in community health.

I've cataloged a range of achievements, and they are significant. But our work is not done; even on fronts where progress has been made, commitment and persistent attention are needed to see the project through. Let me mention some areas of unfinished business and some steps we can take to advance.

First, it is vital that our academic and administrative units all maintain the culture of equity, opportunity, inclusiveness, and respect that the university aspires to as a whole. Going forward, I have asked Provost Lange, Chancellor Dzau, and Executive Vice President Trask to request an annual report from each academic and administrative unit on efforts related to diversity, with plans set for the coming year. The reports will be further reviewed by the vice president for institutional equity and the vice provost for faculty diversity and discussed by the entire senior leadership team. A summary of university-wide issues will be shared with the Executive Committee of the Academic Council and with the Human Resources Committee of the Board of Trustees each year, and a comprehensive report will be published for the Duke community every other year.

Second, regarding students. In a diverse community where people are still growing and discovering, every year will bring tensions and challenges. With respect to this January's controversy I would say the following. I hope all members of this community recognize that it is not the proper function of the university to block expression from its faculty or enforce a correct view. Universities live through free and open debate; when someone thinks someone else has come to an erroneous conclusion, the remedy is to criticize it and offer a better account. On the other hand, I can see why students took offense at what was reported of a professor's work. Generalizations about academic choices by racial category can renew the primal insult of the world we are trying to leave behind—the implication that persons can be known through a group identity that associates them with inferior powers. A further insult was that the paper had been included in an *amicus* brief submitted by opponents of affirmative action urging the Supreme Court to hear the case I mentioned earlier regarding admissions policies at the University of Texas.

In this or any such situation, the university cannot guarantee that students or other community members won't be distressed or angered by the expression of divergent points of view. But we do owe it to those who are distressed to listen to their experience, to promote understanding across the divide, and to pay deep attention to root issues. If Duke students are unable to pursue the educational goals they come here to attain, that's an institutional issue that deserves an institutional response. The everyday experience of students in the classroom is always a legitimate concern for the university, and I'm grateful for the work Laurie Patton, Steve Nowicki, and Lee Baker are doing in listening and working to ensure a supportive intellectual community for our undergraduates.

Let me speak to Duke's philosophy of admissions. When we offer admission to a student, we do so with confidence that the student will succeed and thrive. We pay attention to test scores for what they are worth, but we know they are an imperfect measure: at the end of the day, Duke's goal is not to reward high test scores but to recruit and train the level of talent that will make the highest degree of contribution to the university community and our future society. This potential needs to be assessed by many measures, including measures of character, drive, and good use of prior opportunity. We will continue to draw talent thus broadly assessed from every background. This policy is well within the bounds of current law. Duke will be joining with other universities in filing an *amicus* brief in support of holistic assessment of talent for admissions purposes. Strikingly, in the *Grutter* case, the most trenchant defense of a qualitative selection policy came from a group of twenty-nine high-ranking retired officers and civilian leaders of the U.S. military, including former chairmen of the Joint Chiefs of Staff and former secretaries of defense, who pointed out that for the military to function effectively, it is critical to have leadership that represents America's diversity.

In this vein, the single front where I myself feel the greatest frustration regards senior leadership positions at Duke. Since I arrived as president, I have appointed eight of my ten direct reports, and the provost and I have together appointed every sitting dean. My leadership recruits include two African Americans (Ben Reese and Phail Wynn), one Asian American (Victor Dzau), and one woman (Pam Bernard), but the number of women on my team—another key component of diversity—is fewer than I would wish. Excellent academic leaders appointed in recent years happen to be women, including the deans of Duke's two largest schools, medicine and arts and sciences, but Duke has still not had a black dean of any school.[1]

This is a matter that can right itself only by appointment choices made case by case, each of which must be mindful of the full range of criteria in question. But I am aware that including African Americans in the top academic leadership of this university is a piece of unfinished business, and I pledge that I will give the issue continuing attention. Senior leadership searches are charged to look broadly for talent, and the extent to which they have done so is assessed before a short list is approved. We will report on leadership searches every year to ECAC and the HR Committee of the Board of Trustees.

I conclude with this: The values of diversity, inclusiveness, and respect are core values of Duke University. We embrace them first because they are the bases of any decent, healthy community, and second because they are key to what we do. Work teams are more productive when they embrace a variety of viewpoints and make each player feel included. Classes and daily interactions are more instructive when we engage with minds coming from many different places. That's also crucial preparation for the world our students will be living their lives in. So for the deep work of the university to get done, and indeed to fulfill the mission and the meaning of the university, it's imperative that we make these glowing words a living reality.

We're never totally there; living up to these ideals will always be a work in progress, and the nature of the challenges continues to evolve

1. Happily, by my last year in office, the picture of the senior administration described in this 2012 address had changed considerably. Just a few months after this address was given, Paula McClain was named dean of The Graduate School—the first black person appointed to the top ranks of academic leadership at Duke. In 2014 Sally Kornbluth became the first woman to serve as Duke's provost or chief academic officer. In 2015, Valerie Ashby came to Duke as dean of Trinity College of Arts and Sciences, and Eugene Washington was named chancellor of health affairs and president and CEO of the Duke University Health System; each is the first African American to serve in that capacity. These outstanding appointments show that the values of excellence and diversity need not trade off against one another. They are only well served when they are both served together.

with larger changes in our society. But fifty years ago, Duke made a commitment, and in the whole history of the twentieth century, the change we are about to celebrate is rivaled by only two others for its impact on what Duke has become. Without the move to Durham from Randolph County in 1892, this school would have been nowhere and would probably have failed. Without the transformational gift from James B. Duke in 1924, we would still be a distinguished regional liberal arts college, not a world-renowned university. Without the repeal of racial exclusion policies, this would not be the place where the brightest minds come from every origin to deepen and expand our knowledge of our world. We are exactly that, thanks to the history I have been describing. Let's be proud of Duke's remarkable progress, and let's be resolved to speed this progress on.

Repairing the Broken World

Duke Chapel, May 11–12, 2012

Last month, during the Duke reunions, the small child of visiting alumni was heard to exclaim, "How beautiful is this place Duke." I thought, That's what the Class of 2012 must be feeling. Once upon a time, when you did not know any people here, you must have fallen in love with the look of this school, which is so beautiful, so everything a college should be. Over these four years, you've filled this space with so many joys and friendships, so many challenges faced and met, that this physical setting has ripened into something more profound: a visual image of your personal growth. Now, just when the place couldn't get any more beautiful or full of personal meaning, we have a nasty surprise for you. This beautiful place Duke is about to throw you out. Come back in three months and you'll find that we've replaced you with another. Like your famous ancestors Adam and Eve, whose departure from Eden is pictured in these stained-glass windows, your days in the earthly paradise are over. Next, exile and the Great Unknown.

Friends, are you sure you want to go through with this graduation? Because in your case, the Great Unknown has some pretty scary features. The Class of 2012 has the historical distinction of having settled into college in late August 2008, less than a month before the meltdown of the global financial markets. That was very smart of you: you got to sit out the greatest recession since the Great Depression in the comfy, secure world of college. Three years is usually ample time for a recovery, so that too seemed like good planning on your part—but this time, the familiar cycle has not worked quite right. This time, the recovery has proved anemic and fragile, and the trauma we passed through has cast deep doubt on the strength and even functionality of the underlying system.

This nation has emerged from the recession laden with debt, with so many fixed expenditures as to virtually paralyze the discretionary spending by which we invest in building the future, and with entitlement obligations guaranteed to drive this debt higher and higher as far as the eye can see. This winter Duke had a memorable visit from Alan Simpson and Erskine Bowles, cochairs of the bipartisan commission that proposed a plan to rein in future deficits and secure a margin for investment. But as you'll remember, their plan was not enacted or even seriously engaged. Instead we got to watch our government square up to the crisis of an endangered future only to fall into partisan deadlock and an astonishing failure to act. We've always been proud of the superiority of our form of government—but last summer we presented the world with the spectacle of an almost total inability to engage in complex problem solving and long-term planning. Pundits have a name for this: Washington is broken.

A CNN poll this February revealed that 86 percent of Americans believe the system of government is broken. But of course that's only the start. Haven't you heard? Health care now makes up nearly 20 percent of the U.S. economy while producing health results inferior to many other developed countries. In short, health care is broken. K–12 education is definitely broken; people have been saying that for years. Colleges and universities used to be accorded some measure of respect, but within the past year at least two hundred people have hastened to assure me that higher education is broken. Bad luck, Class of 2012: the world is all before you, but its institutions no longer work.

I wonder if I'm the only one who thinks that our culture's way of talking about our problems might be part of the problem. "Washington is broken": it's a bold, decisive phrase and certainly easy to remember, but the thousandth time we hear the formula, it might dawn on us that we are in the presence of a massive cliché. And we need to ask ourselves, How healthy can it be for a culture when bombastic clichés supply our principal means for thinking about social issues? The "X is broken" mantra bespeaks a mind-set with a number of related features. First, it promotes aggressive, melodramatic simplifications in place of shaded or complex analysis. Second, it combines vast pessimism with a tone of smug self-satisfaction. (You're broken, it implies, but I am not.) And third, it offers no hint of how broken things might be put right, indeed suggests no feeling of responsibility either for the existence of the problem or for envisioning a solution. Hard to see how any of this will be of much help.

But there would be another way of standing toward all the same contemporary facts that puts them in a completely different light. Instead of standing apart from problems and denouncing them, what if you engaged them, took an active role in them, brought your best energies to bear on them? Instead of accepting reductive slogans posing as profundities, what if you used your independent powers of mind to try to understand the complex histories of those challenges and their multiple dimensions and plural causes? And instead of washing your hands of problems thought beyond hope or help, what if you mobilized others, pulled together their different forms of talent and intelligence, and found what you could accomplish together? The litany of problems would not go away, but they would reappear as challenges to our collective imagination and collective action, not shameful failures or dead ends.

Fortunately these are skills you have been building every day the last four years. The deep beauty of this place isn't the architecture: it's the way Duke draws gifted men and women together in a space of engagement where they unleash each other's creative powers. A month ago I watched the production of *Ragtime* with forty-one students onstage and over 120 involved overall. What was this? People who could have been sitting around complaining that life was empty of meaning, who instead got together to fill it through their collective creativity. Pure Duke. I recently had dinner with varsity athletes in the senior class and, by chance, chatted with two who had worked on a DukeEngage project improving childhood health and education in Chile. One form of engagement sliding effortlessly into another: how beautiful is this place Duke. Last summer I visited a rural township in Tanzania that had a medical clinic filled with broken medical devices. In this faraway place I encountered two Duke students, living with a host family without electricity or hot water, who were using their engineering knowhow to fix broken equipment and teach others how to keep it working. Pure Duke: classroom education being carried out in service to real-world challenges. Closer to home, we've been planning the massive redesign of West Union, which will soon reopen as the center of community, connectivity, and engagement it was always meant to be. (In case you didn't notice, West Union is broken.) Members of your class have been active at every stage of the process and have supplied many of the best ideas: making this place better rather than bemoaning what it lacks.

You may be familiar from Judaic tradition with the concept of *tikkun olam*, the Hebrew words for "repairing the world." In this concept, the world is broken not because of anything Barack Obama or John Boehner did, but fundamentally: the essence of reality as it is given us to live is that it is fragmentary, disrupted, incomplete. The human obligation, in this concept, is to struggle against the brokenness we can never finally cure: to use our human powers to help create the better world we imagine but do not see. This phrase is a useful reminder that if today's challenges have their specificity and urgency, we're not the first people in history who have faced difficulty. And it's a reminder that it makes a world of difference whether we meet our problems with negativism and passivity or engage them through an active, constructive approach.

Men and women of Duke, we have a great hope for you: that in whatever career or sequence of careers awaits you, you will be repairers of a broken world. The world needs this; you have this capacity; and your education has fortified this power. But there is one thing more you will need, and neither you nor we can be certain at this time that you will have it: namely, the will to use your powers for this larger good. I say this because we live at a time when education and trained intelligence are more vital than ever to delivering all the things our society needs, from a vibrant economy to skilled workers to quality health care and schooling to sustainable practices, international understanding, and all the rest. But this is also a time when the best educated have shown more and more of a tendency to shut themselves in with one another, in a bubble of smartness and success. In a world where higher education and the culture of success are so highly correlated, there's no way you can fight entirely free of this temptation. So it will matter, over time, that you feel some internal prod reminding you that your gifts and your opportunities gave you a higher calling than personal success alone. That's what Duke could be for you when you leave it: the image of the place where you first took the measure of what you could be, and a summons to live up to that high mark.

A few years back I was taught a saying that I'll share with you as my parting gift. Here it is: Discovering the Use of Knowledge is Education. D-U-K-E. It's an interesting thought. Taken seriously, it would mean that education isn't complete when you finish acquiring knowledge, but only when you find the use of knowledge, learn what you can do with it, learn what you can make happen. That can't be taught; you have to discover it. And how to discover it except through experience and trial, a long life attempting to use your intelligence in active, productive ways. I was not kidding when I said you are now departing for the Great Unknown. But the unknown could be this space of discovery, the place to learn the use you could make of your training and your powers.

College is over; time to start your education. Make it a great one. It has been a joy to share this place with you.

Connecting and Disconnecting

Duke Chapel, May 10–11, 2013

March 27 was the Last Day to Withdraw from Spring Courses. I bet you never noticed. April 24 was the Last Day of Classes. That you noticed, but that was just fun. Then April 28 was the Last Day of Reading Period, and May 4 was the Last Day of Exams—and by this same inexorable progress, you have now arrived at the Last Day of Duke. Face it: when you reach the Baccalaureate service, this whole thing is about to be over, finito, kaput. Repent! The end of your world is at hand.

You're all in black, the color of mourning. No wonder. You're about to leave a beautiful place and a magical way of life and the company of a thousand friends. You were so connected, and you're about to be disconnected. Let's linger a little on that word.

Your fellow alum and Commencement speaker Melinda Gates once recommended a book to me called *Connected*, by Nicholas Christakis and James Fowler. The book takes off from the thought that people live not just as separate individuals or members of abstract identity groups but specifically as creatures of networks. Each of us lives within an architecture of relationships, differently shaped for each person, composed of many different kinds of bonds. The people we have bonds with in turn have bonds with others, and they with others, in ramifying patterns that contemporary graphics can display with beautiful precision.

As social network scholarship has been revealing, once you map these networks, it can be shown that things flow across them in measurable, if surprising ways. One finding is that if everyone on earth can be connected to every other by six degrees of separation (this was demonstrated by sociologist Stanley Milgram in the 1960s), actual influence tends to be focused within three degrees of separation, as far as your friends' friends' friends. And the things transmitted within these network neighborhoods can be quite unexpected. The data trove from the health study conducted for many decades in Framingham, Massachusetts, enabled the discovery that rates of obesity increase noticeably not just for those whose friends are obese but also for those with more overweight contacts at second and third remove. In Christakis and Fowler's words, we influence and are influenced by relationships beyond our direct ones, yet not so far away.

From this study I learned the fascinating fact that the core webs of connection for college graduates are nearly twice as dense as for people who didn't go to college. I am positive that the webs for the average Duke grad would be six, ten, or even twenty times that. Think of it. The students Duke attracts have already shown signs of inordinate human curiosity and eagerness to engage when we first admit them—that's one of the things we select for. Since the historical tipping point in the advent of social media happened just around the time you were choosing a college, you were able to start connecting on Facebook within minutes of your admission, and already had hundreds of friends (well, in a certain sense) before you ever saw each other's faces. When you finally arrived, from the first assault of the smiling FAC brigade, you knew you had stepped onto a campus where people rejoice in each other's acquaintance. Last week a mother in Boston told me her not excessively social son called home his first week at Duke and said, "Mom! It's ridiculously easy to make friends here!"

From this start, think of the connections you made with teachers, with friends, and the people you shared residences or classes with, or activities, or sports teams, or summer experiences, and add in all their friends—that's what it meant to go to Duke: to be connected and reconnected across a multitude of circuits to this lively, inventive community all day for four long years. What Christakis and Fowler helped me realize is that the hyperconnectivity you *formed* at Duke is in no sense separate from what you *learned* at Duke. Information and ideas and questions and angles of perception flowed in to you from contacts both direct and a little distant, shaping your personal understanding, making it steadily richer, and flowed out from you to shape the understandings of others. If you are not the same person you were when you arrived, it's because you've inhabited a culture of connectivity continually at work to open eyes and deepen minds.

And then? Just when the circuits are all lit up, you're about to be un-plugged. What will that be like? A few weeks back I met a graduate two years out who said, "You know, President Brodhead, leaving Duke has left a void in my life. A profound void," he added, with riveting earnestness. At a Duke gathering in New York shortly after, I asked a woman from the same class whether she agreed, and she said, "Oh, I wouldn't call it a void exactly—it's more of an abyss."

She was partly kidding, and so am I. You won't be disconnected when you leave. You'll have exchanged hundreds of texts with each other be-fore you even get home, and once you get where you're going next, you will have little trouble finding Duke enclaves to stay in touch. Like a reli-gious sect renewing communal bonds through ritual observance, Dukies in far-flung cities somehow find each other during basketball season. And alums and their yet-unmet friends may help you in the future in important ways. Friends of friends are an especially significant source of tips about jobs, Christakis and Fowler remind us—also of introduc-tions to people you might someday marry. The alum who found it ri-diculously easy to make friends at Duke is getting married this summer to someone he met nine years ago—a fellow resident of Giles.

So one of my messages to you is, Relax: the Duke connection will not be dissolved; it will deepen and grow. But my other message is, To the extent that this chapter actually is over, that's not all bad. If you're living in some city next fall and every one you know is a former Dukie, that might be fun. But if ten or twenty years from now you don't know anyone except your Duke classmates, that will be pathetic. You will not be a cool person; you'll be a shut-in. You will not be a smartie; you will be a dullard. You broke out of an established life and opened yourself to a host of new contacts when you came to Duke; that was the condition for your horizons to expand as they have. Time to break out of this known, loved world before it becomes a limit to you. Want to learn something that may amaze you? There are very interesting people in the world who are more than twenty-two years old! You have been living in a generational ghetto. Break out, and you can make new connections with new chances to learn and grow.

Your breaking out of this enchanted dream has a social meaning as well. Some while back I heard a memorable phrase—former labor secretary Robert Reich apparently coined it, though I learned it second- or third-hand, through connections: "the secession of the successful." The phrase describes the growing tendency for the affluent and well-educated to shut themselves into little worlds where they can associate with one another, with limited contact with those with different experience. We have long seen this in residence patterns that group the affluent in a cluster. Those have helped produce schooling patterns that group children from similar socioeconomic backgrounds heavily together. More recently the Brookings Institute has demonstrated that college graduates have begun increasingly to settle in hot spots with high proportions of other college graduates, leaving other cities to become educational deserts. Being well-connected is highly compatible with being disconnected, it appears, since even networks have their bounds.

The secessionist temptation is easy to understand, but such choices take a toll. If people like you continue to hang out only with other people like you, there will be a double cost. You'll lose the means to grasp the conditions the majority of your contemporaries actually live in, a cost of knowledge. Plus you lose the chance to bring your powers to bear on the challenges of your world, a cost of influence, since problems will be too far away for you to see or care.

I'm glad you did well here, but you won't have learned Duke's lesson if you seek to extend Duke for life. Duke wants you to keep opening your mind to your world your whole life long. And Duke wants you to be an actor in your world, using your gifts to shape what *is* into what *might be*. Your Duke years readied you for such a career. But that's over now; Duke is done. Now the burden is on you to keep connecting and connecting and connecting, learning your world and the reach of your powers.

It's been a pleasure to be connected to you. We're disconnecting now. Good luck out there. Go well.

Interview with Stephen Colbert,
The Colbert Report

August 15, 2013

I was asked to chair the Commission on the Humanities and Social Sciences created by the American Academy of Arts and Sciences. When the committee's report, The Heart of the Matter, *was published in June 2013, it received a good deal of publicity, including an invitation for me to discuss the report with Stephen Colbert on his popular Comedy Central TV show,* The Colbert Report. *As host, this wickedly talented satirist impersonated an overblown caricature of a certain kind of conservative, with a crazy interviewing manner designed to throw guests off balance. My appearance, certainly my most widely seen performance in all my years as president, aired on August 15, 2013.*

Duke University President Richard Brodhead talks about his report on the humanities, *The Heart of the Matter*.

Stephen Colbert: Welcome back, everybody. My guest tonight has been the president of Duke University for the past nine years. When's he going to graduate and get a job? Please welcome Richard Brodhead!

[*SC runs to the interview table.*]

SC: Nice to meet you.

Richard H. Brodhead: You as well.

SC: All right, sir. Professor Richard Brodhead.

RHB: That would be me.

SC: All right, Duke University, president of Duke, cochair of the Commission on the Humanities and Social Sciences, created by the American Academy of Arts and Sciences. And you have a new report called *The Heart of the Matter*. First of all, what is the American Academy of Arts and Sciences? Is that a taxpayer boondoggle?

[*laughter*]

RHB: You'll be sorry to hear that it isn't.

SC: All right.

RHB: It's a scholarly society that represents people across all the fields of learning.

SC: What's your field of learning, before we get into this?

RHB: My degree is in English.

SC: English major! [*cheers, applause*] All right! You went for the big cash.

RHB: And look: now I'm on your show.

SC: Yeah, it worked out. All right, let's give the humanities the "Colbert bump." Oh, we can do it; we can do it if you want.

[*fist bump, followed by applause, cheers*]

        You lament in this report the fall of the humanities in our universities. People are not becoming humanities majors any more. Why do you think that is?

RHB: Well, you overstate it. It's not so much the decline, as we think that all across American life, starting in kindergarten through twelfth grade, through college and through later life, there's a hunger for things that the humanities supply, and people haven't paid enough attention, haven't given these things enough attention.

SC: Well, of course. We are hu*m*ans; of course we hunger for the humanities.

RHB: Well, because what is the humanities?

SC: I don't know, actually. [*laughter*]

RHB: Well, I'll tell you.

SC: I'm not a humanities major; I don't know.

RHB: Humanities is humans studying the things other humans have achieved and suffered and struggled for in other times and places, and—

SC: But is that how bad our educational system has become, that we have to teach our children how to be human?

[*laughter*]

SC: When I was a kid, you just popped out of the womb, and you knew it. You kinda had a feel for it.

[*laughter*]

RHB: Well, those were the days.

SC: They were.

[*laughter, applause, cheers*]

SC: Now, you say I'm overstating the case. But you also say in here [*gestures to report*] that English majors are at an all-time low.

RHB: The figures about who majors in what aren't the most important thing. It's about how much emphasis—we're talking in support of a broad version of education that arches from the sciences to the humanities, that starts early and continues all through people's lives. That's what gives people the full set of equipment they need for employment, for personal pleasure, for all the things that education is meant to supply.

[*applause, cheers*]

SC: Yeah, but obviously, you're a humanities guy, and so you think we should have the humanities in our lives. But if you were not the president of Duke but instead, were perhaps the president of a technical training institute. . . .

RHB: OK . . .

SC: . . . wouldn't you be talking about the ineffable beauty of draining Freon from an A/C unit?

[*laughter*]

RHB: Well, I'll tell you. This commission that I cochaired had on it some presidents of universities, it had on it some scholars, but it also had the CEO of Boeing, it had the former governor of Tennessee, it had the person who heads the largest community college in America, and all of them argued for the long-term value of the kind of things that the humanities teach us. All of them did. I'll tell you something especially interesting. The former president of MIT who is now the head of the National Academy of Engineering—he was on our committee, and he says engineers need to do more than engineering; they need to be able to communicate in order for the full value of their education to come across.

[*applause, cheers*]

SC: Let me tell you. This is the report. It's called *The Heart of the Matter*. (I see you sprung for the fancy binder to try to get a better grade.) But I want to point out something here. Look at your margins! Look at your margins right here. You're clearly trying to stretch this. If you properly formatted this, this would be like eight pages long.

RHB: All serious readers know that margins are to keep your notes in.

[*audience reacts*]

SC: Glad I'm not a serious reader!

RHB: [*laughs*]

SC: I would feel bad that I didn't know that. Can I talk to you—
      you're a bit of an expert on Melville and Hawthorne, is that
      right?

RHB: That's true.

SC: Can you tell me something about Melville? About *Moby-Dick*?

RHB: Yeah?

SC: That's a big book, OK? I've got a beautiful volume. I don't want
      to crack it open, because that'll ruin the resale value. [*audience
      laughter*] Is *Moby-Dick* a metaphor for the struggle of trying to
      read *Moby-Dick*?

RHB: You missed your calling as a literary critic.

SC: Well, I've got a fallback position. How does that pay?

RHB [*laughs*]: I thought we already covered that.

SC: Well, professor, thank you so much for joining me. The presi-
      dent of Duke University, Richard Brodhead! Be an English
      major! We'll be right back.

Receive, Connect, Engage

Duke Chapel, August 21, 2013

The freshman convocation at Duke typically begins with the presentation of the class to the president and the faculty by the dean of Undergraduate Admissions, who highlights in witty fashion some of the more unusual accomplishments of the students.

I love the fact that Christoph Guttentag starts this assembly. The treasure hunters in our admissions office found you, so he deserves the chance to gloat. Plus he sets a good tone for the start of college. Official Duke could have been pompous, intimidating, overbearing—instead, he was relaxed, unpretentious, friendly, and fun. That's a good message to learn about Duke. This is a place where highly talented individuals live together in a state of mutual appreciation and enjoyment. You've come to a good place.

But fun and friendliness aren't the only moods this day should inspire. Did you see this sublimely beautiful building soaring around you? Did you feel Duke Chapel vibrate to that solemn organ tune? Do you see your president, regally dressed and obviously equipped with supernatural powers? Our welcome is genuine, but I hope you also feel some awe at what is about to begin. Today you make a fresh start on an altogether new life. This will be the first chapter of life that envisions you as an adult, no longer a child. And today you enter a life in which you'll have one and only one mission: to become the person you have it in you to be, a person equipped to lead a fulfilling life and to give the world the benefit of your gifts.

Now how are you going to perform this exalted task? Let me share an insight from one of Duke's great teachers. Last fall Duke was delighted to learn that our longtime faculty member Robert Lefkowitz had won the Nobel Prize in Chemistry. He was honored for discovering the so-called G protein-coupled receptor, the mechanism on cells that detects a chemical change in their environment and produces a corresponding change inside the cell. You see a bear; your body secretes adrenaline; its molecule fits like a key into the receptor, unlocks it, enters the cells, and sets your heart racing. The discovery of the action of receptors now forms the basis for hundreds of drugs, including beta blockers and antihistamines.

I got to interview Dr. Lefkowitz last year—he is another funny, unpretentious person—and I asked him, "What can a teacher really do for a student?" He said, "I try to get them to reach the point where they feel absolutely absorbed in the inquiry they're involved in. Once they've felt a taste of that, they'll never be willing to give it up." He added, "President Kennedy used to cite the ancient Greek definition of happiness: 'the full use of your powers along lines of excellence.'"

You know, I hope, what he was talking about. Does this sound familiar? You're doing something that began as homework, a task set by someone else performed to please someone else, when suddenly you find you're engaged with the question, propelled forward by your curiosity, moving to pull together things you already know to help understand the thing you don't yet know. This does not happen only in academic work. Great coaches help players find how to release their full powers in excellent performance; that's why athletics can have a role in a university. Or you're in a musical or dance group, or debate team, or tutoring program in local schools—you begin doing what you think is expected, but then some internal power switches on, and now it's you playing or teaching or performing, you're living inside the activity, reaching levels you did not know you could attain. Or you're talking with a friend, paddling in the shallow waters of casual conversation, when suddenly you've both moved deeper in, sharing something that matters, helping each other inhabit unfamiliar points of view, seeing together what neither of you could have seen on your own.

President Kennedy was paraphrasing Aristotle, and they both had it right: "Happiness is the full use of your powers along lines of excellence." There's pleasure to be found in knocking off or lying about, but the height of pleasure comes through engagement, through the activation of the self's full powers. We want you to be happy at Duke, so we need you to be engaged. But even more, engagement is the precondition for learning and growth. The things we do in an uninvested, half-hearted way leave no mark on us, even when we're extremely good at them. We do them, we forget them, it is as if they had never been. The things that inspire your deep participation are the things that expand you and transform you, releasing the recognition of what you can be at best.

Under the influence of Dr. Lefkowitz, I am visualizing Duke as an organism pumping thousands of stimuli out at you, things that can wake you up, shock you into responsiveness, and call forth your full powers of aspiration, curiosity, creativity, and concern. These stimuli are partly academic but not exclusively so: everything you do here, every course, every activity, every conversation at a place so rich in intelligence and spirit, can be a chance for self-expansion and self-discovery. But just being at Duke won't guarantee you this enlargement. If you insulate yourself, if you hold back or shut yourself in from Duke's provocations, your Duke will be a land of missed opportunities. To receive what Duke can give you, you need to be a receptor, actively opening yourself to the opportunities around you.

So if you ever face a choice between hanging back and leaning in, remember what your president told you: receive, connect, engage. And if I could give one other tip, it would be to engage broadly, reaching far beyond what you've done before, even at the cost of taking risks. Duke students have always done so well in high school that when they arrive here, there's a danger that they will feel constrained to do only things they are already good at, to keep up the picture of the Perfect You. Taken to extremes, this can even lead to premature certainty about what you're going to be for the whole rest of your life—a restriction parents can be guilty of abetting. But smart people seldom stick to scripts composed in their teens. More often, they only begin to find what they might do or be while they're in college, or even later. As a dutiful son, Dr. Lefkowitz set off to be a doctor; only later did he find that his true calling was to research. My newfound friend Stephen Colbert was a philosophy major when he started college. Only in college did he discover the love of theater that released him to his later career.

People are always telling students "Follow your passion," but you're a little young to know what passion should direct your whole life. I loved it when I heard a variant on this advice: not "Follow your passion" but "Give your passion a chance to find you." That's what college is for. Your horizon is about to be thrown open wide, to possibilities intellectual, social, global, and local that you have scarcely imagined. So why stay trapped in the little world you used to inhabit? Step out, step up: let Duke help you find who you might be.

Friends, we've been living through a sour-toned debate on the value of education, with many claiming that costs are out of control, learning could be delivered as well and far cheaper online, and the measure of education is whether you get a well-paid job the day you graduate. I don't minimize the cost issue, and your parents will be quite right to expect you to support yourselves. But though the media has pretty much restricted itself to reporting the college-bashing line, there is another view: that the value of education is different from the cost; that a valuable education equips you for your whole life, not just your first job; that while this can be assisted by technology, it fundamentally works through human interaction, teachers and students, students and students unlocking each other's potential through living, face-to-face exchange.

When you chose Duke, you and your family put your bet on this second value proposition. You made a great choice, and that's what awaits you: a chance to build your whole person through personal interactions in a lively learning community. But to realize this value, you have to do more than pay the price. To get the value of Duke, you have to give yourself to it, throw yourself into every chance to learn and grow. Are you prepared to do that? Awesome! By the powers vested in me, I now declare you students of Duke.

Remarks at the Opening of the Center for Sexual and Gender Diversity

September 27, 2013

The opening of Duke's new Center for Sexual and Gender Diversity was the occasion to speak of a revolution in values at Duke and in the nation and the broader vision of humanity the university embraces today.

This week Duke is concluding its year-long celebration of the fiftieth anniversary of the enrollment of the first black students at Duke. That event marked a playing-out in our local world of a drama from the larger world. That drama is well known: After the end of slavery, civil rights that had been newly won by the black population were systematically withdrawn, officially in the South and de facto in much of the United States. Blacks lost their chance to vote, were excluded from first-class education and medical care, and were made to endure a host of daily humiliations designed to mark them as different and inferior.

The civil rights movement that opened Duke's doors was based on the recognition that every human is equally human, and every human is entitled to the same human rights—not just technical legal rights but the same fundamental opportunity for personal fulfillment. The further teaching of the civil rights movement was not only that it's wrong to deny opportunities to others on prejudicial grounds like race but that the whole community is impoverished when some are excluded from full membership. When anyone is treated as less than fully human, there is a cost to us all.

The civil rights movement unfolded during my teens and my college years, and I well remember how a cause first focused on race began to broaden its concerns. The women's movement gathered steam in the 1960s as an attack on another form of prejudice. Later still, civil rights found a new cause in fighting the oppression of gays and lesbians.

It would be hard to describe today how deeply entrenched prejudice on grounds of sexual orientation and gender identity was in this country at that time. Homophobic prejudice was everywhere, with its aggressive mockery and crude repression. Further, people thought it a requirement of their virtue to uphold this prejudice.

The gay rights movement started later than the other chapters of the civil rights movement—the Stonewall riot, the first rallying cry, occurred in 1969—and the progress was slow and the opposition intense throughout the next three decades. In the first years of this new century, there has been marked progress, more progress than anyone could confidently have predicted a decade ago. But we all know that this struggle is far from over.

As an institution within a larger culture, it's not surprising that the Duke of older times was saturated with homophobia. Last year, students in Blue Devils United brought forward evidence of official intolerance and active repression of homosexuality at Duke from the 1960s. They also shared personal testaments from graduates of that time. These Dukies testified that they could not be the people they knew themselves to be while they were students, could not have the love lives and personal lives they wished, were pathologized—and even when the situation improved slightly, the pressures of swimming against the stream were dispiriting and exhausting.

I've read these histories, and I'm sure we'll uncover many more in the future. As president of this university, I would like to say today that this university regrets every phase of that history. There is nothing in that past that I will not now confidently and totally repudiate. I regret every act that ever limited the human life of anyone who came here.

But the history of the world can't be told only as a history of bad things, because that makes it seem as though the struggle for a better world meant nothing. In the depths of segregation, this university was designed by a black architect. So too in its most homophobic period, Duke drew strength from its gay community: the most famous teacher at this university in the twentieth century was Reynolds Price, a gay man who was not always open about his homosexuality but who never denied it, and who wrote a celebratory memoir of it in *Ardent Spirits*. More recently, my predecessors made Duke the first large employer in the state to give same-sex partner benefits. My predecessor Nan Keohane agreed that same-sex unions could be performed in Duke Chapel long before such things were common anywhere. Today, alumni who could not be gay when they were students are able to return to Duke in honesty and to have their talents recognized with the university's highest honors. Tom Clark, who spoke earlier in this program, was an outstanding president of the Duke Alumni Association. Blake Byrne is about to receive the Distinguished Alumnus Award at Founders' Day for his crucial work as the founding chair of the Nasher Museum's advisory board. As an even more recent sign of progress, I would cite the video Duke student-athletes made last year with the message "If you can play, you can play."

And now, to crown this history of progress, I come to this new Center for Sexual and Gender Diversity. Janie [Long], I've been to your place before, but it wasn't quite as nice as this. It wasn't as large as this. And it wasn't as central, or as visible. Now, anyone walking from the Chapel to the Bryan Center is going to walk right past this space. Anybody walking into the student center of Duke University is going to walk right up to this recognition of the value of sexual and gender diversity. We've always known the phrase "out of the closet." Today this Center comes "out of the basement." We've heard of things being "marginalized." Today this Center been centralized, placed at the visible center of Duke University.

This Center will give a safe community place for students, faculty, and staff who self-identify in non-heterosexual ways, but just as important, it will give a gift to every member of this community. A university is a place for learning, and if there are two lessons Duke University wants everyone to learn, they are, first, that everyone must be free to define the life they are meant to live and to respect that right in others; and second, the human family serves us best when we allow ourselves to be human together rather than make some people victims of artificial discriminations.

I'll say a word of thanks, and then I'm done. I thank Janie Long and her staff and the many people in Student Affairs, not least Larry Moneta, who worked on the planning for this Center. I thank the students and faculty and staff who had input in the planning process. But my deepest thanks goes to all those who built this community over the years. It could not have been easy to be one of a handful of advocates for a then-unpopular cause—but thanks to that struggle, look where we have arrived. Now, let's go forward together.

The Value Debate in Higher Education

New York, October 24, 2013

Having chaired the American Academy of Arts and Sciences Commission on the Humanities and Social Sciences that issued the 2013 report The Heart of the Matter, *I was asked by David Coleman, the president of the College Board, to give the Presidential Address to nearly two thousand admissions officers, college counselors, and others at The College Board Forum in 2013, in the middle of a heated—and in my view, deeply misguided—national debate about the value of liberal arts education.*

I am honored to have a chance to address The College Board Forum. David, I am especially pleased to speak in the first year of what I trust will be a long and happy reign. To my audience today: you perform one of the most significant functions in American life, and I salute you. Since the military draft ended forty years ago, the chief experience that people from different backgrounds go through together as an age cohort is the college admissions process. In this great transition, you are the border patrols and the crossing guards. As secondary school leaders and college guidance counselors, you urge students forward, help them visualize their options, and encourage them to present their accomplishments in a compelling light. Those of you on the college and university side enlighten students and families as to what college is and why it matters, help them make the finances work, and select and shape an admitted class.

Put it all together and the scale of the process is astounding. I'm told that of the 3.2 million young people who graduated from high school in 2012, about 2.1 million, or 66 percent, were enrolled in college in the fall. It matters profoundly how well this transition is managed. It matters to individual students and families, who regard you as holding the keys to life or death; it also matters to the nation. Our wisdom and productivity in the future are directly dependent on whether, in earlier life, the greatest possible number of men and women can get the education that lets them live up to their potential. If quality higher education is richly available, we'll be prepared for any future. If people don't get the full measure of educational enablement, we'll lose their potential and we all will pay a price.

Deployed as you are along the perimeter of higher education, you are uniquely equipped to register the hopes and dreams that drive the quest for college admission—and, equally, the negative emotions that have strengthened in recent times. Never has college been sought with such desperate eagerness as the route to fulfillment and success as it is today, but never has there been so much cynicism and mistrust. You know the litany. College is our only hope, yet college costs too much. You can borrow to help pay the cost, but then you're saddled with disabling debt. Some colleges admit students with no realistic chance of completion, and they end up with the worst of both worlds: the debt and not the degree. But those who do graduate may fare little better. Students may have learned little or nothing in college (journalists eagerly adopted this message from Arum and Roksa's *Academically Adrift*) and so may have no better shot at quality employment after they graduate than if they had never gone.

As I trust you know, this litany represents a mix of fact and wild distortion. In sober truth, unemployment is significantly lower and lifetime earnings significantly higher for four-year college graduates. But media organs prefer the lurid version of the tale, which their repetitions have come close to establishing as accepted truth. In May 2012, right around graduation weekend for many colleges, the Sunday *New York Times* ran a lead story featuring a student from a four-year liberal arts college who emerged with $120,000 in debt. She was working two fast-food jobs to pay it down, and her mother had taken out insurance in case the child died and she became liable for the loans. Right there on page one, the poster child for college education in the scammy days of cost, debt, unemployment, and disablement! Only in the sixth paragraph did the story reveal that the median debt load of graduates was in the $20,000 range, one-sixth of what the front page implied was "typical."

As you also know, however, the new negativism is not solely a media creation. At bottom it is a by-product of an economic downturn followed by a recovery that has lacked the lift of a true recovery, especially for the middle class. Barbara Ehrenreich long ago explained that the middle class is that class that can never amass enough wealth to secure its children's well-being through inheritance. Instead middle-class parents strive to assure their children's success by hyperinvesting in education. When costs go up for families whose incomes aren't rising, and postcollege employment prospects grow uncertain, this strategy comes under massive pressure, with its hopes shrouded by a sense of betrayal.

We see one result in the rush to hold higher education accountable for the value it no longer seems to deliver. When the president began a virtual campaign tour this past August, he sought to connect with the public's hopes and fears by preaching federal accountability for higher education. After the State of the Union address, the Obama administration issued report cards measuring cost of attendance, debt rates, and completion rates for every institution of higher education. Virginia law now requires all institutions to post the starting salaries for their graduates broken out by college major, so parents can know what course of study leads to what result.

The anxiety that higher education may not lead to a secure, prosperous future is the great new fact of our time. There's no wishing it away: if we are living through a structural change in the distribution of wealth and opportunity, as many fear, it will be with us for a long while to come. In this new circumstance, we have work to do to mitigate cost increases and teach the public the real facts of price and choice.

But that is hardly the end of our challenge. A peculiarity of recent years is that as the debate over the value of college has grown more heated, the concept of this value has grown narrower and more impoverished. The White House website may tell you the effective cost of attending Dartmouth or Arizona State, and this is useful information, except that it leaves the impression that the value of a college education is identical to its price. The Virginia website makes it easy to calculate the benefit derived from attending any institution, provided you assume the benefit equals the salary paid by your first employer.

As such reductive metrics gain ground around us, the friends of higher education have a job to do. Without ignoring or minimizing economic realities, we need to say loud and clear what the value of a good education actually consists of.

Now, there are many different versions of postsecondary education, some of which do involve learning specific workplace skills, and these may be adequately measured by near-term employment statistics and rates of pay. But much of American higher education draws on some version of the liberal arts model, which has an altogether different value proposition. Liberal arts education is not just a matter of requiring students to visit random unrelated fields and check the curricular boxes. Beyond its formal requirements, this education aims to engage multiple forms of intelligence to create deep and enduring habits of mind, an active, integrative, versatile spirit that's naturally disposed, when it comes upon a new fact or situation, to use existing knowledge to try to grasp it, while updating preexisting understandings in this new light.

The value of this habit of mind is not measured by income alone. It is, in the fullest sense, equipment for living. Its value is that it supplies enrichment to personal lives, equips students to be thoughtful and constructive social contributors, and prepares them to participate fully and creatively in the dynamic, ever-changing world that awaits them after college. It's easy to see why people might get anxious about something so difficult to calculate, and might want a straighter line to the payoff. But the fruits of such education can only be reckoned over long-time horizons, as they enable people to rise to challenges and seize opportunities they could not foresee at first. The lives of successful people almost never involve continuing to do what they prepared for. As their lives unfold, they find that by drawing on their preparation in unexpected ways, they're able to do things they hadn't intended or imagined.

I am describing a situation where, thinking they are securing real value from education, people are tempted to pursue narrow and short-sighted versions of that value, and so short-change themselves and the world. One favorite target for those who want a bang for the buck has been the humanities. All federal research investments have been constrained in the days of high deficits and sequestration, but humanities budgets have been cut disproportionally. Between 2010 and 2013, the appropriation for the National Endowment for the Humanities was cut more than 16 percent. In those same years, allocation for the Title VI foreign language programs fell a whopping 44 percent. Shortly after his election, the governor of my state said that public dollars should support only education that leads straight to a job. If students want to study more rarefied subjects, he said, they should do so at private institutions at their own expense.

As David mentioned, this is my tenth year as president of Duke, but I started my life as an English teacher, and at heart I am that still. At present I'm involved in a campaign to promote the liberal arts and the humanities, and I want to share some lessons from this adventure. The story starts more than ten years back, when, at the request of two senators and two congressmen, the National Academies commissioned the report called *Rising Above the Gathering Storm*. This report made an urgent, cogent case that to prevent a disastrous loss of competitiveness in the global economy, America needed to strengthen its training in science, technology, engineering, and mathematics. It's a measure of this report's success that STEM has become a national byword, and bipartisan majorities supported the America COMPETES Act.

Now, no one I know doubts the need for STEM initiatives, but one can ask whether the nation's needs can be met through STEM alone. When the National Research Council commissioned a new report on research universities focused solely on STEM fields, I voiced the thought that the humanities and social sciences, equally key activities of universities, needed to be included as well. That didn't happen, but later, with its own charge from two senators and two representatives, the American Academy of Arts and Sciences launched the Commission on the Humanities and Social Sciences, and for my sins, I was asked to be cochair.

Inviting people to serve on this commission was great fun. We eventually asked fifty-five extraordinarily talented and busy people. All but one quickly accepted, saying the effort was important and well worth their time. Among others, the Commission included the presidents of Harvard, Stanford, Penn, and Notre Dame, the chancellors of UC Berkeley and the University of Texas system, and the head of the nation's largest community college, also business leaders, military leaders, a former governor, a federal judge, the heads of major libraries and museums, an actor

(John Lithgow), a filmmaker (George Lucas), and a great architect (Billie Tsien).

Over a year and a half, the Commission met for a series of highly engaging conversations. What was interesting in these discussions was that the most eloquent voices on behalf of the value of the humanities and liberal arts often came from nonacademics. James McNerney, the CEO of Boeing, told us that high-tech manufacturing requires skilled engineers, but that beyond a certain level, people will not advance if they do not have a broader array of skills, especially skills at communication and interacting with culturally diverse others—liberal arts training par excellence.

General and ambassador Karl Eikenberry, who headed military and diplomatic efforts in Afghanistan, testified that in the globalized modern world, weapons can do only so much to protect national security. Equally essential are the understanding of foreign languages, foreign histories and cultures, and beliefs and ethical systems different from our own: classic humanities fields within a liberal arts education.

Norm Augustine, longtime head of Lockheed Martin and the principal force behind the *Gathering Storm* report, argued that collecting evidence, weighing interpretations, and making arguments are core skills for creative workers and good citizens and that these require broad training across the arts and sciences. The father of STEM said he thought America's single greatest educational deficit is in history, a prime teacher of the skills he cited.

Eduardo Padrón, president of Miami Dade College, reminded us that one-third of all undergraduates in the United States are in community colleges, where their aims are not exclusively technical. Miami Dade serves 175,000 students, 90 percent minority, more than 60 percent low income, many of them immigrants or first generation—as Padrón says, "We take the people who can't pay or be admitted elsewhere." But even when these students seek training for a particular job, it's the broader training they receive that typically helps them to the next job—with Miami Dade's liberal arts curriculum launching thousands into careers in public service, law, business, and education. "If there is one area where the social sciences and the humanities are important," Padrón has said, "more than the Ivy Leagues, more than the Smithsonian, it is right there, where the masses of Americans have their first chance to achieve the American dream."

In addition to arguing for the utility of humanistic training, Commission members across all sectors agreed that that the humanities need to be studied because they broaden and deepen human awareness. Humans are the only species capable of entering into the hopes, fears, strivings, and wisdom gained by others across space and time, a radically enhanced experience available to us through art, music, film, and the written word. As humans, we can see, feel, and know things we could never have grasped on our own by entering into the transmitted imagination of others, a magnificent expansion of consciousness. We turn our backs on this legacy only at the cost of condemning ourselves to the harshest of poverties: imprisonment in our narrow present, seeing by our own unaided light.

After many months spent learning from one another, this summer the Commission was ready to issue its own report, titled *The Heart of the Matter*. Like the report that launched the STEM crusade, this one aims to make a compelling argument for the public need for the humanities and the social sciences—and to outline practical steps to advance the cause. The report makes the case that the humanities require support along the whole arc, from K–12 education through college into community cultural life and lifelong learning. It also makes the case that the separate parts of this effort will each be more effective if they work together.

The Heart of the Matter first calls for a deepened commitment to literacy. "Reading and writing are the building blocks of learning, making possible all the rest of our education and development," the report says. "From being able to sound out words on a page, we advance to be able to analyze, interpret, ask questions, make connections, and express our thoughts in words. . . . Even in a digital age, the spoken and written word remains the most basic unit of our interactions, the very basis of our humanity." If we are to expect any later development of this range of powers, we must lay a strong foundation in early life.

The Common Core Standards Initiative emerged from the National Governors Association while our Commission was deliberating. While we do not claim expertise in the details, we recognized the Common Core as an attempt to institutionalize such a deeper version of literacy, where learning to read is not the end but the beginning of an unfolding process of interrogating the world and building critical thinking powers. It is our hope (as it is the College Board's) that, started early and continued from year to year, this approach will bring many more students to the end of high school prepared for the higher-order work they will do in college. We were forewarned that raised standards would initially lead to lowered test scores, but the road will still be the right one if it leads to deeper enablement for many more people. When I asked his thoughts on the expected dip, Bob Wise, former governor of West Virginia, said that when his high school football coach would make him lift heavier weights, at first it was hard, but eventually it made him stronger.

A broad, cumulative development of powers rooted in literacy won't work without teachers who can live up to this aspiration. So as we raise the literacy bar, our report calls for a parallel emphasis on teacher training. This is a place where closer collaboration between high school and college and university teachers is needed. These two segments of our educational system are commonly separate worlds, each absorbed in its own task. But it's hard to see how high school results can be better aligned with college expectations if there is not more communication across this line. Furthermore, higher education could help provide resources to enrich curricula and help teachers open their lesson plans for active exploration. Ten miles down the road from me in North Carolina is the National Humanities Center. It's a refuge for scholarly reflection and research, but importantly, it has also spearheaded an outreach to high school teachers through online seminars and toolkits of primary materials for historical inquiry. The different segments of our educational community will all be stronger as we see more cooperation across institutional bounds.

At the next level, the report is mindful that the distinctive American strength in higher education—a strength envied and admired around the world and which many Asian countries are currently trying to replicate— is based on a plan that opens minds in multiple directions, engages our curiosity in a variety of ways, and puts us in a position to synthesize bits of knowledge to form new insights. This broad, integrative training that reaches across the arts and sciences is the American alternative to the early specialization that many countries require, and it is widely perceived to support the nimbleness, innovativeness, and creative versatility that give the American economy its dynamism.

Public understanding of this model of education may be eroding at the very moment when this form of education is becoming more necessary than ever. So the report calls for colleges and universities to make a far greater effort to communicate the enabling power of liberal arts education, sharing this message in many ways with their many publics, and we call for colleges and universities to make sure they maximally deliver what we claim to provide. Specialized curricular offerings can be life-altering experiences for students and are one of the great luxuries of a great education. But if we're to lay claim to developing the broad-based, integrative skills I've been describing, we need to take trouble to offer the courses that accomplish those goals and to help students understand how course choices can build to a thoughtful educational whole.

I will leave our many further recommendations to your careful reading of the report, which can be accessed at HumanitiesCommission.org. I want to turn to say something about tactics—that is, how we plan for our work to have an effect. Reports like ours can lie around unread, and many, perhaps most, have met this fate. But they can also make a difference, as was the case with *Gathering Storm*. So we were eager to consult Norm Augustine and others of our members who served on both commissions about the grounds of that success. What we learned was that, even after coming up with a persuasive rationale and a list of practical measures, there was a long interval spent carrying the message to multiple audiences before the result began to take shape.

That's the stage we're at now. We were delighted that the launch of *The Heart of the Matter* received enthusiastic coverage in the media. Thousands of people visited the website to download the report, pbs *Newshour* and *The Colbert Report* introduced it to television audiences, and papers around the country continue to publish op-eds and follow-on articles engaging with its ideas.

To me this is evidence that the report hit a nerve. In truth, it's actually not a hard sell to remind people that literacy is the foundation of all communications and analytical skills, that citizens of a democracy need some understanding of history, that in a globalized world it's dangerous to know so little about foreign people and cultures—*and* that STEM is a crucial component of a balanced diet but not the whole of what we need; *and* that it's not only good for people to study humanistic subjects, but that humans naturally love and crave this kind of nourishment. (Why else does the Museum of Modern Art have more than a million follow-ers on its Twitter feed? How else could Oprah have managed to mobilize the Oprah Book Club to read Faulkner and Toni Morrison and *Anna Karenina*? What else could it mean that the Coursera professor with the highest enrollment to date has been a humanist, the philosopher Walter Sinnott-Armstrong, whose online course "Think Again: How to Reason and Argue" has reached more than 400,000 students?) So far from bear-ing an unpalatable message in the "Eat your broccoli" mode, we've been telling people something that made sense to them, indeed that they al-ready knew and believed, or would have if our public discourse was not so clogged with other, contrary messages.

Eventually we will be looking for the federal government to play a role in support of the humanities. It's hard to believe this is an auspi-cious month for seeking new appropriations, but the defunding of the National Endowment for the Humanities, which supports arts and his-tory projects in every state across the country, is scandalously short-sighted. Restoring adequate funding for the study of foreign languages and cultures through Title VI and the Fulbright-Hays Program is another obvious goal.

But unlike the sciences, the humanities aren't fundamentally depen-dent on federal support, and to succeed, we will need to mobilize actors at every level of American life, including states and local communities. With the American Academy coordinating and in partnership with state humanities councils, our Commission continues to carry the message out in this way. Former Supreme Court justice David Souter came out of retirement to lead one such humanities event in Albany, New York. To my great delight, Carnegie Mellon University, the computer science and technology powerhouse in Pittsburgh, featured *The Heart of the Matter* in its freshman orientation this fall. Two weeks back I attended an event in Charlotte, North Carolina, honoring support for the humanities by two particularly active citizen leaders and a local historian who has given presentations in nearly a hundred towns. Three hundred people came, and they cheered loud and long. As I say, the humanities have plenty of friends, if we remember to remind them of the fact.

Meanwhile, in the wake of *The Heart of the Matter*, the American Academy continues to engage in mass dissemination of information, some of which might take the average American quite by surprise. Did you know that three-quarters of American employers "want new hires with precisely the sort of skills the humanities teach: critical thinking, complex problem-solving, as well as written and oral communication"? Did you know that humanities majors scored 9 percent higher on the Graduate Management Admission Test than business majors? It makes you wonder if useless things might have their uses after all.

Now I turn my eyes to you, members of the College Board. More than two thousand in number, you are today's evangelizing target for this great cause. I know you are besieged by parents who want to do right by their children and don't want to fall for a scam. I know you know the legitimate concerns and frequent economic pressures they face. And we all know that colleges do not always make it easy for students to get the glorious experience they've seen advertised, especially when their families don't have the tradition of navigating college and knowing how its value is extracted.

There's plenty of work to do to close the gap between the real and the ideal in higher education. We all need to be part of that solution. For all that, a great harm we can do to today's students is to limit their reach by siding with their anxieties and letting them settle for an education that's light on ambition. The great question of education today is how to promote the fullest realization of potential in the young men and women who will be the productive and creative citizens of tomorrow—or could be, if their education lets them. The humanities aren't the whole of the answer, but they are certainly a part of it. The humanities are not a luxury; they are a core dimension of our humanity and a crucial basis for human power. You're all counselors of different sorts. Let's counsel students to build all the sources of their potential strength. That's where the value resides.

Interconnected Knowledge and the Twenty-First-Century University

January 14, 2014

It is a great pleasure for me to return to Tsinghua University, and I thank you, President Chen, for your welcome. The last time I visited this campus, Tsinghua awarded me an honorary degree, one of the greatest honors I have ever received. Since that visit, I have taken pleasure in watching Tsinghua continue its remarkable ascent. I was delighted to read in the news recently that Tsinghua had unveiled China's first domestic cloud computer, and that Tsinghua and one other Chinese university were ranked as the top universities in the emerging BRIC economies. Now in the United States, people feel that their personal status is raised when the status of their university goes up. So as a degree-holder from Tsinghua University, I say: Keep it up!

Chinese universities have been very much on my mind in the last few months. Let me mention a few salient events. In September 2013, China's Ministry of Education gave establishment approval for Duke Kunshan University, a joint-venture university being created by Duke, Wuhan University, and the Municipality of Kunshan that will open its doors in August 2014. In October 2013, the Schwarzman Scholars program, on whose advisory board I serve, had its groundbreaking on the Tsinghua campus. Also in October, an ambitious document was issued by the associations of leading academic institutions in the United States, Europe, Australia, and China describing the characteristics of research universities and the policy environment needed to support them. In November 2013, I traveled to Chicago to meet with twelve Chinese university presidents and a comparable number of American university presidents at an event featuring a speech by Vice Premier Liu Yandong. A few days later, Madame Liu and U.S. Secretary of State John Kerry spoke at the Fourth Annual U.S.-China Consultation on People-to-People Exchange in Washington, DC.

As this list suggests, China is scarcely foreign territory any more for the president of a major American university. Far more than when I came to Tsinghua in 2006, the Chinese and American higher education systems have become deeply interconnected, linked through a web of personal relationships, interinstitutional projects, and national initiatives.

In fact, Chinese-American university relationships have gone far beyond finite collaborations for fixed purposes. My experience these last few months makes me feel that we are arriving at a new stage in which these sets of institutions have begun to help each other *think*. Today the universities of China and the United States confront a shared paradox. We've arrived here for different reasons, derived from the different phases of social development we have currently attained, but we have a similar landscape before us. On the one hand, it is clearer than ever that research universities are critical to continued social and economic development; on the other hand, there is a growing perception that universities face challenges delivering the full value the public expects from them. To meet this heightened expectation, universities can't only stick to established practice. They need to think afresh about the good they have the potential to supply and then ask how they can best supply it. One key benefit higher education institutions can offer each other around the world is to help with this work of *thinking* about education's methods and goals.

The document issued last October by the American Association of Universities, League of European Research Universities, the Go8 in Australia, and the C9 in China is a case in point. (Its formal title is the "Hefei Statement on the Ten Characteristics of Contemporary Research Universities.") I am unaware of anything like this document in the history of higher education. It is remarkable not just for the global breadth of its signatories but for its depth of reflection on the function and value of research universities.

As background, this document understands that modern development and higher education have a complex symbiotic relationship.

Across the world, the progress of development has opened the doors to education to multitudes who formerly lacked such access, enriching their lives and equipping them to participate in more complex economic and social processes. Meanwhile, the increase of trained intelligence in the population has fueled the economic dynamism that, along with other products, creates growing educational opportunity. The massive expansion of higher educational opportunity that marked what economists Goldin and Katz have called "the Human Capital Century" gathered steam in the United States in the decades following World War II. In China this expansion has happened at an even more accelerated pace in the years since 1998. Now both countries are busy asking how educational access can be yet further expanded to prevent the hardening of social inequalities, and how the quality of broadly distributed education can be assured as well as the quantity.

Within the general landscape of higher education, research universities occupy a distinctive niche. Major research universities are relatively few in number and serve a relatively select portion of the population, but their impact on their societies is disproportionately large. Research universities are where the great discoveries have been made that lead to new economic activity and improved quality of life: work conducted at research universities has enabled the crucial innovations in modern information technology, environmental sustainability, and health care, to name only a few. And far more important than their specific research results, major research universities have a key role in producing a certain kind of person or citizen. Students trained in great research universities have gone on to play leadership roles in virtually every sector of modern societies. The same schools that are leading places of inquiry and discovery are also the training ground for habits of creative problem solving that are key requisites of modern life.

The Hefei Statement is a powerful piece of thinking because as it articulates the value research universities produce, it recognizes that these values exist in tension. Specifically, the Statement argues that while societies everywhere demand short-term benefits from research universities, the most profound benefits societies derive from universities are of a different nature and are not so easily named or defended. In the words of the document, "Universities also are storehouses of knowledge and broad capabilities that provide an underlying state of preparedness—a kind of information- and capacity-based insurance and broader vigilance—that business, government, and communities can draw upon to help deal with the unexpected and the unknown. This ability to respond quickly and creatively drawing on a significant breadth of capabilities . . . becomes more important as the volatility of the world increases and the unexpected becomes the norm."

In this way of thinking, universities do not exist primarily to produce answers to specific questions or people equipped to do specific things. They are a space of exploration, places where questions are asked and mental skills are developed without reference to immediate use alone, thus laying down a body of powers and understandings that can later be activated, brought into new combinations, and put to uses that could not be foreseen at the time they were first developed.

Since the public pays for research and education, it will naturally want to see the return on its investment, and there is no avoiding this expectation. The key challenge for research universities, therefore, is how to win a margin of public protection for their deep mission, how to fend off short-term pressures so they can do the unique things that meet society's long-term needs.

The university presidents' meeting in Chicago, which took place soon after the Hefei Statement was released, was a frank discussion of this problem in China and in America. The comments of the Chinese presidents made clear that the issue of university autonomy in China is not of concern just to foreigners. The Chinese leaders spoke freely of this need. They identified achieving the appropriate degree of independence as an unsolved problem that will have to be addressed if their universities are to reach their fullest potential. Though details have yet to be worked through, in principle your state partner does not disagree: Madame Liu's speech at that meeting cited the recommendation from the Third Plenary Session of the 18th CPC Central Committee that more autonomy be given to school authorities in the running of schools.

Through our longer history, American universities have established habits of independence not yet fully achieved elsewhere. But at this meeting, American presidents made clear that we too are beset with pressures: decreased state funding for public universities, an uncertain funding environment for basic as opposed to applied research, and a general public inclined to measure the worth of education in terms of immediate job placement and starting salaries for graduates.

None of these questions is easy, but even were we to get the problem of external relations—what the Hefei Statement calls the "policy environment"—right, universities still face another, internal question: If we require some freedom from the world's short-term demands in order to deliver a greater long-term value, are we delivering that value to the fullest extent, and how could we do better? How can the education we supply today be best designed to supply the world's needs tomorrow?

I have worked in higher education for nearly forty years, first as a scholar and teacher, then as a dean in charge of undergraduate education at Yale, and now this is my tenth year as a university president at Duke. The longer I have worked in this field, the more I have come to think that higher education's important goal is not the mastery of distinct subject fields but the development of deep habits of mind. For purposes of academic organization, we divide the university into natural sciences, social sciences, and humanities; we divide it further into physics, economics, philosophy, and the rest. But to name the traits that education should cultivate, we need very different words: active engagement; strength and breadth of curiosity; the urge to pull separate bits of knowledge together into new insights and to apply old lessons to new problems in new ways; the ability to think independently but also to work in teams; the will to use one's intelligence for the common good.

What if, instead of starting from the familiar map of academic disciplines, we started with this list of goals, then worked backward to ask how such habits of mind could be developed? I believe we would design university education somewhat differently. There is no set formula for cultivating these mental characteristics, but in the United States, putting the question this way has led to renewed interest in the idea of liberal arts education. Liberal arts education isn't just a matter of requiring students to visit random unrelated fields and fulfill their curricular obligations. Beyond its formal requirements, this model of education aims to engage multiple forms of intelligence to promote an active, integrative mind that's naturally disposed, when it comes upon a new fact or situation, to use existing knowledge to try to grasp it, while updating preexisting understandings in this new light.

The push for shortcuts and quick payoffs has produced negative talk about the liberal arts in the United States in recent years, and defense of the university's mission has required defending the value of this broad preparation. Two years ago, members of the U.S. Congress asked the American Academy of Arts and Sciences to convene a Commission on the Humanities and Social Sciences, which I was asked to cochair. The Commission was composed of fifty-three men and women of high achievement from every sector of society, including educators, businessmen, diplomats, judges, elected officials, artists and actors, and filmmakers. When the committee met, it quickly agreed that its real mission was to make the case for the foundational social value of a broad and inclusive concept of education that equips students with multiple skills. Although this commission contained many distinguished scholars and academic leaders, among them the presidents of Stanford, Harvard, and the University of Pennsylvania, some of the most eloquent voices on behalf of liberal arts education came from nonacademics. James McNerney, the CEO of Boeing and former chair of the U.S.-China Business Council, told us that high-tech manufacturing requires skilled engineers, but that beyond a certain level, people will not advance unless they have a broader array of skills, especially skills at communication and interacting with culturally diverse others—liberal arts training par excellence. General and ambassador Karl Eikenberry, who headed U.S. military and diplomatic efforts in Afghanistan and who, incidentally, holds an advanced degree in Chinese history from Nanjing University, testified that in the globalized modern world, weapons can do only so much to promote national security. Equally essential are the understanding of foreign languages, foreign histories and cultures, and belief systems different from one's own: classical social science and humanities fields within a liberal arts education. Norm Augustine, longtime head of Lockheed Martin and a principal proponent of improved science and technology education in the United States, argued that the single greatest weakness in U.S. education is in history and that the study of history develops core skills for creative workers and good citizens: collecting the evidence, making persuasive arguments, and weighing the value of conflicting interpretations.

If I were to look for a classic product of liberal arts education, I could find one in Chinese history: Yung Wing, Yale Class of 1854, the first person from China to graduate from an American university. As he recounts in his autobiography, Yung Wing had an offer by a benefactor to pay his full way through college if he would agree to return to China as a missionary. He declined, on the grounds that he did not want his life's work delimited in advance. After he graduated, he returned to China, where he worked rather aimlessly as a translator, then a clerk in a tea house, where—in recognition of his verbal powers—he was asked to write an appeal for foreign aid following a major flood. This, plus his entrepreneurial ventures getting tea out of rebel-held areas, won him notice as a clever man. In consequence, Yung Wing was asked to advise the Chinese government on how to close the knowledge gap in the field of technology. At this point he returned to the United States to buy machine tools for China, equipment that, on Yung Wing's advice, could manufacture not just specific needs but the machinery to meet many further needs— steamboats, for instance, in addition to rifles. Having established a base for technological education in China, he was then asked, in an early human rights initiative, to document abuses of Chinese migrant workers in the New World. This report ended the virtual slave trade in coolie labor to Peru. Later still he drew up plans for a national bank.

How was Yung Wing able to participate so constructively in so many different domains? Not by having been trained in a narrow, specialized way in any of them. He could move from one newly arising situation to another and play a role in building his nation in each because he was smart and enterprising and because he had a highly various, highly mobile set of skills. He perfectly exemplifies what the Hefei Statement means when it speaks of "a storehouse of broad capabilities that provide an underlying state of preparedness . . . that business, government and communities can draw on to help deal with the unexpected and unknown."

If we want a more contemporary example of the versatility broad preparation breeds, we could find it, paradoxically, in the twentieth century's most famous dropout. Steve Jobs, the founder of Apple, enrolled at Reed College, then one of the most noted liberal arts colleges in the United States, but he soon dropped out. But we would be wrong to think that college had no value for him. It's no surprise that Jobs was an early student of information technology and computer gaming, but he himself claimed that the most valuable thing he ever studied was a calligraphy course he took at Reed. It's the combination of technology with aesthetics, the power of design that Jobs first learned to appreciate through calligraphy, that gives Apple products their visual distinction and functional appeal. When Jobs first introduced the iPad, he showed an image of a crossroads at the intersection of two streets called Technology and Liberal Arts, and he announced that innovation is the product of conjunctions. "Technology alone is not enough," he said. "It's technology married with liberal arts, married with the humanities, that yields the results that make our hearts sing."

There is no magic formula for the form of education I am advocating. No university or national system has devised the surefire secret for training the sort of thoughtful, versatile graduate who will make a difference in the world. But what I find striking nowadays is the recognition by universities that they need to ask themselves the question, and the willingness to experiment in exploring possible answers. At Duke this year we are introducing a program called Bass Connections that will create, alongside the traditional school and department-based curriculum, a complementary curriculum based not on disciplines but on contemporary problems. Students in our undergraduate and professional schools will be able to access a broad, integrative curriculum addressing the issues of global health, energy, information, education and human development, and the study of the human brain. Each will draw on the range of disciplines that must play a part in successful solutions in these domains, including the sciences, economics, ethics, psychology, law, policy, and the study of culture. As students become deeply engaged, they will be able to pass from enrollment in courses to active participation in research teams and firsthand experience in real-world settings.

We do not regard this as a replacement for traditional training, but we do believe it will have an important effect in producing students who are wide ranging, skilled at integrating perspectives and domains of knowledge, and committed to using their intelligence to solve real-world problems. Though still in its pioneering phase, I have already met undergraduates working on teams with faculty, graduate students, and postdocs to test the success of programs to prevent school dropout in rural areas, to devise smartgrid elements, and to explore the boundaries between good and bad forms of stress. Our programs at Duke Kunshan University will feature the same cross-disciplinary, problem-solving pedagogy.

On the Chinese side, I am seeing a similar exploratory engagement with a version of education not limited to traditional disciplinary specializations. In the past decade, many leading Chinese universities have devised their own experiments in "interconnected knowledge." Here too, instead of adhering to a single model, different schools are trying different things—the ambitious Education Scheme for Arts and Sciences at Fudan University, the great books model at Sun Yat Sen University, the new experiments at Zhejiang University, not to mention Tsinghua's own liberal arts curriculum. In reading the reforms agreed to at the Third Plenary Session, I see what appears to be a national commitment to this broader, less rigidified model of education. The announcement pledges to examine a "multi-evaluation system" to make college admissions less dependent on a single test's metric for success. Another reform states that "efforts will be made to cultivate all-round students," a recognition of the special value that is produced when different dimensions of intelligence are developed in a single mind.

My point is that the challenge of having to face hard questions about the trained mental powers societies need can be a good thing for research universities, a spur to exploration and innovation. In this period, we have a great deal to learn from each other's efforts, since none of us is guaranteed to have the right answer in advance. Higher education has always advanced through the sharing of bright ideas and best practices across national boundaries. The system we in the United States regard as "American" is a hybrid of elements derived from medieval France and Germany, Reformation England, nineteenth-century Germany, and, more recently, the imported brainpower of faculty and students from East and South Asia. At the meeting of Chinese and American university presidents in Chicago, I saw an emerging forum for just this sort of exchange. We will all benefit by being good trading partners in ideas.

This leads me to a word about a final form of education sorely needed in our time: learning to understand and work productively within the context of cultural differences. We are all aware of China's rapid emergence as a global power, of which the rise of your universities is both an effect and a cause. After the Berlin Wall fell and the Soviet Union dissolved, many in the West predicted that we were entering a new global order that the United States would dominate as the single superpower.

Like many sage predictions, this one, if it ever was true, did not stay true for long. What Fareed Zakaria calls "the rise of the rest" has created a multipolar world, in which both China and the United States can claim superpower status.

History has taught that the collision of great powers can be highly destructive if they become trapped into defining one another as enemies. It is my hope, as it must be the hope of every thoughtful person around the globe, that we can do better than to replay the Cold War with a substitution in the cast. The United States and China are bound to be competitors, but it is not yet settled whether their competition will take a mutually damaging form or, perhaps, the sort we speak of in business and athletics, where competition makes every player better.

Education will be of the essence in determining how this question is settled. The chief guarantee of a positive future is for large numbers of people on both sides to have a chance to experience each other, to trade simplistic caricatures for a subtle understanding of each other's cultural particularities, and to learn how to work together on a basis of mutual understanding and respect. It has been thirty-five years since the U.S. and the PRC established diplomatic relations, and the People-to-People Exchange our governments have committed to involves many levels of exchange, but given how deeply people's mind-sets are shaped in their youth, the bilateral flow of students is the most critical element.

In the current generation, large numbers of Chinese, including virtually every Chinese university leader, have had the experience of studying in the West. I am glad that the traffic flow is in the process of becoming more two-way. The Schwarzman Scholars program will be a prestigious, highly competitive honor drawing future Western leaders to study in China. At Duke we are happy to have nearly one thousand Chinese students studying at our campus in North Carolina, but we will be even happier when our best students and your best students can learn together at Duke Kunshan University.

I close with a quotation that I have always found inspiring. Wilhelm von Humboldt was one of the principal inventors of the new-model research university created in Berlin in the early nineteenth century, from which all modern universities are derived. Humboldt defined the essential spirit of the research university this way: "Everything depends upon holding to the principle of understanding knowledge as something not yet found, never completely to be discovered, and searching relentlessly for it as such." This claim—that no one has the whole truth yet, that the truth is something that can only be progressively discovered, advanced toward in better and better approximations through an ongoing act of inquiry—this is the creed that animates the modern research university; the Hefei Statement eloquently restates it, but it scarcely improves on it. In this concept, faculty members are explorers and discoverers, not primarily authority figures; students and teachers are there to search together; and every idea, however final it may seem, not only can be but needs to be questioned, tested, reconsidered, for knowledge to keep advancing.

No research university ever perfectly lives up to this ideal, but all universities become better when they remember this ideal and strive to make it real. For all their challenges, this as a moment of opportunity for universities, to the extent that we are pushed to keep asking and coming up with better answers to the question of what a university at its best can be. None of us can find the answer alone, but we can make progress if we work together. I welcome all Chinese partners in this shared quest.

Leadership Transitions, Rebuilding the Campus, the Role of Philanthropy

March 27, 2014

Friends, for the past several years, some single issue has been so important to this community that I have made it the sole subject of my faculty address. One year I spoke of Duke's strategy for coping with the economic downturn. Another year my subject was Duke's approach to international engagements. As we began to celebrate the fiftieth anniversary of the enrollment of the first black undergraduates, I addressed the history of Duke and race. Last year I talked about college costs and the value of liberal arts education.

This year no single subject clamors for attention to the same degree. So with your permission, I thought I would share some thoughts on three issues. I remember learning in grade school that nouns were the names for people, places, and things. In hopes of securing your attention through to the end, I propose that my topics today will be People, Places, and Funds.

First, people. This spring I am completing my tenth year as president of Duke. It is a notable fact that for this entire decade, I have worked with the same executive leadership team. Victor Dzau, chancellor of health affairs, was hired a few months after me and started work on the same day. Peter Lange, the only provost I've known at Duke, had already been in office five years when I arrived. Tallman Trask, my only executive vice president, had come to Duke earlier yet, in 1995.

These have been good years for Duke, and while I know that administrators have not been the sole cause, the stability and experience of this leadership team has certainly contributed to Duke's success. But nothing lasts forever, and this year, we knew, things would begin to change. Since the time when he accepted a third term as provost, Peter Lange and I had looked to this, his fifteenth year, as the time when he would step down. Peter has been here for so much of the modern history of Duke and has put his energetic mark on so many aspects that it would scarcely be too much to say of him, as the epitaph of the architect Sir Christopher Wren says in St. Paul's Cathedral: "If you seek his monument, look around you." So deep has his impact been that we've all had moments of asking, How can Duke be expected to survive without him?

But it's the mark of healthy institutions that they're built to withstand leadership transitions, and the great question mark we all faced at the start of this year has been answered in a reassuring way. As you will recall, after consultation with ECAC, I named a search committee last August. At Josh Socolar's wise suggestion, the committee and its chair, George Truskey, spent an hour this September meeting with the Academic Council and listening to your hopes and fears. On this basis, an excellent document was drawn up articulating what Duke needed in its next provost. An outstanding pool of talent found this job attractive and entered the field as candidates. We tested the candidates against the institution's needs, and at the end the choice was surprisingly easy.

Many of you know Sally Kornbluth, the James B. Duke Professor of Pharmacology and Cancer Biology, but since she is here for the first time in her new capacity as provost-elect, I hope you'll allow me to say what the search found so compelling. Sally is a scholar's scholar who has been widely honored for her research, including by election to the Institute of Medicine. She has also been a devoted mentor, seeing twenty-five PhD students through to completion of their degrees. As vice dean for basic science in the School of Medicine, she has helped build a shared infrastructure for biomedical research, first for the basic sciences, then also for the clinical departments. As she has taken on wider and wider responsibilities, she has won high marks for her "people skills," specifically her skill at listening to people articulate their needs and the creative problem-solving skills with which she then welds people's separate ideas into something none of them quite suggested that ends up benefiting them all. Add to her imaginativeness and problem-solving gifts that she has an immense love of this institution and total dedication to its values, and it's clear that Duke will thrive with Sally Kornbluth as our new chief academic officer. Sally, I thank you for your willingness to serve.

As I say, it had been long foreseen that this would be the year for a provostial transition. Though we knew that we would face a change in the Health System before long, I did not foresee that that change too would arrive this year, but with the announcement that Victor Dzau will be the new president of the Institute of Medicine, Duke now faces another issue of leadership succession. Victor has presided over extraordinary successes in Duke Medicine and has emerged as a leading voice regionally, nationally, and internationally, advocating new solutions for health care challenges. For a Dukie to be chosen to head the IOM is a well-deserved honor for Victor and an honor for us all, and I offer him our thanks and congratulations.

But as with the provost's, the prospect of a vacancy in this key position can be a little anxiety-inducing, since it reminds us just how broad and rare the skills are that will be required in a successor. The chancellor for health affairs needs to be adept at understanding the business of health care *and* completely in tune with the research aspirations of a world-class academic medical center, *and* he or she needs to understand how these potentially rival commitments can be made to serve and support each other as complementary elements. In addition, like the provost, the chancellor has to be deeply devoted to the existing world of academic research and education yet also unusually alive to the changing landscape in which these activities take place, and has to be able to lead us in seeing how to protect the best of the present while innovating in ways that will guarantee our long-term success.

It's daunting to draw up the list of such requirements in the abstract, but I am confident that we'll find a person as capable of leading Duke Medicine forward in the next chapter as Victor was in the last. In the coming weeks, I will be announcing a search committee, which will have ample faculty representation from the School of Medicine's basic science and clinical departments, from the School of Nursing, and also from the university side. By custom, given the institutional importance of this position, a trustee or recent trustee has headed health system chancellor searches at Duke, and I am delighted to report that

Rick Wagoner, who stepped down as chair of Duke's Board of Trustees last summer, has agreed to chair the search. By custom we have also had a distinguished faculty member as the vice chair, and I'm grateful that Bart Haynes, former chair of the Department of Medicine and lead investigator on the multi-university grant in pursuit of an HIV-AIDS vaccine, has agreed to serve in this role.

I am expecting the search to begin in April and to conclude in late 2014, with the new appointee taking office as early in 2015 as can be arranged. Victor will remain in office through June 30, but that will leave a gap of some months, so I should say a few words about interim arrangements. I do not plan to appoint an interim chancellor. Instead, Bill Fulkerson will have broad leadership on the Health System side and Nancy Andrews on the School of Medicine side, with both reporting to me during this interim, and I will be involved in making system-wide decisions. Duke Medicine is in excellent shape to weather this transition, and all parties are committed to making things work. By this time next year, I expect to introduce the new chancellor to this body.

In truth, universities renew themselves through change, and for all the anxieties change can inspire, at the end of the day leadership transitions are opportunities for institutional renewal. I now want to turn to another dimension of institutional change and renewal, this one involving our physical setting. The campus of any great university is the result of a long, complex process of accretion, but that doesn't mean that change is constant or steady. In general, changes in the built environments of universities track the ups and downs in the larger economy. With the infusion of James B. Duke's transformational gift in the 1920s, Duke sprouted the Georgian campus on East and the Gothic campus on West, including the newly founded School of Medicine and Duke Hospital. We've never experienced the physical remaking of Duke on anything like a comparable scale—I once read that at the time, the building of Duke University was the largest construction project under way in America—and after this prodigious start, Duke added little new for several decades. What was added, be it said, was not always built to the highest or most eternally enduring standards. The 1970s and 1980s, financially hard times for American universities, gave Duke the Bryan Center and the Central Campus apartments: not exactly Duke Chapel.

When I arrived in 2004, there were cranes everywhere. In fact, building off the unprecedented run of prosperity that continued (with occasional punctuations) from the mid-1990s through 2007 or so, Duke was then in the middle of the second-largest physical transformation in its history. Almost every school got more adequate, handsome, and contemporary space through this process: Engineering's Fitzpatrick CIEMAS Center was dedicated in the fall of 2004; we are meeting in the major Divinity School addition that was completed in 2005, the year that Sanford added Rubenstein Hall; the Nursing School, previously housed in parts of five separate structures, got a proper home of its own in 2006; Arts and Sciences added the French Science Center in 2007; the Law School, whose building was once unkindly likened to a midwestern high school forcibly crossbred with a branch bank, completed its major renovation and expansion in 2008.

As it opened the door to growing academic excellence in our different units, this time also saw the building of shared structures that drew the university together and enriched our common life. The renovation of Perkins Library, including the addition of the Bostock and the von der Heyden Pavilion, completed in 2005, took Duke's central knowledge repository and carried it forward many decades in a single bound, giving Duke state-of-the-art services for information sharing and knowledge creation and causing a revolution in student study habits. (Library use increased 40 percent when the renovated Perkins opened.) The Nasher Museum, also completed in 2005, gave this community high-end access to the experience of art that has enhanced our lives and put Duke on the artistic map. You will recall that the Nasher's *El Greco to Velázquez* exhibit, based on the scholarship of its now-director Sarah Schroth, was ranked as one of the top ten shows in America in 2008, a new kind of national news for Duke to receive. The *Archibald Motley: Jazz Age Modernist* exhibit currently hanging at the Nasher, similarly based on Duke faculty expertise (in this case Rick Powell's), will continue from Durham to the Los Angeles Museum of Contemporary Art and then to the Whitney's new facility in New York—an event that never could have happened had Duke not created the Nasher Museum.

In sum, the Duke we now take for granted was in significant measure built in relatively recent times. For reasons you may be able to discern, that building boom ceased rather abruptly in 2008. For the next several years, with few exceptions (one at Fuqua), the cranes vanished from the university side of campus. Since the health care sector of the economy followed a different trajectory even during a catastrophic downturn, building activity in this next phase took place largely on the medical side of the house, with the stunning creation of the Duke Cancer Center, completed in 2012, and the Duke Medicine Pavilion and the Trent Semans Center for Health Education, which both opened last year.

Here let me stop and say that, to my mind, building a building can never be the goal of a university. Buildings are means, not ends. A university should have a strong presumption against investing resources in physical entities unless there is a strong case that the things that are our real ends—research, teaching, the work of knowledge creation and education broadly considered—can be reached only with the help of a physical structure. The boast Duke deserves to make about our second big building boom is not just that we returned to a higher standard of architecture and construction, but that we met this test for capital investments.

The point is worth emphasizing because now, a little unexpectedly, we find ourselves in another building phase. I'd like to think that for every project currently under way on campus, Duke could concisely and convincingly explain not just what is going up but what that facility will facilitate: what high end of a university will be made reachable by this means.

For a quick tour of the campus taking shape around us, I'd begin with the new environment building being built out the back of the Levine Science Research Center, which will be dedicated next month. The Nicholas School of the Environment is the single Duke school that did not benefit from the last building boom. The new building will give expansion space to a school that's currently massively overcrowded, and, at least as important, it will allow the three academic units that were merged together when the Nicholas School was created to lead a fully unified, physically integrated life at last.

Proceed down Circuit Drive and turn left on Towerview and you will come to the major academic building put up at Duke in the 1960s, Gross Chemistry. When I had occasion to look up press articles on the opening of this building in 1968, I learned that it was said to be designed in the "modern Gothic" style—Gothic became "modern," apparently, by substituting heavy, dark, and low for the light, airy, aspiring style we used to know. Well, every university has its Gross Chem. But implausibly yet wonderfully, even Gross Chem has now been touched by the magic wand of transformation. New windows now let light and life into a structure that used to have the forbidding gloom of a tomb. Inside, the dead, empty atrium has been transformed into a bustling, attractive interaction space, drawing people together across the many cross-school initiatives that now have a home here: the Energy Initiative, the Innovation and Entrepreneurship Program, the "big data" project, and the Social Science Research Institute. With its strategic location near the Law School, Sanford, Fuqua, and the sciences and engineering, the refurbished Gross Hall has the capacity to be the innovation center our campus never had, an experimental space where new questions can be explored, drawing faculty and students together in new configurations, at the junction of Duke's separate schools.

Skipping to East Campus, I invite those of you who haven't done so to attend a concert at Baldwin Auditorium. Forming the focal point of East Campus as Duke Chapel does of West, Baldwin has always had a lovely, dignified appearance, but as with many original Duke buildings, when you walked inside, it all fell apart. Linoleum not stylish since the 1950s covered the floor; black plastic bags shut out the light and hid the graceful interior dome; plus the hall, a concert hall, was a veritable graveyard of sound. I give Tallman Trask the lion's share of the credit for remaking Baldwin into the jewel it is today. While perfectly preserving the traditional exterior, a new concert hall has been built inside that's strikingly beautiful and has state-of-the-art acoustics, acoustics that are tunable night by night to the needs of different forms of musical performance. The Baldwin renovation was recently honored with an Excellence in Construction Award from the Associated Builders and Contractors group, the first national award of its kind given for a Duke building. At the opening concert last September, I heard a compliment that touched me quite as deeply: a faculty performer told me that Carnegie Hall was the only other hall he had ever played where each musician could hear the other musician play. These things matter, and not only in an ornamental sense. People's minds are opened and their powers of attention and appreciation are decisively expanded by the experiences they have at university. Thanks to the Baldwin renovation, Duke now has one more place where people can experience the revelatory power of excellence, an education that will touch thousands of students, faculty, and community members for decades to come.

I turn last to two large projects at the center of Duke's campus. You have all seen the massive crane looming over the library, and with a well-trained guide, you might have seen the large hole that's been made where the 1928 Perkins Library's insides used to be. The latest construction will complete the Perkins transformation, creating new study spaces, new means for retrieving and sharing Duke's vast collections, and a new place to encounter Duke's extraordinary and growing archive of primary source materials. As with Baldwin, the library's classic, familiar appearance will be lovingly preserved on the outside even as a state-of-the-art new facility is created on the inside. If these buildings give the message that education has something to do with conservation and perpetuation and something to do with innovation—the two understood as partners, not opponents—that will be a powerful signature of Duke.

Across the Chapel Quad from the library, another piece of surgery is under way that will write this message in a comparably central fashion. West Union is the central shared student space at Duke, but if ever you toured its quite confusing floor plan, you know that this building was a hodgepodge of random architectural accretions aggravated by incoherent space assignments, the whole in massive need of tender loving care. The chance to radically rehabilitate West Union gave us a chance to think of the whole precinct ranging down the Plaza to the Bryan Center and to ask how the whole could be coherently redeveloped to give maximum benefit to student life. If you've followed the detours, you've seen the first fruits of this emerging project. These include, first, the Bryan Center, shorn of its gloomy exterior panels to create light, visibility, and an air of modernity and reorganized to give prime space to the most widely used student activities; second, the beautiful Penn Pavilion, in the short term a swing space for dining displaced during West Union construction, and in the longer term, a large, central, flexible events space of the sort this university has sorely needed; and third, the extended West Union plaza, our High Line, an expansion of the outdoor space that's proven so successful as our pedestrian Main Street since its opening in 2006.

These are all preludes, however, to the main event: the construction that will restore and renovate West Union's great historic spaces, replace its incoherent core with well-designed places for gathering and dining, and open the whole for maximum connectivity both to the plaza and to a new garden space to be created on the lower level toward Kilgo Quad. Tallman will remind you of the plans in detail if you like. My point is that we are continuing the building of this university, and doing so not just to add snappy amenities but in service to our deepest educational mission.

The heart of the ideal of residential education is that a community of engaged, spirited, intelligent people educate each other all day long, stretching and inspiring each other through every encounter, including those marked "academic," those we term extracurricular, and those that might be labeled merely "social." The challenges to higher education in recent years typically refer to this idea as passé, but in truth, current trends are increasing its value, not diminishing it. When "everything" can be learned online, there will still be profound things that can be learned only face-to-face, by living people interacting with other living people in the fullness of their living humanity. How many in this room can trace some major transformation in their personal and intellectual life to something a teacher or classmate said or did in college, some spark they struck, some trouble they took, or some attention they paid? In the world at large, the vibrant, successful places are ones that offer the richest chance for smart people to collide with each other in person, to bump into and interact with each other in a host of unprogrammed ways.

Schools like Duke have the precious potential to anchor education in direct personal interaction across a massively diverse range of talents and experiences. But we can't take for granted that this benefit will automatically be delivered. To realize this potential, we have to create the enabling conditions for maximal interaction, our own collision spaces, places sufficiently attractive that any student or faculty member in the university might be drawn there on any day, at any hour, with no particular plan, and have the chance of running into people they know, or half-know, or are about to begin to know. For all the beauty of this campus, Duke has not had an overabundance of such unowned, collective spaces, though virtually every construction project has added to the stock (think Twinnies in the Fitzpatrick Center, or Star Commons in the Law School, or the Jo Rae Café in the Trent Semans Building, or the Nasher Café), all with instant success. The restored West Union will be Duke's chance to put this sort of space at the literal center of the campus on a scale that can accommodate the whole community, saying to everyone who looks, "Come to Duke and step into a place of endless connection and interaction, a place where people live together and learn together in the most profound way possible."

So you got my message about People: transitions aren't scary; change is renewing! And now you have my message about Places: we're building, but it's not about the building. To close, I will say a word about Funds. I made it sound before as if building trends on campuses track the general ebb and flow of the economy, and in a general way they do, but this account leaves out the crucial intermediary: philanthropy. In many public universities, building trends tend to track the generosity of legislators with the taxpayers' dollars. In private universities, private generosity tends to be the crucial variable and enabler. Think back with me. No James B. Duke, no East Campus and no West Campus. No Ray Nasher, no Nasher Museum. No Michael and Patty Fitzpatrick, no Fitzpatrick Center; no Roy and Merilee Bostock, no Bostock Library.

Duke's last great wave of building was borne on the back of the Campaign for Duke, which raised $2.3 billion by its close in 2003. And Duke's new buildings benefit from help from our friends in the same way. The West Union project, Baldwin Auditorium, and, in the fullness of time, the refurbished Page were made possible by a gift from The Duke Endowment, the private foundation in Charlotte established by James B. Duke. Rubenstein Library, the rare book and archive facility now being created within Perkins, was enabled by the generosity of David Rubenstein, current chair of the board of trustees. Penn Pavilion was made possible by a gift from Robert and Katherine Penn in support of Duke's dream of student community.

When we officially launched the Duke Forward campaign in September 2012, we had already recorded gifts and pledges of $1.3 billion on our way to a $3.25 billion goal. I am thrilled to announce that earlier this week we crossed the $2 billion mark. As significant as the dollar total, the Duke Forward campaign has had extraordinary success in bringing the case for Duke and the vision of its future out to alumni, parents, and friends. Since launching the campaign on campus in 2012, we have taken its message to nine major cities with crowds that have broken all known records for Duke gatherings, often by a considerable amount. Over five hundred people came in San Francisco and Los Angeles, a thousand in New York City, four hundred in Chicago, two hundred plus in London, to events offering inspiring exposures to Duke faculty and students from every school, at the end of which people have been so jazzed that they stayed well beyond closing time. I'm grateful to all who have participated in these events, because they have done something far beyond—also logically prior to—the raising of actual funds. They've shared the intellectual excitement of what we're doing here and reminded our friends and donors of this university's ongoing trajectory—a story they can help create, a mission they can help us to fulfill, through their investments in this university.

This is the final lesson, then: we're building, but it's not about the buildings; so too we're fundraising, but it's not about the money. I have told you our dollar target, but the best "sell" I know how to make in this campaign is to say that the dollars are not the goal: dollars are the means to our real goal, which is in every part educational. The buildings piece is, in reality, a relatively small part of what we're seeking to support. Our primary goals will always be investments in people. We seek support for faculty—the funds to draw top minds and to help them reach new heights in teaching, research, and clinical care. We also seek support for students—the means to fund our commitment to make Duke financially accessible to all students of high talent, regardless of family background. That commitment, while expensive, is central to our notion of what a university can be—a diverse community of people brought together by their potential, not by their means—and what a university should do— namely, to help our students to live up to that potential and release it for the world. These financial targets, then, have a real and human goal, which is to continue to populate Duke with the kind of faculty and students who bring its mission to life. With your help, we've created a vision of education that people are eager to invest in. Now let's make that vision a reality. There's work for all of us in this cause.

Opportunity Changes Everything

May 3, 2014

President Padrón, President Oroza, members of the state board of education and the state legislature, trustees and members of the faculty, happy families whose sacrifices have paid off at last, and graduates from the Kendall Campus whose dreams come true today: good evening! I can't think of a prouder occasion. Danielle Rose, I congratulate you on your outstanding accomplishments and thank you for your kind words. I also want to acknowledge Pascale Charlot, the new dean of the Honors College here at Miami Dade, a graduate of my own university.

Colleges are a wonderful invention because colleges are in the human potential business. Colleges exist to help you become the person you have it in you to be, so that you can deliver the full measure of your promise to your world. By the evidence before me today, in the shining eyes of graduates who have overcome every challenge and are ready to take on the world, this college is entitled to say, "Mission accomplished Graduates, you did it! Waiting world, look out!"

Now I'm a sucker for graduations, and I've seen a lot of them, but it's especially inspiring to experience this moment at Miami Dade College. Every person who has been president of the United States for the past twenty years has come to speak at a Commencement here. To the best of my knowledge, that record is unmatched at any other institution of higher education in the country, with the understandable exception of the service academies. So why is Miami Dade the place to go? When Miami

Dade calls, why does no one refuse? It's partly due to the respect President Eduardo Padrón commands across the nation: I can tell you, this is not a man you want to say no to. But he enjoys such prestige because of the institution you all have created, which is unique in this land.

From the day this school first opened its doors, it was designed to create opportunity where opportunities were hard to come by. This year we're celebrating the fiftieth anniversary of the 1964 Civil Rights Act, the law that made it illegal to discriminate on the grounds of race, sex, religion, or national origin in hiring, housing, education, and public transportation. That law rolled back the hateful legacy that maintained a separate and unequal racial regime a hundred years after the Civil War had ended. This is the law that introduced the language of equal opportunity into American life.

But Miami Dade did not wait for Congress to act; in the early 1960s, you stepped out in front. While some groups were still striving to maintain racially segregated schools in the South, your founders opened the doors of educational opportunity to African American students, creating the first integrated junior college in the state of Florida. The Miami of that time also hosted another population that lived on the margins of American success: the thousands of refugees who fled here in the wake of the Cuban Revolution. Immigrant children too found welcome here and a place to launch American careers.

From this remarkable origin grew a school with highly distinctive characteristics. Already by 1967, Miami Dade was the largest institution of higher education in the state of Florida. Today Miami Dade College has the largest undergraduate enrollment of any U.S. college or university—175,000 of you, enough to fill a fair-size city. Immigrant-friendly and international from the first, this college's students represent 185 countries and speak ninety-four languages: the parade of flags at the Olympics was poor stuff compared to the signs of national origin displayed here today. More than half of Miami Dade students are the first in their family to attend college. Two-thirds are low income. Miami Dade confers more associate degrees than any other college in the country and ranks first in degrees awarded to black and Hispanic students.

If you want to see democracy in action, people of every origin lifting themselves by their own hard work, you could not do better than to witness a Miami Dade Commencement. That's why President Bill Clinton came here to speak. That's why President George W. Bush came in 2007. That's why President Barack Obama came in 2011. And that's why President Richard Brodhead came in 2014. I am honored that I too am about to receive a Miami Dade degree. A person who believes in democracy could boast of no higher distinction.

Given the history I've just traced, it is not surprising that the motto of my new school is "Opportunity Changes Everything." That's a great saying, and Lord knows, it is true. A major paradox of our time is that fifty years after the passage of the Civil Rights Act and the creation of the Equal Opportunity Commission, we are living at a time of deepening inequality; the law made a difference, but it didn't make all the difference. Throughout the history of the United States, education has always been the main vehicle for people to rise higher than their circumstances of birth would dictate. A hundred years ago, high school was still a novelty, and a person with a year or two of high school had dramatically improved employment prospects. In the decades after World War II, college enrollment rose steeply in the U.S., and attending some college became a way to get a better job. Today high school skills don't get you very far in the American labor market—if you stopped there, the doors of advancement are closed pretty tight—and college training is needed for jobs that never had that prerequisite even a short while back. Complex manufacturing needs smart workers, the brains as well as brawn; jobs with a technology component need workers who can manage the technology; service careers need advanced communications skills; employers everywhere want people who are creative problem solvers, who can see how to reinvent the job and do the work in better ways.

If there had been no college for you to enroll in, there would be no open door, no ladder to help you rise. Instead, Opportunity Changed Everything. But let's remember the funny nature of opportunity. The dictionary tells me an opportunity is "a favorable juncture of circumstances," "a good chance for advancement and progress." True, but that's only half of the story. For the whole truth is that opportunity makes absolutely nothing happen by the sheer fact of its existence. An opportunity creates a possibility, but a possibility turns into a reality only when some man or woman seizes the opportunity, capitalizes on the favorable circumstance, and drives the progress to make it happen.

In short, opportunity requires a shrewd and timely action from someone who might instead have held back. Mark Twain once said, "I was seldom able to see an opportunity until it had ceased to be one." And what we celebrate as you complete your degrees isn't just the existence of Miami Dade College; it's that when the possibility of college was afforded to you, you seized the opportunity and saw it through.

Let me tell you a little story from where I come from. About two years ago, I was at a meeting discussing opportunities for professional training that we have for our staff at Duke. It was all very informative but a little abstract until someone gave it a human face. An employee in our library named Jameca Dupree told us her story. She had been a single mother of a six-month-old baby, with no college training, holding down two part-time jobs, one of them clearing trays in our hospital cafeteria. A person who would have had every excuse to go home every night downhearted and too tired for any further effort instead found her way to Duke's Professional Development Institute, where she began to learn about financial and record-keeping systems, business writing, and other administrative skills. From there, she took advantage of Duke's employee tuition benefit, in which Duke reimburses its employees for tuition expenses if they choose to deepen their skills and improve their qualifications. While continuing to work a full-time job, Jameca finished a four-year degree in business administration at a local college in two and a half years. Armed with her new degree, she is now a financial analyst in our library system, married, the mother of two sons and a daughter, and she and her husband have purchased their own home. Jameca ended her story on a note of obvious pride: "I am an example to my children." And I thought, no—you are an example to us all.

Now, Jameca is, I admit, a bit of an overachiever, but I learn something important about you from remembering her tale. Here is the point: Opportunity Changes Everything, If You Actively Seize Opportunities. If Jameca Dupree had not had access to a professional development program or to the tuition benefit, her advancement may not have happened—though knowing her, I'm betting she would have found a way. But the mere fact that those programs existed didn't guarantee that anything would change for her; she must have had dozens of coworkers who had the same opportunities around them who didn't make those uses of them. So what did Jameca have, what's the specific content of this word I keep using, *to seize*? Well, she had the drive, the desire, the sheer ambition to be something more for herself and her children; she had the strength to keep that dream alive on the many days when it must have seemed just too hard; she had the discipline to manage her life's complex obligations each day so as to leave room to keep advancing toward this goal; she had a commitment to a better future and the grit and determination to make it happen.

My friends at Miami Dade College, you and your families know it far better than I: those are the virtues it took for you to be here today. Your diploma does far more than certify the programs you've passed and the subjects you've mastered, important though those are. Your diploma is an announcement to the world of the character, discipline, persistence, and commitment that you have shown in completing this course of study. College didn't just teach you subjects: it was a trial through which you have built new strengths for yourself. And that whole character, not just the little bits of specialized knowledge, is what you can offer the world now.

Are you following me? It's getting complicated! So let's review. (1) Opportunity Changes Everything. But more accurately, (2) Opportunity Changes Nothing If You Don't Seize It, But Everything If You Do. Then further: (3) Seizing Opportunities Changes Everything, and Especially Changes You. And now that you've become a more capable person through your work acquiring an education, what else can you change? Well, I hope, your personal circumstances—your job, your ability to contribute to your family, the example you set to your children and family and community. I wish you this success in ample and abundant measure. But that's not all a capable person can do.

What if the Opportunity of education changed Everything? Could it really change Everything? Well, the world is changing every day, changing for better and changing for worse, and it doesn't change by some fated process—it changes through the steps humans take and the choices humans make together day by day. Ask yourself about anything that's important to you in our society. You know it could be about to break in a bad direction or, possibly, in a good one. We'll come to better outcomes to the extent that people believe in their power to shape the outcome and pitch in to make the better alternative win out.

Think with me. Recent studies have shown that children with early exposure to a rich learning environment start school far ahead of those who lack such an environment, that they acquire full literacy more easily and progress faster in school, and that they enjoy better health and experience fewer bad health outcomes for the whole course of their life. It's a profound inequality rooted in the earliest years of life. So is it just fated that children will be born to radically different life chances, and that's the end of that? Or could citizens use every power we have, first in our own families, neighborhoods, and communities, then in our state and national lives as voters, to promote better and fairer starts in life for all of our children?

At the other end of the age spectrum—and I know this is especially relevant in Florida—I'm thinking of our senior citizens. You probably know that the social safety net erected in this country in the last century has begun to have the effect of shifting public resources more and more into the support of older people, with less and less available to invest in creating future opportunities for younger Americans. If nothing is done to change the current system, this disparity will grow more gravely serious with each passing decade, and none of us will escape its consequences. This is a wicked hard political problem—but it's made harder by the assumption that there's nothing anyone can do about it. We'll all be gainers if concerned citizens come together to find the thoughtful balance point between the needs of the older and the needs of the younger generation. Leave it to someone else and you're unlikely to enjoy the results. You're an educated person: what if you take responsibility to create the world we'll inhabit together, and not just passively inhabit it? You'll never know the extent of what you can change until you try.

My theme today is opportunity, and my point is that opportunity isn't a historical constant. At this moment there are many open questions in our society. The way we answer these questions will help determine what kind of opportunity exists in the future and how widely that opportunity will be shared. I look before me at the inspiring spectacle of representatives of all the world's people, through your hard work and belief in your promise, stepping forward to claim your place as full members of American society. But please remember, education is good not only for opening the door to personal success. It also equips you to be a shaper of our shared world, so take that power seriously. Graduates of this college that's been such an agent of opportunity, I congratulate you on the opportunities you have seized and the new ones that await you now. I wish you wonderful lives. *Que Dios los bendiga.* Now go help create opportunities for others.

On Comfort True and False

Duke Chapel, August 20, 2014

Parents, your children are sitting in regal splendor in Duke's glorious Gothic chapel, but you are seated far away, in Cameron Indoor Stadium. Why the distance? Well, Duke Chapel has just enough room for our entering class, so we put you in an overflow zone. But you might have suspected a deeper, darker reason: we are rehearsing you for a great separation. You have loved and nurtured these children, you have given them every means to develop their gifts, and they made your dream come true: today they enter one of the world's great universities. Now there's one last thing you as parents need to do: go home, back off, give them space to build an independent life. Dean Nowicki and I will be out front of the Chapel after this ceremony, and I cordially invite you to come find us, but after lunch, it's time to go. If that's sobbing I hear, here's the comfort: if you stick around, your children will just find you annoying; leave, and they'll miss you and love you all the more.

Now for you, Duke Class of 2018. I trust you've found Duke comfortable. I saw you moving into those cozy East Campus rooms with your cars full of pillows and personal effects, all the comforts of home. There you met a concierge staff keen to see to your every need, our bizarrely numerous FACs and RAs.

As the manager of this fine hotel and minister of comfort to Duke Nation, I now want to go the final step and remove the very last twinge of discomfort remaining. Is anyone a little homesick? You may feel you alone are experiencing this emotion, but it's a common thing to feel when you enter a strange new world, and behind their masks of cheerful well-adjustedness, many of your classmates are feeling just the same. Duke psychologist Mark Leary, one of the world's great experts on homesickness, notes that unlike some other animals, primitive humans lacked the bodily means to protect themselves on their own. Our earliest ancestors needed groups to survive, so in evolution, it was an adaptive trait to feel pained when stepping out of known social worlds. So if you experience such pangs, you need to say, "Oh, I remember! That doesn't mean anything; that's only human!—a transition emotion that will quickly fade."

Now let the Comfort Doctor probe a little deeper. Tell me the truth: Duke is great and all, but in your heart of hearts, might you not be finding it a little daunting? I watched your faces as Christoph Guttentag spoke. You laughed, but I could detect another response: "Uh oh! I don't come from a place with a cute name. I was not the Tae Kwon Do champion of Myanmar. I was not conducting promising research on the Ebola virus when I was in tenth grade. What am I doing here? How am I supposed to compete when everyone else is a certified miracle of adolescent achievement? Plus what if I should be unmasked, what if some Edward Snowden got access to my private messages and uncovered the awful truth that, contrary to the big brags of my college application, I am at some level a fairly ordinary person?"

Have any of you had such thoughts? How many—maybe twelve hundred of you? Friends, you disappoint me. How can you be so unoriginal? That anxiety isn't proof of your special deficiency. That's what every smart person thinks when they step up the level of their game. The fun thing about Duke is that it's a community of talent where talent manifests itself in a thousand different forms, yours cheerfully included. Duke students aren't interested in exposing each other's limitations. They rejoice in each other's gifts and accomplishments; they lift each other up.

You will do fine here. You will thrive. I want you to feel completely comfortable in that assurance. Very comfortable. Very, very comfortable. But let's not make comfort your only goal.

For the first time in human history, modern consumer culture has come to hold out the ideal of comfort as a plausible full-time expectation and worthy human aim. We live in the time of comfort foods, comfort zones, humidity comfort indices, being comfortable in your own skin.

But there are values that are not compatible with comfort, and those include values crucial to the adventure you're about to undertake.

Those of you who are serious athletes or musicians know that you didn't get to the level you've reached by being told that you were already perfect, or that good enough was good enough. You learned to visualize an ideal of high performance and to embrace the discipline required to raise yourself toward what you could be. That's what you're invited to join at Duke: a community of aspiration, a place where people work and play together to reach the highest level of their capacities. Stick to what's comfortable and you will miss that fun.

But the fact that comfort promotes mediocrity is not the only problem. I will be amazed if you are not carrying around in your head a chatter of voices assuring you that you should already know what you're going to be in later life and should plan your Duke career to enable the systematic acquisition of all the merit badges that will assure your arrival at that happy goal. There are many contributors to this inward chorus—natural anxieties, an unreliable economy that has heightened the perception of risk, a media and political chorus convinced that education has no value unless it aims straight for a job, parents who crave assurance that you will be set for life. These voices all reinforce the idea that there is one sure ultimate comfort: a career that will purge your life of uncertainty and risk. But allow me to say: you're still very young, you can't possibly already know for certain the eventual career that you are meant to occupy. To find that, you need to open your horizons, learn the range of possibilities, and find what fulfills and motivates you. Duke can be just the space of exploration and discovery that you need, but only if you free yourself from the need to know the answer in advance.

Then further, whatever it is you find to do, there will be a richer and a poorer version of the self you bring to that eventual career. The really successful people in our world don't just know how to do a job. They bring a fund of knowledge and wisdom to their life, a wide awareness of the great, wide world, various and versatile tools for understanding what's around them, the capacity to see things from others' points of view, an active mind that's always integrating new perceptions and putting the world together in new ways. Those are the traits that make people thoughtful, adaptable, creative, and humane. Without these, any job will be a dead end. With them, you're equipped for a lifelong adventure.

Those are all skills Duke can develop in you, but you won't gain a single one of them by following the path of comfort. The comfort imperative is to avoid challenge. To be comfortable, you're going to want to be pushed as little as possible beyond what you already know and believe. You'll seek out subjects you already "get"—that's so comfortable! You'll stick to the people whose lives have been most like yours and who share the same life attitudes—no pressure there! If you take enough trouble, you might emerge from Duke not very different from what you are today.

Alternatively, you could court everything that challenges you: try new things, study things you don't already understand, seek out friends not already certified to agree with you, try the Duke opportunities that expose you to the world outside the bubble of elite education. Then you'd have four years of growth and empowerment—a big return for having been willing to risk some small initial discomfort.

My Duke colleague Gregory Jones once said that the trick for students is to learn to be comfortable in the right ways and uncomfortable in the right ways. That's what I wish for you. *To comfort* can mean "to soothe," "to solace," "to make you less frightened and upset," and as you arrive with everything so strange and new, I want for you the full measure of reassurance. But in its root the word *comfort* bears a different meaning: it comes from *cum*, Latin for "with," "together," and *fortis*, Latin for "strong," known to you from the words *fort, fortress, fortify,* and *fortitude.* I wish you enough happiness at Duke to embolden you for the adventure of Duke. Use these next four years to make yourselves strong together. Then you'll know comfort in its deepest sense.

....

Choices That Made Duke—Medicine, Athletics, Durham

March 19, 2015

In my annual addresses to the faculty I've tried to lay out my thinking about large questions facing the university. In recent years I've talked about Duke and race, globalization, and the cost of education at selective private universities and the value proposition of the liberal arts. Last year my address was about leadership transitions in the senior administration, the construction boom on campus, and the goals of our fundraising campaign—people, places, and funds, as I called it for short.

The number three seems to have stuck in my head, for this year I want to speak to three areas that aren't strictly academic but that have been involved with this university since its founding. To end your suspense, I'll name the three adjacencies: health care, athletics, and our home city of Durham.

Medicine was built into the founding act of envisioning Duke University, and in its early years medicine did as much as anything to make Duke known. As part of his plan to revive the school's fading fortunes, John Franklin Crowell, the graduate student recruited to be president of Trinity College when it was still located in Randolph County, had the idea of starting a medical college and teaching hospital at Trinity in 1891. After Trinity moved to Durham, the idea continued to be talked about, and when President Few conspired with James B. Duke to transform Trinity College into a fully ramified research university, they planned for a medical school to be added when there were sufficient funds.

When Mr. Duke died in 1925, a codicil in his will provided an extra $4 million for this project, with Mr. Duke's indenture to The Duke Endowment underlining his commitment to bring high-quality health care to the Carolinas. Armed with this funding, Duke built a medical complex continuous with the new West Campus and welcomed the first class of medical students in 1930. As Crowell had foreseen, an academic medical center required a teaching hospital, and Duke Hospital also opened its doors for patients in 1930, in July.

Of all the acts of outrageous optimism and pure nerve that accompanied the founding of Duke, none quite exceeds the thought of building from nothing, on the site of a cleared pine forest, a medical center that would vie with the best in the land. But that's what happened here. There were of course favoring conditions: the professionalized, research-based model of medical education projected by the Flexner Report in 1911 was still relatively new at this time, and Duke had the advantage of being able to build to this model unencumbered by baggage from an older medical world. The level of aspiration at which Duke Medicine was pitched and the financial resources that accompanied that aspiration made it possible for President Few to recruit top leaders from leading schools, specifically the brilliant young doctors whose paths to advancement had been blocked at Johns Hopkins.

In consequence, Duke Medicine did not start off humbly and slowly evolve, as had been the case with Trinity College. It appeared full blown as a high-end, up-to-the-minute medical facility (an accreditation agency placed Duke in the top quarter of American medical schools only five years after its opening), and major national advances began to come out of Duke very early on. Deryl Hart, the Johns Hopkins doctor recruited as the first chair of surgery, introduced ultraviolet lights into operating rooms at Duke in 1936, a major step forward in controlling postoperative infections. When this upstart university began to win a national reputation, Duke Medicine led the way.

But in order to become a home to high-end medical research and education, Duke had to go into a business related to academics but not identical with it: namely, the business of health care. Fast-forward eighty years, and Duke is as eminent as ever in medical research and patient care, and we are ever more deeply involved in the business of health care delivery—and thus subject to the vicissitudes of that rapidly transforming sector.

A curiosity I have been well positioned to observe is that while the Great Recession of 2008–9 had an almost immediate impact on the university side, the medical part of the Duke economy was at first not so badly hit. You may recall that during the first two years of the recession, when there were no raises in the university, employees of the Health System continued to see salaries advance, and the ARRA stimulus bill, which disproportionately benefited medical research, further hid the bad news to come. As things began to rebound on the university side, medicine has entered its own, belated period of economic challenge, with storm clouds menacing every phase of its operations: new uncertainty about the funding of graduate medical education, a changing health care system certain to cut reimbursement levels to which we have long grown accustomed, and a continued slump in research funding from federal agencies that has been aggravated in the postsequester era. (The NIH reached its high-water mark in 2003, with research funding declining over 20 percent in real dollars from then to now.)

This confluence of challenges was sufficiently concerning that in February 2013, Chair of the Board of Trustees Rick Wagoner appointed an ad hoc committee led by trustee Jack Bovender to study the impact of known and potential challenges on the Duke University–Duke University Health System relationship. Questions to be considered included the following: As the current health care transformations unfold and operating margins grow thinner, will the Health System be able to support academic research in the School of Medicine at a sufficient rate? If the Health System needs to grow the scale of the population served to be competitive in the market, might we need to contemplate new partnerships as a means to expansion? And if we grow in this way, how can we assure that the priority Duke gives to the research mission would be protected? At the outer limit, might the business end of Duke Medicine finally become so large and so responsive to its own different logic that the idea of a symbiotic relation of university and Health System might finally prove untenable?

At the end of a deep dive I've never seen equaled in comprehensiveness, the ad hoc trustee committee looked dire possibilities in the face but came to a cautiously reassuring conclusion. A stress test conducted by outside experts predicted that the Health System would be able to manage whatever changes are brought by the Affordable Care Act without disastrous impact on its finances. This meant that while the Health System needs to continue to build its competitive position, there is not a strong case for us to grow on terms that would dilute our academic mission. So far from seeing our health care business and research activity inevitably growing further and further apart, this group reaffirmed their inevitable interdependence and called for clearer provision for financial support of the academic side. To optimize these reciprocal benefits, the committee concluded that we need to take better care to coordinate strategic planning in the medical school and Health system, and to strengthen the coordination of governance on the university and Health system side.

In effect, the ad hoc committee report represented a reaffirmation of the core dream of an academic medical center. Academic medical centers are sites of health care delivery and medical research and the training of expert future medical practitioners, but the point is, these things do not just happen side-by-side. In the ideal version, patients get their care in a place where people are asking the fundamental questions that lead to new and better models of care, and research is practiced in such a way as never to lose sight of the human condition it can aim to ameliorate. Every part of the academic medical center equation is under fierce new pressure that could lead to a fracturing of their fragile alignment. This makes it more essential than ever for these activities to be *managed* so as to be mutually supportive.

Let me mention two more or less direct consequences of the trustee study. In response to its deliberations, a key step has been taken to make surer provision for academic support. Through a transfer of more than $500 million from the DUHS balance sheet, the university is planning for the creation of a permanent quasi-endowment to support the academic mission of the School of Medicine. Augmented with $200 million from SOM reserves and $40 million from the university's earnings on its reserves, this fund will generate roughly $45 million in annual support to the SOM for the indefinite future—a measure of predictable, long-term security our School of Medicine has never had.

Second, the deliberations of this committee were enormously useful to me in a task I've had this past year: finding a new chancellor for health affairs. When we learned that Victor Dzau would be leaving to become president of the Institute of Medicine, I took preliminary soundings on the proper shape for this key leadership role. Among others, I spoke to presidents of other universities noted for their biomedical strength. Many, as you know, have a separate dean for the medical school and CEO for their health care business who report up through different paths, and I was eager to learn what they saw as the advantages of different organizational structures.

One helpful colleague told me that having one person over both of these operations is the ideal arrangement if you can find the perfect person, but in the normal run of things, it just makes more sense to have two separate chiefs. Then how do you manage things that have high institutional value that require collaboration across domains, I asked—things like our Cancer Institute or Translational Medicine Institute, to name no more? With commendable candor, he replied, "Oh, we don't have many of those."

I put this together with the lesson of the ad hoc report, and the conclusion seemed clear: just for the reason that the health care delivery business and academic medical research are threatening to pull further apart, the highest success will come to the place that is able to hold all the parts together, to make the components of an academic medical center work together in a mutually beneficial fashion. So when we began to look at chancellor candidates, we were looking not just for impeccable professional credentials but specifically for people who could manage to this sense of shared mission and common purpose.

Eugene Washington, our new chancellor, who will start at Duke on April 1, has every qualification one could imagine for this wide-ranging position: a distinguished researcher and department chair in OB/GYN, he became the first provost at the biomedical research powerhouse UCSF, then dean of medicine and CEO of the health system at UCLA, and national cochair of PCORI, the Patient-Centered Outcomes Research Initiative, one of the key visualizers of a new national practice based not on treating illness but promoting health. To this all, I'd add that he is a proven uniter and inspirer, someone with a long track record of listening to others to elicit their best thought, then making them want to work together for the highest communal good. We will not be spared the challenges of health care reform or the newly difficult environment, but Gene Washington's leadership will give Duke the best possible chance to face new facts with creativity, imagination, and a keen sense of our ultimate goals.

I promised three items, so let me hasten to my second. In the history of this university, a domain that has a surprisingly close structural analogy to medicine is athletics. Duke elected to have a medical school and hospital in the act of defining itself as Duke; put another way, Duke built medicine deep into its institutional identity—and exactly the same is true of athletics. You may not remember that football, then the ultimate high-visibility college sport, was banned at Trinity College by President John Carlisle Kilgo in 1895, a ban reluctantly continued by President Few until 1920. But when Trinity College was reborn as Duke University, a crucial part of the planning involved the restoration of high-end athletic competition. The football stadium, the first structure put to use on Duke's newly built campus, holds down the south end of West Campus as medicine holds down the north. And just as Few went to the celebrated Johns Hopkins, the frontrunner of new-model medical schools, to hire a leader, Wilburt Davison, to create a tradition of excellence and put the new university on the map, Few went to Alabama, the Johns Hopkins of intercollegiate football, to recruit the football coach who would take Duke to the front of the pack: Wallace Wade.

William Preston Few was no fool. He knew that to establish its name and its claim to greatness, Duke needed strengths in addition to its strictly academic strengths, and he saw athletics as a means to build a sense of internal community and to win this school national acclaim. Thanks to this deep incorporation of athletics in the establishment of Duke's identity, this university has had a continuing interinvolvement with another world that's not wholly academic—with the result that, as with health care, we are subject to the dynamics and vicissitudes of the intercollegiate athletics market.

Perturbations in the intercollegiate athletics scene have brought challenges to the schools that play Division I sports. This is not a new story, but in the last few years, the money available through media contracts has put college sports increasingly in the entertainment business, with pressures on university priorities that can be highly distorting. We can all name universities that have savaged academic budgets while continuing to build sports facilities with embarrassingly large price tags. We can all name universities that admit students to play high-visibility sports who have no realistic ability to benefit from educational opportunities or interest in doing so.

Given the potential of sports programs to sully academic reputations, some ask, Why not get out of this business altogether? My reply would be, If there are self-defeating ways to link athletics to academics, those aren't the only ways—and we would lose a significant richness from our mix if we were to subtract this portion of our program. I myself was not a student athlete, but in twenty years of presiding over residential universities with highly miscellaneous programs of activity and engagement, I have come to understand that athletics can be far more than just a pastime or recreation—can be a mode of education complementary to more strictly intellectual ones. Men and women learn things through athletic competition that aren't so easily learned in other ways. These include the pleasure of high performance; the ability to recognize excellence and to embrace the discipline necessary to achieve it; the logic of teamwork; the ability, in success or failure, to keep getting up and trying again; the ability to start with a strategy and revise it improvisationally, on the fly, as circumstances change. These aren't the only things worth knowing, but they are highly valuable life equipment. It's not for nothing that in ancient Greece and parts of Europe a seat of learning *and* athletic competition is called a gymnasium.

The problem is that for a university, there's no embracing athletics at the highest competitive level without becoming involved in contemporary intercollegiate practice. But even as we participate, a school has choices as to how to manage its participation. I am proud to represent a university where student athletes have graduation rates as high or higher than nonathletes and where the great preponderance of athletes are serious, accomplished students. You will recall my mentioning that of Duke's 640 varsity players, 495, or 77 percent, were included on the ACC Academic Honor Roll.

Keeping the balance requires continual attention as new threats and opportunities emerge in the intercollegiate scene. You will remember that this past year, the sixty-five universities in the five so-called power conferences were recognized as having semi-autonomous standing within the NCAA, able to pass regulations in some areas that will affect their students alone. It is easy to see how autonomy could open the door to abuse. This could be the means for the schools with the highest media revenues to shower funding on athletes in revenue sports in ways that would make them little different from paid performers, with less and less in common—and less and less contact—with the student body at large.

This January I attended the first meeting of the Autonomy Conferences to cast votes on Duke's behalf. I am cautiously pleased to report that at this first outing, the power conferences avoided such measures and favored more constructive ones. The measures that were approved include tighter policies on athletic concussions; permitting schools to offer athletic scholarships that cover the full cost of attendance; and the one that mattered most to me, a measure that forbids universities from revoking a student's athletic scholarship for reasons of athletic performance. If a school can withdraw students' scholarships the day they are no longer strong contributors to the team that recruited them, it's a naked confession that the school had no interest in or commitment to the students other than for what they could do on the court or field. In a better world, the offer of an athletic scholarship is a commitment to stand by a student until he or she finishes his or her education, as has long been the case at Duke.

My larger point is that over the course of their histories, different universities court involvement with their own sets of extra-academic activities, such that when these relations grow problematic, severing the Gordian knot is seldom an option. The art is to make the relation work. This is certainly true for my third example, the city of Durham.

Most universities are located where they were founded—Harvard is in Cambridge, Stanford is in Palo Alto, UNC is in Chapel Hill—but one of Duke's peculiarities is that this school was founded elsewhere, in rural Randolph County, and operated there for over fifty years. Just as it chose to have health care and chose to have big-time sports, Duke's ancestor Trinity College chose to be located in Durham. The ambitious little college packed up its bell and the several thousand books of its library, loaded them onto a boxcar, and moved to this city in the 1890s in order to be connected to more dynamic parts of contemporary America (Durham was a New South city) and, not coincidentally, to have access to philanthropic support from New South wealth. The consequence was that here again, Duke acquired an enduring codependency through an originating choice.

For many years, Duke must have appeared little connected to its chosen home. In the early twentieth century Durham was a vibrant center of black culture and commerce, was indeed so prominent in the world of black business enterprise that it was known as the "Black Wall Street." But in the depths of segregation, any Duke connection with black Durham—beyond the manual labor force that it depended on—must have seemed tenuous at best. When the Georgian East and Gothic West campuses were built in the late 1920s, they were separated by a mill village attached to the factories on Erwin Road. This was a territory equally alien to the university culture of that time.

When the tobacco and textile economies collapsed in Durham, Duke's lack of urban connectivity became paradoxically a kind of asset, at least in the short term. In the 1970s and 1980s, as cities became focal points for social pathologies, universities that were more visibly urban in setting and signature—Columbia, Chicago, Penn, Yale—paid large public relations prices for their dangerous, depressed locales. When Duke hit the cover of the *New York Times Magazine* as the new "it" school in 1984, it was partly because it was set in a Gothic wonderland, standing apparently clear of its urban surround.

But as urban decline abruptly reversed course in the U.S. in the past twenty years, Durham's missing downtown became a serious negative for this university, and a century after moving here, Duke came to understand the need to invest in its place. During Nan Keohane's presidency and with John Burness in the lead, Duke began investing to reverse cycles of social decay in twelve proximate neighborhoods through the Duke-Durham Neighborhood Partnership. Through the genius of Tallman Trask, Duke also invested in rehabilitation projects downtown with decisive effect. Duke's commitment to lease one-fourth of the one million square feet of the abandoned American Tobacco site led to the securing of the rest of financing for the ambitious project that reignited Durham as a commercial attraction. Comparable Duke participation helped advance the building of the Farmers' Market and the Durham Performing Arts Center, which opened to the public in 2008.

From this start, with a brief timeout for the economic downturn, Durham has become a veritable boomtown for investment and activity. Two thousand three hundred residential units have been built within two miles of downtown within the past three years. Four hotels have opened or are soon to open within a mile of downtown. Durham's locavore food scene, the subject of much free publicity and national acclaim, continues to recruit new restaurants virtually by the week. (Your president enjoyed being informed at one of these on a January evening that he could happily have a table if he did not mind the three-hour wait.) As new residents and new entertainment and nightlife bring new dynamism to the downtown, the last undeveloped bits are coming to new life as scenes of commercial activity and employment.

In a choice that would have seemed unimaginable a short while back, the Duke School of Medicine decided that instead of building a new research building on campus, it would rehabilitate the last great tobacco warehouse, the Carmichael Building in West Village, into high-end lab space where it could co-locate faculty doing research on metabolomics, physiology, and human genetics—one attraction being that private sector companies could locate in adjacent space to share research projects and commercial development of discoveries. The new tenants in the Carmichael Building have raised the number of people for whom working at Duke means working downtown to north of twenty-five hundred. The Chesterfield Building, long Durham's greatest eyesore, a dead, dull tomb for the vanished age of the cigarette, is under construction now and will soon form part of a new archipelago of biomedical research and development spaces mixing academic and industry participants. Start-ups, which spring up most luxuriantly in high-density collision spaces with highly educated, innovative neighbors, will have a natural new home in what is being called the Durham Innovation District. Duke's own Innovation and Entrepreneurship Initiative will open such a space of connectivity in downturn Durham within the year.

As we help bring these new realities to life, we can glimpse a Durham that never was but that will benefit us immensely as it comes into being: a center of economic and cultural vitality that draws smart people from around this country and the world and gives their creative ideas a place to develop. If Duke and Durham are bound to each other in a shared fate, we've entered a chapter where both sides can see newly positive prospects, possibilities both parties have helped create through a vision of constructive partnership. Durham is not yet the new Austin, let alone the new Silicon Valley, but the selection of this city as one of four new sites for Google Fiber development shows that it is not only we who see the potential concentrated here.

Duke has an important role to play in every aspect of this city's and this region's development. It was dismaying to learn that in the school grading program recently mandated by the North Carolina legislature, many Durham public schools got grades of C, D, or F. There can be no great surprise here. Since the principal insight of these grades seems to be that affluent towns already known to have the best public schools do indeed have the best-performing public schools, with the converse holding true for areas of concentrated poverty, the exercise seems at once punitive and stupefyingly tautological. But even if we do not like the grading system, we all have a role to play in advancing more equitable schooling for this city and its people. Duke cannot do this alone, but our partnerships with the Durham Public Schools in early education programs, summer and afterschool academies, and our many shared research and literacy initiatives are crucial contributors to a better civic future.

With health disparities having emerged as one of the most devastating and intractable forms of social inequality in America in our time, Duke and Duke Medicine and even Duke Athletics have a crucial role to play in partnering for a healthy community. Eugene Washington, who has won recognition for his work on behalf of community health in Los Angeles, will find many willing and innovative partners in Durham. If we want to benefit from our home, we must be active to make it the community it can be.

I conclude with this: We are the inheritors of choices made long ago on Duke's behalf. There is no unchoosing those choices: they are so deeply woven into the fabric of this place that the theory of their separability is a simpleton's mistake. But just because these choices have been so decisive in their impact, it is essential that we manage their consequences toward this university's greatest good. That's our work here together every day. Thanks for letting me share a few glimpses from where I sit. And I thank you for your concerted work to lift this university toward its highest purpose.

Remarks at a Community Forum
on a Racial Incident

Duke Chapel Steps, April 1, 2015

Universities are inspiring places, but, being communities of humans, they cannot guarantee the elimination of all vestiges of stupidity and intolerance. They can, however, use such occasions to deepen education in the meaning of inclusion and human respect and their essential role in a university. These remarks were given before about one thousand students, faculty, and others gathered in front of Duke Chapel to express their outrage over a racial incident.

My friends, I'm Dick Brodhead, and I'm the president of Duke.

This is a beautiful day, and this is a beautiful place. But we are gathered here because something ugly happened on this day and in this place. Duke is a place that is very fun and inspiring in many ways, but something happened today that was dispiriting and depressing in the extreme. You know the news as well as I do. Last night around two o'clock in the morning, a rope noose was found hanging in a tree on the Bryan Center Plaza.

Let me say a few things. One: we don't know who did that. I hope we will know who did it, and if you have any idea who did it, I hope you will help us find out. There's been an investigation going on since the middle of the night, and I hope it will come to a clear resolution. Two: we don't actually know for sure what the person who did this deed had in mind. It might have been the most awful thing one could imagine; maybe somebody thought it was funny; maybe somebody had no idea what this meant to people. In my experience, when you get to the end of the story, things aren't always exactly as you guessed.

But if there is uncertainty about how this arose, there's no uncertainty about what that symbol meant to the audience that saw it, or why people had the response they had. A noose hanging in a tree in a southern state of the United States is a symbol, an allusion to the history of lynching. If you don't know the history of lynching, let's take the chance to learn a little bit about it—and please go find out more afterward.

After the end of slavery, other ways were perfected to assure the inferiorization of the black population in the South, even after this population had won technical legal rights. People were kept from going to equal schools; people had their voting rights repealed. At the extreme, violence was visited on black bodies. Black people were hung from trees—that's what a lynching was—through an extrajudicial process. This was not typically a spontaneous community act. Lynchings were often planned and advertised days in advance, and the images of the lynching were circulated widely throughout the community.

Lynching was a way of demonstrating to black people that violence could be visited on black bodies at any point—it was visited on some people's actual bodies—but the circulation of that image was what was really powerful. Seeing this image gives you the message: If you are a person who belongs to a certain category of people, this could happen to you at any time. Black people were made to experience not only the denial of civil rights and of equal standing before the law; they were made to bear the psychic burden of feeling continual vulnerability on grounds of their race.

If anybody didn't know this history, it would be good to learn it, because otherwise you can't explain why this image is so upsetting. This was not simply rope. This was a symbol that evoked the whole legacy of racial oppression in the segregated South. As a person, and as the president of Duke University, I find this symbol and what it symbolizes abhorrent. This university condemns the display of this symbol and repudiates the message that it gave about the kind of place this is. This university repudiates racism in all its forms, as it repudiates every other form of discrimination based on thinking of people as members of abstract categories you can treat as if they are somehow inferior to you.

It wasn't so long ago that these things were realities in this place. If they are not now, if there's not a contemporary history of lynching, it's because people, actual humans, North and South, white and black, fought and fought, decade after decade, to repudiate the world in which inequality was the law of the land—inequality before the law, inequality of rights and personhood. It was only fifty-two years ago that Duke accepted its first black undergraduates. It was only fifty years ago that the Voting Rights Act was passed in this country. Men and women worked to create a world in which people would not be marked as inferior on the basis of the prejudice and bigotry of the people who felt they had the power to do so.

We fought to make that different world. This university was created in the crucible of that struggle, and we have no intention of going back now. Somebody may think today's image is a symbol of Duke's present or future, but that's not the Duke I know. That's not the Duke I want. That's not the Duke I'm here to help build. And as I look at the multitude—what a pleasure for me, to see one thousand faces stretching as far as I can see—you came here for the reason that you want to say, with me: This is no Duke we will accept. This is no Duke we want. This is not the Duke we're here to experience, and this is not the Duke we're here to create.

This would be abhorrent if it happened anywhere in the world, but there's something especially abhorrent about it happening in a university. We who live in universities are inestimably privileged. We get to live a life where our work is to try to improve our understanding of ourselves and the world. And we're able to do it because we have the greatest of all luxuries: the highest talent brought to us, not from the world we already know but from every part of the human world—from every country, every race, every community, every origin—brought together so that we can teach each other and learn from each other and open our limited perspectives to benefit from the perspectives of others. But there's a precondition to having that work successfully. For us to get the benefit of the education that a diverse community embodies, people have to make other people feel safe here. People have to make other people feel welcome here. People have to treat each other as if each other person here has just the right to be here that you do, is here for the same purposes, and is going to be part of a project of education through community.

In the wake of an incident like this, there are things for the administration to do. I do understand that. By chance I met this morning with the leaders of the Black Student Alliance—the appointment had been set up before we ever knew this would happen—and they had suggestions about ways that orientation programs could be improved. I think those and other suggestions could be very valuable, and we'll be looking to see how we can implement them. There is a proposal about discussions that could take place in the residential houses on campus; I think that's a great thing. I would only echo the words of the first speaker here today: learning about our duties to an inclusive community isn't a vaccine you get once that renders you immune forever. This is an ongoing human challenge, so we all need to keep educating and being educated about its meaning. The Duke administration is committed to work on eliminating all forms of inequality and discrimination at this university.

But I'm also going to call on you, because getting this right can never just be the work of the administration. That isn't something you can delegate to other people to take care of. It has to be all of our work to make the community all of us want to live in. So, as you would be respected, show the respect to others that you would want to receive. As you would have someone understand you, take the trouble to extend yourself to understand where that person is coming from.

Duke may seem like it's all finished, but we're making this place every day, and we have a choice about what kind of place we're going to make. One person put up that noose, but a thousand people came together to say, That's not the Duke we want, that's not the Duke we're here for, and that's not the Duke we're here to create. Thank you.

....

The subsequent investigation determined that this incident stemmed from ignorance and poor judgment. A Duke undergraduate student acknowledged responsibility for the action, received a sanction through the university conduct process, and wrote an open letter of apology to the Duke community. Unfortunately, 2015 saw further incidents of intolerance on Duke's campus, with attendant campus and community reaction. In response, I created the Task Force on Hate and Bias Issues; the university is currently implementing the recommendations of this task force in an ongoing effort to create a more inclusive and welcoming community for all.

Constructing Duke

Cameron Indoor Stadium, August 19, 2015

My friends, this year we are staging your official welcome in a different way. Usually the Freshman Convocation is held in Duke Chapel, a majestic space suited to solemn ceremony. This year we've decamped to Cameron Indoor Stadium, the boisterous home of Duke school spirit, where fans go crazy and foes wish they could just go home.

Why the change? Well, the talent of our famous basketball team is just shorthand for the talent of our whole student body, so maybe we're here to introduce the whole Duke team, all 1,750 members of the Class of 2019, in Cameron Indoor fashion! At the top of the alphabet: A freshman from Cairo, Egypt, who enjoys ballet, writing, and tennis, HADEEL ABDELHY! Fast-forward to the end: An engineering freshman from Mendham, New Jersey, MATTHEW ZYCHOWSKY!

The real reason for the change of venue is far more prosaic. We're gathered in Cameron because Duke Chapel is closed for repairs. Indeed just about everything at Duke is closed for repairs. If you came to campus last spring or summer, you saw a wilderness of cranes, construction fence, and beep-beeping earthmovers. As you faced Duke Chapel, closed for repairs, to your right you saw the Rubenstein wing of Perkins Library, closed for repairs; to the left, Page Auditorium, our largest lecture and performance space, closed for repairs; then West Union, our central eating and social collision space, closed for repairs. The great West Campus quads were closed for repairs; you couldn't get through to the plaza, our other great gathering spot—that entrance was closed for repairs. Up behind West Union, our future student wellness center is a big hole surrounded with construction fence. Cameron is open, but don't try using the south exit: it's closed for repairs, part of a construction project encompassing the football stadium as well.

I'm grateful that you chose Duke, given that when you came for a campus visit, all you saw was construction. Today I ask, What does it mean to have all this construction going on at your new home? For one thing, it makes you a witness to history. When Duke's Gothic West Campus and the brick Georgian East Campus were built at the start of the Great Depression, this university was the largest construction site on the North American continent. The reconstruction we're engaged in marks the biggest building boom on campus since Duke was created. You are seeing it with your own eyes.

Second, you're the lucky ones. We're not just doing fix-ups; we are engaged in a transformational renovation of this campus, restoring beautiful exteriors while creating new interiors to meet the needs of today's education in extraordinary new ways. There has been disruption galore on our way there, but you will enjoy the fruits of our labor. Lots of projects are finished and waiting for you. The West Campus quad is green again; the renovated library will open its doors on Monday; Page will soon be hosting the sorts of speakers and performers that make it a luxury to go to a great university; the football season will kick off in the renovated Wallace Wade Stadium; and there's plenty more to come. The East Campus Marketplace, closed for renovation all summer, reopened Monday, and when the basement is completed, we'll have virtually doubled that shared activity space for our freshman class. A new student arts center is about to arise on Campus Drive, across the street from the Nasher.

But I have a third thought, and it's my real message to you. Please sear the sight of all this construction indelibly in your mind as an image of what your work here could be.

Duke exists for two purposes. We are here to push the boundaries of human understanding through our research activities, and we are here to help talented young people develop the most broadly knowledgeable, thoughtful, capable, resourceful version of themselves that they can become. We take trouble with physical structures because they serve the real construction project this great university is engaged in: the building of capable men and women, eager to deliver on their promise in the life of their times. Buildings are inanimate; we can renovate them whether they want it or not. But we can't work that transformation on you unless you actively reach for it—unless you come here with the will to be the builder of your best self.

Here are some tips for you as builders. One thing contractors know is that the materials assembled on the worksite were put there so you would use them. Walking past a handsome new library won't do much to change you; for that, you have to go inside, learn how to frame an interesting question, and seek materials that might help you to answer that question. Why come to a school with great faculty if you don't seek them out? With these, as with every Duke resource, you have to engage the opportunities around you to unlock the door to future growth.

Next, we've done a ton of demolition here, accompanied by a lot of noise and inconvenience, because we couldn't build the things we're creating without disrupting what had been there before. I am not recommending that you take a jackhammer to your life, but if you want to make room for a new, improved version of yourself, you have to tolerate disruption—of your personal habits, of your preexisting networks, even of assumptions that seemed certain because you have never heard them challenged. If nothing here is disrupting you, that probably means that you are stuck in the status quo. Disruption is not fun, but it is the opener of possibilities, so don't be scared when it approaches.

Last, there may be solo architectural geniuses, but construction is always a massive group effort, and if you want to build a fully empowered self at Duke, you should be thinking how this community can assist in that project. Duke has succeeded in drawing top talent in a hundred forms from across every known social boundary—regional, national, racial, cultural, religious, political, socioeconomic, and more. As sociologists of knowledge have long recognized, from Renaissance Florence to the start-up hotspots of today, the places where smart, energetic people from different starting points have been drawn together and allowed freely to collide have been the places where world-changing ideas are hatched and new human energies released. Today you become a citizen of just such a place. From today, every one of you will contribute to the dynamism of a massively diverse community, and every one will get a growth boost from the others here with you.

You could not insulate yourself from this energy if you tried. But if you want to build to your full potential, you're going to have to use this resource in an intentional fashion, seek out and open yourself to this human richness, even if that means venturing outside what's comfortable. After the first diversity buzz wears off, you'll face inevitable temptations to fall back on communities that you subliminally perceive as "like you." And in even the healthiest communities, things can happen that pull people back from the things they share.

Duke is committed to being a community where everyone is respected and has an equal right to thrive. Therefore Duke requires that each of you take responsibility to build such a community, treating every other with the respect that you wish for yourself. But since no human world could guarantee you a life free from all social ills, if frictions do arise, I hope you will find a more constructive way to engage with differences than recoiling in resentment or withdrawing in defensiveness, human as both impulses powerfully are. In this country and around the world, we see the price millions pay when differences harden into conflict and estrangement. Let's do better than that at Duke. Let's make it be part of your education to learn how to enter into points of view fundamentally different from your own and open your own point of view to those not already equipped to grasp it, and to practice this hard human skill not just on good days but even in times of challenge. This will make Duke a better place and will equip you to be a constructive social contributor long after you leave this place behind.

Let me close with a personal word. I was drawn to Duke by its distinctive builder's spirit. This school has always taken pleasure in what it was, but kept reaching for the further thing it could become. In this spirit, the Durham fairground—today's East Campus—was rebuilt as Trinity College. In the late 1920s, that college threw up a comprehensive university on what had been a forest and an adjacent pig farm. Over the past ninety years, that school has built itself into a global beacon in a hundred fields. By now Duke is rich in tradition, but we're not conservators of tradition. We're still reaching, trying to envision the even better form research and education could take, and using our power to put those dreams into practice. That's the spirit that has fueled Duke's construction. I welcome you into the company of that spirit. We admire and applaud what you are already, but you didn't come to Duke to stay the same. You came to catch sight of further possibilities and to win strength and joy from the struggle to reach them.

That construction starts today. I welcome you to Duke.

On the Fate and Fortunes
of Public Goods

Loyola University, Baltimore, Maryland, September 25, 2015

I wish a happy fiftieth birthday to the National Endowment for the Humanities. For fifty years, the NEH has helped scholars open the human record to new understanding, made our shared past accessible to a broad democratic public, and, in partnership with state councils, kept the humanities alive at the local level in all fifty states, reminding us that history has happened everywhere and bears the imprint of us all.

Fifty years back, this familiar agency was a profoundly new thing, and the meaning of that novelty is my subject today. Let's remember how it came to be. The agency was officially authorized when President Lyndon Johnson signed legislation creating national endowments for the humanities and the arts in a Rose Garden ceremony on September 29, 1965. This legislation implemented recommendations from the National Commission on the Humanities, which had been set in motion in 1963 by three scholarly organizations: the American Council of Learned Societies, the Council of Graduate Schools in America, and the United Chapters of Phi Beta Kappa. The commission's report, published in 1964, speaks to a nation in confident possession of superpower status, a status that brings new risks and new choices.

Global dominance can take two forms, the report explains. One is a dominance of economic might, military power, and technological superiority. Alternatively, together with economic and military supremacy, a nation could exert a different order of power, in the ideals and image of civilization it projects—in which case, other nations would eagerly follow its high lead. Get enough economic and military superiority, and you are at best a muscled-up hegemon; add the humanities, and you could become an aspirational civilization. That's the opportunity before the United States, and seizing it is not guaranteed. How to assure this better outcome? What's needed is help advancing "things of the spirit"—help on the artistic and humanistic side.

As the cochair of a recent humanities commission, I marvel that when a comparable group sat down in 1963–64, they arrived at a single recommendation: the creation of a federal agency to support humanistic activity, federally funded but with independent decision-making power. President Johnson embraced this proposal in a speech at Brown University in September 1964. Within a year the legislation had passed with bipartisan support, the bill was signed, and the NEH was born.

So the question I ask myself is, How did it happen that a proposal in this exact form was so persuasive to both academic and political leaders in the 1964–65 season? There is a relatively easy answer. The 1964 report is jealously mindful of the creation of the National Science Foundation in the early years of the Cold War, and science envy is the proximate cause for wanting a foundation of our own. But the idea draws on forces and developments reaching well beyond NSF, and I'd like to share the story of how I came to understand them.

Please be patient as I take you on a humanist's excursion. Last summer—this is how I spent my summer vacation!—I read Sven Beckert's book *Empire of Cotton*. Beckert traces the long history of the industrialization of cotton around the globe across five centuries, underlining the dependence of free markets on coerced labor. Once the labor of slaves on plantations in the American South supplied the cotton to English, then also New England mills. Three or four decades after the Civil War, cotton manufacture moved to the southern states that had once been sites of cotton growing, with women and children cast in laboring roles.

History, the recovery and reinterpretation of the past, is one primary humanistic form. The study of visual culture is another, and images brought me the next stage of my journey. When I got to this point in Beckert's book, it put me in mind of Lewis Hine's classic photographs documenting child labor in the North Carolina cotton mills in the early twentieth century. These images bring history vividly to life, such that we can *see* the faces of individual children, *see* the relation of small bodies and large machines that Beckert had evoked.

These photographs brought something else to mind, this time retrieved from the world of law. Law is nothing if not the humanities applied: an affair of texts and interpretation and arguments over meaning, an attempt to align values and precedents with contemporary situations. Four or five years back, David Levi, the dean of the Duke Law School and a former federal judge, and Jed Purdy, a Duke law professor and political philosopher, asked me to join them in teaching a course. The course was a consideration of how the law had negotiated key moments of national crisis in American history. This was great fun, since it gave me a chance to be back in the classroom, my primary passion, but it was also a lot of work, since I had to master tons of material from the U.S. Supreme Court.

One of the cases we worked through was called back to mind by the idea of cotton mills in North Carolina. The case was *Hammer v. Dagenhart*, decided in 1918. In 1916 Congress had passed a law prohibiting interstate commerce in goods that had been produced with child labor. (The age in question was fourteen.) A father of two minor sons employed in a mill in Charlotte was upset that his family should lose the children's earnings, so he sued, arguing that the law exceeded federal authority. The case went all the way to the Supreme Court.

In judging between a federal law and the father of child mill workers, perhaps playmates of the ones imaged by Hine, the Court reasoned as follows. It recognized that by 1918 public opinion had undergone a powerful shift toward viewing child labor as dehumanizing and unethical. It acknowledged that many states had passed laws limiting the practice—North Carolina itself forbade child labor under the age of twelve. But the judges could not be persuaded that child labor was a proper subject for federal regulation.

Here's why. By the Tenth Amendment of the Bill of Rights, the Constitution reserved for the states all powers not delegated to the federal government. Regulation of interstate commerce was one of those delegated powers. But by the analysis of the Court, "the making of goods . . . [is] not commerce, nor does the fact that these things are to be afterwards shipped or used in interstate commerce make their production a part thereof." This conclusion arises from a segmenting cast of mind that sees parts as more real than the wholes they form; in this case, it sees the differences of phases of production as far more significant than their continuities. Manufacture is over and done with before cloth leaves the mill to enter trade. Ergo, manufacture is not commerce. Ergo, its practices are not subject to federal legislation. (In his tart dissent in *Dagenhart*, Oliver Wendell Holmes rolled his eyes at a nation that could figure out how to federally prohibit the sale of alcohol but not the exploitation of children in factories.)

These habits of mind derived from an older world where local things were not experienced as part of larger integrations and where the federal government's sphere was correspondingly small. (Remember that only in 1913 was Congress's right to impose a federal income tax established.) These were once common, mainstream understandings, and they continued their mental hold as the world around them changed. During the Great Depression, the scale and duration of national economic dysfunction made it desperately obvious that local remedies were of no avail. With the ascendancy of Franklin D. Roosevelt and the New Deal, problem after problem was visualized as having a federal solution and so received federal regulation of its own. Hence the birth of federal agencies: the Farm Security Administration, the Civil Works Administration, the Federal Deposit Insurance Corporation, the Federal Housing Administration, and many more.

But through Roosevelt's first presidential term, the Supreme Court continued to balk at these innovations, for reasons wholly familiar to a student of *Dagenhart*. In the case that ruled the National Industrial Recovery Act unconstitutional, Chief Justice Charles Evans Hughes retraces the familiar logic. The kosher slaughter of chickens at the Schechter plant in Brooklyn was a localized, self-contained activity. Even if they came from elsewhere, when the chickens reached the slaughterhouse, "the interstate transactions in relation to that poultry then ended." Since the work involved was not in interstate commerce, it was not subject to federal regulation. Don't you get it?, Chief Justice Hughes all but says to New Deal adherents. I know you are dealing with a damnably difficult problem, but our national system does not permit your solution. "Extraordinary conditions may call for extraordinary remedies. . . . [But] extraordinary conditions do not create or enlarge constitutional power."

The 1935–36 Court decisions mark one of the great impasses that have defined the history of this country—a moment when a set of rules and understandings perfectly well-established in one cultural world are unable to cope with powerful new facts. An earlier impasse—over the federal government and slavery—was not resolved short of civil war. This one was resolved by a change of understanding that took place between 1936 and 1937.

FDR won an electoral landslide in November 1936 on a scale the country had never seen. The next spring, probably not in response to Roosevelt's Court-packing proposal, the Supreme Court began finding by 5–4 margins that the truth had changed sides. In a March 1937 decision in a minimum-wage case involving chambermaids in Washington State, the Court found that the federal government had a far larger power of regulation, with the same Chief Justice Hughes commenting that, although the Depression emergency had not created new constitutional powers, "recent economic experience" has brought heretofore overlooked chains of cause and consequence "into a strong light," justifying a federal role where none had seemed warranted before. Within a year, the bare majority thinking became a new consensus. (The *Dagenhart* decision was unanimously overturned in 1941.) From that point on, the United States had entered a new normal world where virtually no challenge was outside the federal government's sphere.

I may seem to have made a long detour, but, to my mind, we cannot understand where the National Endowment for the Humanities came from without understanding how the sphere of federal authority expanded in the first half of the twentieth century. There was no federal role in support of the humanities before this transformation. Without the conceptual transformation forged in the crucible of the Great Depression, it is inconceivable that a national commission could have envisioned a federal solution to the challenge of the humanities in 1964.

When the NEH legislation was adopted, of course, this was not an act by itself. It formed an integral part of the Great Society program, Lyndon Johnson's revival and extension of the New Deal amid 1960s American preeminence and prosperity. The NEH proposed to do for the nation's humanistic yearnings what the Economic Opportunity Act (signed in August 1964) did for employment, what the Voting Rights Act (March 1965) did for participation in the political process, what

Medicare and Medicaid (July 1965) did for the health needs of the elderly and seriously disabled.

The public roared approval. Johnson was reelected in November 1964 by a popular vote margin that exceeded Roosevelt's largest percentage. Nor did this support go away when the optimism began to dim. Just as both the Republican and Democratic parties contained progressive wings in the early twentieth century, both parties shared a big-government vision in midcentury. Johnson launched the NEH with a $2.5 million appropriation. It was under Richard Nixon, then Gerald Ford, then Jimmy Carter that the NEH received major new increments of funding, just as it was under Nixon and his successors that federal environmental programs—another new aspect of the general welfare now enforced through a federal role—saw their greatest growth. There is no understanding where the NEH came from without understanding how the American dream of government got big.

That change having been accomplished, the world, of course, did not stand still. Coming forward from the NEH launch to the world of today, three changes are especially salient.

First, that day's confidence in America's mission to lead the world has certainly not vanished, but it has grown more complex. I find it striking that the Gulf of Tonkin Resolution authorizing military action in Vietnam passed Congress in August 1964, right before Johnson's embrace of the national endowment idea in September. I entered college at that exact time, and I can testify that few saw the toll the war would take on belief in the government's integrity and in America's benevolence abroad. Even after many reversals, American civilization is still unparalleled in its global attractiveness, but this has not functioned as the report envisioned.

A fascinating section of the report spies a new danger Americans are facing in the 1960s, a novel access to superabundant leisure. If the humanities do not fill this leisure with rich materials for "man's questioning and his need for self-expression," the 1964 report sternly cautions, "men and women [will] find nothing within themselves but emptiness" and "turn to trivial and narcotic amusements." Materialism, trivial amusements, and gadgetry define this report's nightmare of a deficient civilization. But as our culture has continued to hold sway over the global imagination, this has worked through, not in spite of, consumerism, personal technology, and popular entertainment: Think of the stream of popular music, film, video, and iconic brands that have held the world enthralled via iPhones and other American-born devices.

As this suggests, a second great change between the NEH's debut moment and today involves the public standing of the humanities idea. The 1964 report is confident that there is a body of knowledge that connects individuals to a rich heritage and rich domains of existential meaning. This body of knowledge is spread through a model of education with roots in classical antiquity that aims to develop the whole person, what we call the liberal arts. As you know, this confident, unitary vision of the humanities has suffered self-questioning and fragmentation among its adherents in intervening decades and no longer commands wide public persuasion. When the Commission on the Humanities spoke, Johnson answered in the idiom of humanistic high-mindedness. When claims for humanities and the liberal arts are made today, they're often met with skepticism, if not scorn.

The core conviction of the NEH's launch was that the federal government was the right player to advance the humanities. In a third change, this tenet too has grown uncertain. In New Deal and Great Society historiography, the age of big government is here at last, so happy days are here again. But there was always an alternative that, if eclipsed, never lost its power. In the election of November 1964, the scale of Barry Goldwater's defeat seemed to confirm that his version of conservatism was a freak development that would never be seen again. Of course, this conservatism had older roots than many at the time cared to note. In the late 1950s and 1960s, Henry David Thoreau, a writer for the first time enjoying vast popularity, gave validation to the civil rights movement through his essay "Civil Disobedience." But, as is often forgotten, the same works by Thoreau set forth an antistatist gospel. In the first line of "Civil Disobedience," Thoreau repeats the adage "That government is best which governs least" and then offers this improvement: "That government is best which governs not at all."

Such conservatism came roaring back with Ronald Reagan's election in 1980, returning to power a philosophy of small government that produced the first large cut in NEH funding in constant dollar terms. (The second, fundamentally unreversed to this day, came with the Republican-led 104th Congress, elected in 1994.) In our time, big-government and small-government forces have reached a long-running political deadlock, with one byproduct, sequestration, inhibiting virtually any increased investment in the discretionary portions of the federal budget, humanities and research funding prominently included.

Put together the waning power of the dream of the humanities and a waning belief in the positive role of government, and you arrive at the most salient novelty in the past fifty years: the decline in the belief in public goods. The Great Society's heyday was charged with confidence that the quality of life for every American could be improved along every axis, civic, economic, medical, educational, aesthetic, and spiritual; that these improvements would be enacted through federal government activity; and that if there was a cost to the public in taxes, that was a small price to pay for the value derived. The idiom of that day was one of sacrifices for the larger good. "Ask not what your country can do for you. Ask what you can do for your country."

Fifty years down the road, that way of speaking sounds quite dated. Today's public has a seriously thinned-down concept of what social goods are worth having beyond personal happiness, and an even weaker notion of why it should incur any sacrifice to fund such abstractions. The revealing figure here is not the decline of NEH funding but the decline of state funding for public higher education. The Center on Budget and Policy Priorities has documented that since the 2008 recession, adjusted for inflation, state funding per student for public university systems has been slashed, with fifteen states reporting cuts of 25 percent or more and sixteen additional states with cuts north of 20 percent. Tuition costs to students and their families have risen to fill the gap. In the days when higher education was thought of as a public good worth investment from all taxpayers because an educated population increased the quality of life for all, students and their families paid around 25 percent of public higher education expenditure. Today the personal share is near 50 percent and shows no sign of falling.

So, how is a believer in the humanities to proceed at this time? This cause is more, not less, urgent because of the changes I have described. But there is no use ignoring the new facts we have to contend with. Our need is to find out how to advance this cause in the world that we actually inhabit.

Let me say what this means in tactical terms—and if I do not sugarcoat things, it is because, like Emerson, "I have set my heart on honesty in this chapter." First, the federal government is not the prime target for this moment's appeals. The American Academy of Arts and Sciences commission that I cochaired was authorized by two congressional leaders from each party, Lamar Alexander and Mark Warner in the Senate and David Price and Tom Petri in the House. They have been thoughtful advocates, and they spoke compellingly when our report was launched. It is important to have such voices on our side and to get as much support as we can possibly win for the NEH. But major new federal initiatives are unlikely now, and though we might hope for restoration (for instance) of Title VI funds for foreign languages and cultures, the things that most need doing are not federal affairs.

In truth, the humanities are sustained by a continuum of institutions, very few of which are federally funded: elementary schools, high schools, colleges, universities, and community colleges; libraries, museums, performance halls, and other places of artistic presentation; local history centers and book clubs; and a thousand others. Since World War II, science has inevitably looked to Washington because government alone can supply funding on the scale and with the long-term horizon that scientific research requires. But the humanities were never principally a federally supported activity, and their advocacy needs to be decentralized.

If there is one single thing humanities lovers need to press for at this time, it's a stronger, more equitably distributed foundation of elemental literacy, the root of democracy and every humanistic power. President Johnson said in the Great Society speech, "Our society will not be great until every young mind is set free to scan the farthest reaches of thought and imagination." "We are still far from that goal," he added— and we are equally far from that goal today. But funds to attract and retain great K–12 teachers are still overwhelmingly state and local appropriations. In North Carolina, 66 percent of the public instruction budget comes from the state, 26 percent from localities, and a mere 8 percent from federal sources. So advocates need to work nearer to home.

Further, if championing the humanities is a multifront battle now, we also need to think a great deal harder about how persuasion works. In our long time of troubles, too many humanists have been guilty of making our case the way some travelers repeat an English phrase louder and louder to an uncomprehending foreigner, as if with a little more volume the imbecile is bound to understand. But as rhetoric (one of the oldest humanistic disciplines) might have taught us, persuasion does not involve restating what I already believe. It involves engaging with others, entering into their different frame of reference, then thinking how I could make my point in terms that make sense to another. This challenge should not be beyond our collective wits.

From my experience, it helps to recognize that there are different bands of audiences, each of which might respond to a different approach. First, there are the believers: not just professional humanists, but lovers of art and visitors to art galleries, lovers of music and attendees of musical performance, lovers of reading, history buffs. This is not a small group. If every one of these people spoke up for their passion, we might gain massive public traction. If every museumgoer actively advocated for art exposure for children in public schools, if every book club member spoke to a school board member or state legislator about the human needs satisfied by this means, we would have a chorus for the humanities the United States has not heard in years.

In a second ring are what we might term lapsed believers. One of the most frustrating features of recent years has been the number of highly educated people, some paying small fortunes to send their children to liberal arts colleges, who say that such things were great back in the day, but we can't let people waste time with liberal learning now: the only education of value is the one that lands you a job. I used to find this perverse, but I've come to understand that it's just a repetition of sayings heard so many times in "serious" media outlets that they have entered many minds as received ideas. If I ask such a person, Did you find that the things you studied that were directly instrumental led to your later success?, the answer is invariably no. If I then ask, Can you name a single successful person who had just one job-related skill, and did not instead start with a broad education that opened the mind in varied and unexpected ways?, the answer is usually no again. (Even Steve Jobs, the poster child for dropouts, studied calligraphy in college, with decisive effect on Apple design aesthetics.) A lot of people beyond active converts know the value of the humanities but have forgotten. We will do ourselves a favor if, with patience and good humor, we remind them of what they already know and love.

A third ring, those who don't have a latent belief to be reactivated, need a different approach. One thing humanists should be eager to do nowadays is to connect with people working on other problems who can be made to feel what the humanities has to contribute. In a recent project on pandemics at Duke, it was not surprising that ethicists from philosophy departments were of crucial value, since a key question in pandemics is how to allocate scarce medical resources. Less predictable was the help a literature professor could supply by explicating the role of narrative in pandemics: the storylines that get established, then giddily revised, as the emergency takes shape. It is hard to see how we will make new friends and allies if we fail to reach out.

Another thing I have seen work with the unbaptized is what I have learned to call "third-party validators." My humanities commission, like the one in 1964, contained people of visibility and accomplishment who were not in the academy or professional arts. Their voices carried special weight in the rollout because they were not known to be presold. Jim McNerney, chairman and former CEO of Boeing, has said that while his company principally looks for engineers, no one will rise beyond a certain level if they don't also have other skills: skills in communication and cross-cultural sensitivity, the products of humanistic training. Karl Eikenberry, military commander, then ambassador in Afghanistan from 2009 to 2011, has said that military weapons will never be strong enough to solve global conflicts. At least as critical to national security are the understanding of foreign histories, foreign languages, foreign religions, foreign cultures— humanities subjects par excellence. We need to keep recruiting friends like this.

Then let's imagine a really hard challenge: people for whom terms like *the humanities* and *the liberal arts* carry not the slightest residual meaning, are intimidating or off-putting or even just a bore. What to do with the hard nuts to crack? I have two thoughts. First, the humanities can take highly evolved forms, but they are rooted in our most fundamental human powers and needs. When other lines of appeal aren't available, we need to reconnect with the forms that are familiar to people and start from there. A Duke student I know taught debate last summer to ninth graders in the Mississippi Delta. When he asked why debate might matter, one student was quick with a reply: Debate was the key to the antislavery and civil rights struggles; plus if you can argue well, you can persuade your parents. That's a great base to build on.

And if you couldn't get even that much of a purchase? As a last resort, we could just subject someone to the power of the experience. For instance, take them to the hip-hop musical *Hamilton*. The composer-performer Lin-Manuel Miranda read Ron Chernow's biography of Alexander Hamilton on vacation and saw how he could translate Hamilton's transcultural itinerary into a modern, transcultural music-and-dance idiom. Miranda has brought history to life and brought added richness to the performing arts by fusing them with the historical past. But there's no need to know or care about any of that in advance. Anyone who has heard "Hey, yo, I'm just like my country / I'm young, scrappy and hungry" will have *lived* the energy of the humanities. Later, there might be a chance to find that this creation has complex cultural sources that can be analyzed and might even deserve support. Start with that point and you'll get nowhere. Start with the experience and you'll have better luck.

The start of this discussion might have sounded like a familiar story of humanistic decline, but let me say bluntly: It is not helping us to cling to the myth of the lost cause. We live at a particular moment of social history. Other times may have been more auspicious; if so, lucky them. But there's no point pining for what we do not have. The only thing that will move us forward is to understand where we are, to assess the challenges clearly, to spot opportunities with imagination, and to use all our intelligence, passion, and ingenuity to figure out how to restore the perception of a value that has grown dim, to our collective cost.

At the end of *The Prelude*, Wordsworth said to Coleridge, "What we have loved / Others will love, and we will teach them how." We care about what we value because the ability to feel that value was nurtured in us by teachers of many sorts. Let's have the confidence to teach the humanities in that sense. People crave it more than we imagine.

I Learn by Going Where I Have to Go

Duke Chapel, May 13–14, 2016

This winter I had lunch with a Duke couple in the Bay Area. The husband had recently retired at an early age from success in a demanding position. When we met, he was still catching his breath, marveling at the unfamiliar experience of freedom. He summed this up by quoting a line he had learned in meditation: "There is nowhere you have to go, nothing you have to do, no one you have to be."

When he said it, this line hit me like a slap in the face. I have a fascinating yet demanding job. I had just led an event for six hundred alumni in L.A., then rushed to Orange County for meetings there, then flown to San Francisco to confer with more Duke friends, then come down the peninsula for this meeting, to be followed, that evening, by a gathering for 350 in Palo Alto where I was to interview Duke faculty who had created a research app to enable early diagnosis of autism. Each stop on my trip was absorbing, even inspiring, but the schedule involved such a hurtling rush that these words felt like a reproach from an alien world.

And then I thought of you. Here you are gathered at the site of your Freshman Convocation, with Duke Chapel renovated just for you. After four strenuous years, you are all done with college and its demands. No more running around to complete two majors along with a certificate in journalism or entrepreneurship or ethics, or to practice with your club sports team or dance group, or seek start-up funds for the company you're launching, or do tutoring downtown. That's all done now; not a single expectation remains for you to meet. What bliss! There's nowhere you have to go, nothing you have to do, no one you have to be.

But though some contrary evidence has emerged from your escapades at Myrtle Beach, I doubt that you'll do well on the leisure test. The people who were starting out here four years back had been selected for certain traits. The students Duke seeks don't just test well: we look for people who are driven to activity and achievement because they delight to use their gifts to the fullest. The hyperactive life you've led here gave four years' reinforcement to your habit of setting, then meeting daunting expectations. Our species has christened itself *Homo sapiens*, the wise human, but you and I come from the species *Homo occupans*, the ever-busy, ever-occupied human: you could not sit still doing nothing if you tried. This very day, your kind parents and unkind inner demons are urging you past this pause, clamoring for a new answer to the question Where are you going to go, what are you going to do, who are you going to be?

You may expect me to urge you to resist this question. For sure, a dimension is lost when we live only in the future-oriented ethic of achievement. Whatever your religious outlook, entering a serene space of contemplation like Duke Chapel has the effect of pulling you out of the rush of busy time, making you feel yourself to be right here, right now, attuned to an underlying profundity. And yet what we "are" is not accessed solely by slowing down and purging ourselves of worldly expectations. There are dimensions of who we "are" that can be discovered only through the striving to achieve.

You are the same person who arrived here four years back, but you're also different—you have a broader sense of what there is to take an interest in in the world and a clearer sense of where your interests actually lie. How did that happen? Let two brief stories stand for a thousand. I know a student from the Class of 2015 who came to Duke expecting to be premed. But she found those courses only mildly interesting until she took a class studying the result of high-velocity impact on the human body, as from a car crash or an explosion. Right away she knew that she really wanted to be an engineer, pivoted to a major in biomedical engineering, and is now doing graduate work in injury biomechanics. I know another student who came to Duke interested in economics and East Asia. But at some point he began volunteering in the Cancer Center, then studying health economics, and came to the sense that medicine was what he really wanted to do. After graduating, he spent a year studying hospital management practices in China, then enrolled in a postbac program to pick up the premed courses he had missed. He aims to start medical school next fall.

Now, the details of these stories aren't yours, but I trust that you recognize the plotline. People usually arrive at Duke with some vague plan of what they're going to do—in many cases, with emphasis on the word *vague*. But then they start trying things, trying a course here, an activity there, a new friend group here, an internship or research project there. By doing so, they encounter things that kindle a deeper interest, make them feel more fully engaged, causing a new plan to come in view.

The huge privilege of a liberal arts education is that instead of fixing you at an early age on the narrow road to a predetermined career, it allows exploration and self-discovery. You are the fruit of that process. If you are feeling anxious about what comes next, I beg you to remember the lesson of this last chapter. It wasn't your initial plan that made your education happen. It was your willingness to try things out, to throw yourself into things and see where they led you, then revise your plan based on what you discovered. The poet Theodore Roethke caught this precisely when he wrote, "I learn by going where I have to go." You may wish you already knew where you were supposed to go; you may be punishing yourself for not knowing your life destination in advance—but how could you? The goal is found by means of the journey and in no other way. I learn by going where I have to go.

When we see people in positions that we envy and admire, it's easy to imagine they were always headed to that very place, but that is almost never true. Steve Jobs said that you can't plan your life, but looking back, you can connect the dots. He should know: at one stage in his life, he was fired as CEO of Apple, the company he later rejoined and led to become the most successful company in the history of the world. The most impressive speaker I heard on this campus this year was Deborah James, a Duke alumna who is the secretary of the air force. She is responsible for a workforce of 664,000 people and a budget of $140 billion, and she has dealt with extraordinary challenges, including a cheating scandal and security breaches with nuclear weapons, to bipartisan praise. When she came to Duke, she liked languages, got interested in Latin America, and chose to major in what is now called international comparative studies. By the time she graduated, she had gravitated toward an interest in the Foreign Service, and she went to Columbia to get a masters in international affairs. Which was all very prudent, except just when she prepared to enter the workforce, federal budget cuts meant there were suddenly no positions open in the Foreign Service. But having arrived at this dead end, she summoned some resilience, her inner GPS device recalculated, and she found a way to put her talent to work in the branch of government that was expanding in the early Reagan years: defense. From that point forward, she worked her way through a mix of public and private sector positions to the role she occupies today. Her advice to you is "Be prepared to zigzag, because whatever your original idea was may not work out."

Later on the day when I heard the line "nowhere you have to go," I met a graduate from two years back who was relearning this lesson from scratch. While he was a student, he had shared his vocational anxieties. He had come from a background where not everybody had a college education, so advice on career paths was thin. He was majoring in chemistry and thought perhaps he would go on in chemistry, which sounded logical, if uncompelling. Some while later, he told me that he was now interested in going into consulting, but he was clearly not totally sold. When I met him this January and asked how consulting was going, he replied that, oh, he had actually not gone that route; he had joined a start-up promoting research on cures for rare cancers, a decision that had made him quite radiant. He has probably not taken his last zig or zag, but these have not been random ventures: each move has led to a clearer sense of what he wants to do and increased his confidence to make that choice. He learned by going where he has to go.

Friends, you are entering so-called real life at one of the most confusing periods in the history of work. On the one hand, statistics show that the economic returns on college education are higher than ever; on the other hand, people now seem vastly uncertain as to how such education actually delivers such value. Meanwhile, for the first time in history, a recovery that has cut unemployment from 10 to 5 percent has left a country feeling strangely hopeless about the future, a negativism suggesting that you'd better grab some good thing and hold on for dear life. Yet entrepreneurial disruptions have turned many sure things into dead ends, while generating new jobs whose long-term security is a total question mark.

How are you to navigate through this treacherous fog? There are no safe harbors in this new world. Building a life now will take versatility, resilience, a confident willingness to zig and zag, in which you use new moves to win a clearer sense of what fulfills you, then tack toward the thing that holds the most of that.

Shouldn't I be telling you to make a difference and make the world a better place? Isn't that a mandatory message of graduation speeches everywhere? I do want these things, but in my experience, people can't make the world a better place until they have first learned some things about the world. Plus in order to make a difference, you have to know what the difference is that you have it in you to make. And how to know that except by using experience to help reveal to you what you are called to do?

All your life you have been called gifted, but gifts are meant to be given, not just smugly enjoyed. There really is somewhere you have to go. You have to go on the journey to learn what the gift is that you peculiarly could give to the world and how you can deliver it. You don't know this yet, and you will never know it once and for all: you will learn by going. Time to leave Duke now—you got what you could from this stage of your journey. I wish you the courage to keep journeying toward the life you could lead at best. Go well.

Citizens of Duke

Duke Chapel, August 24, 2016

Twenty-twenty signifies perfect vision. And you, Class of 2020, make the perfect sight. For us, you embody the renewal of this university, the surge of energy that will lift us to new heights. On your side, this ceremony marks a great transition. As of today, childhood is over and high school far behind. By the powers vested in me, I now proclaim you a student at Duke. Or let me reach for a stronger word: I now proclaim you a citizen of Duke. Let's think what difference that word makes.

A citizen is more than a resident. A citizen is a member, someone who fully belongs. Belongs to what? We don't speak of people being citizens of their families or a citizens of a club. Citizenship means membership in a social entity that's big enough to contain lots of people you don't personally know. The word derives from the Latin *civitas*, "city," which also gave us the words *civic* and *civil*. When a city-state was the largest effective social unit, a citizen was a member of a city. Nowadays citizenship mostly refers to membership in a national community. Your entering class contains citizens of seventy countries.

Citizenship brings privileges, like the right to vote or the right to serve on a jury, and it brings duties too, which vary from place to place. If you are from Switzerland or Singapore, you may already have performed national military service. If you're a naturalized citizen of the United States, you have pledged to support and defend the Constitution.

This sounds pretty simple, but as this summer taught us, the concept of "citizen" can be quite contentious. I was in England on the day of the Brexit vote. It was going to be close, but those in the "Remain" camp were feeling confident, until, in the early hours of June 24, the count revealed that the United Kingdom had voted to leave the European Union, without anyone knowing exactly what that would mean.

The European Union is a remarkable creation of the second half of the twentieth century in which a score of nations, on the continent where the strife among sovereign nations has engulfed the world in world war not once but twice, concluded to join in a supranational entity, giving up some separate rights to win the benefits of a larger union. Under the Treaty of Maastricht, citizens of EU nations also became citizens of the European Union, entitling them to the free flow of peoples and economic activity across national borders. The union that has brought peace and prosperity to a once war-ravaged Europe was a work of hope, but fears always shadowed that hope. This June, the majority of British voters decided that their fears of lost sovereignty and an influx of "outsiders" outweighed the benefits of an open community.

We know such hopes and fears closer to home. The United States, a country whose culture and economy owe their dynamism to the continual inflowing and intermingling of peoples, is going through one of its periodic bouts of nativism, marked by the will to raise barriers against immigrants and to define citizenship by who we exclude.

The history of citizenship is a fascinating subject, but if I have the word on my mind, it's because of you. Here you are today joining Duke Nation. What does it mean to be a citizen of Duke?

Citizenship always entails some definition of who's in and who's out and how a person can become included. In most countries, if one or more of your parents was a citizen at the time of your birth, then you are a citizen by *jus sanguinis*, by right of blood. In a few countries, most of them in the Western Hemisphere and the United States prominent among them, you also become a citizen by being born in this country whatever the status of your parents. This is called *jus soli*, citizenship by right of soil.

So what determines citizenship of Duke? There is only one way. You may have been born in Duke Hospital, but that did not get you in. You may have had a parent who went here, and we welcome that continuity when it occurs, but no one has a hereditary right to attend Duke. No one is admitted to Duke who has not passed through a searching assessment that starts with tests and grades but goes much further, asking how you took advantage of opportunities you had and whether your achievements evince real curiosity and intellectual engagement, which are very different from the mere knack for "doing well." Plus we consider the sum of your involvements to see if you have the will to live up to the full measure of your talents, with the hard work that entails, and if you have an inclination to use your gifts for the benefit of others.

You are here today because, in your own way, under your own circumstances, you demonstrated the promise that Duke seeks. If you're proud thinking you alone really deserve to be here, you shouldn't be. Each person here passed the same test as you. If you're anxious because you think everybody belongs but you, don't be. You have proved yourself just as fully as any other new arrival. You are entitled to citizenship because you earned it the only way it can be won: by being a person of promise eager to live up to your full potential.

So, what privileges does this new citizenship bring? That's an easy one. Duke offers opportunities for self-discovery in virtually every known form: academic, artistic, athletic, entrepreneurial, social, spiritual, local, global. You will never hear of a university where more things are on offer to undergraduates. Your admission is your ticket to explore every opportunity this university affords.

And the duties? That's where modern concepts of citizenship often fall down. As I noted, there are countries where national service is compulsory. This country has no such requirement: within my lifetime Americans have gotten out of the habit of being asked to sacrifice anything for the larger good. Did you know that in Australia, voting is obligatory? Here it isn't, and since it's optional, the primal democratic right, the right of citizens to choose their government, has undergone partial atrophy from lack of use.

You can decide how well citizenship as passive enjoyment of goodies has served the larger society. But I'm here to tell you, passive citizenship has no place at Duke. For this place to work, you have the responsibility to participate. Let me name four ways.

First, going to a university whose programs are being copied around the world won't do you any good if you don't try to learn about those programs, see which ones might serve you, and make an effort to participate. But second, enrolling in programs is just the start. Duke exists to transmit the store of human understanding, but our real work is continually to increase that store. We take truths that seem final and challenge them, interrogate them, with teachers and students partnering to achieve an ever fuller understanding. But this only works if you participate: if you pitch in, join the discussion, ask your question, share the part of the truth you've been gifted to see.

Third, at a place so rich in talent and perspectives, every classmate and every social interaction could enlarge the understanding you've achieved to date. We have just rebuilt this university's great common spaces, including the Marketplace and West Union, because we know that in a great residential university, informal personal exchange, the unstructured interaction of teachers with students and of students with their fellows, is the essential medium of education. But to get this benefit, you have to have the courage to enter into conversation with strangers, and not just superficially, but risking the deep sharing in which deep understandings are forged.

Fourth, students have told me that they went through rough patches here at first. Is that surprising? No real world ever guaranteed perpetual, stress-free bliss, and if it did, no human ever grew except by seeking and facing up to the challenge. These same students have shared that hard days got easier once they found a mentor, an upperclassman, or a member of the faculty or staff who would take an interest in them and cheer them on. There is no university where more people are willing to play this role for you. But to find your natural advisors you have to reach out, to do your part to make the connection.

Take seriously your responsibility to be active in your education, and this place will give what you came to find. But there's one more thing Duke citizens have to do: you have to help create the atmosphere in which everyone can have the same rich experience. Any way you could victimize someone, or humiliate someone, or silence someone, or exclude someone takes away that person's rights and robs you of their contribution. Every way you learn to respect others, listen to them, and encourage their participation builds their power and equips them to teach you. This is not a care some of you owe to some others. It's the care each of you owes to all.

My friend Dean Guttentag lifted your spirits with pleasantries, and here I am, loading you down with expectations. My excuse is, you actually need to visualize and embrace the commitments I've described: lower your expectations when you arrive and you will lower the quality of the experience you take away. A government website I consulted says that "citizenship is a unique bond that unites people around civic ideals." I've asked you to bond around the aspirations Duke is built on: the ideal of individual personal development, the ideal of education through community, and the ideal of the active, ongoing pursuit of truth.

So let's do this right—this could be fun. Have you ever seen a citizenship ceremony? If not, you can watch a thousand online. Raise your right hand. Do you solemnly swear to pay allegiance to the values of this university by living up to them in your daily life? If so, please signify by saying "Aye." Congratulations! You are now a citizen of Duke.

INDEX

....

and Applied Sciences (CIEMAS), 24, 53, 187, 191, 192; Forging Social Ideals FOCUS program, 66; Franklin Humanities Institute, 111; French Family Science Center, 53, 187; Haiti Lab, 111; Kenan Institute for Ethics, 96; Levine Science Research Center, 188; Nicholas Institute for Environmental Policy Solutions (NIEPS), 39, 47–48, 58; Professional Development Institute, 197; Sanford Institute of Public Policy, 22, 39, 48, 51, 58, 82, 96–97; Trent Semans Center for Health Education, 188, 192; Visual Studies Initiative, 111

Duke University Health System, 137n1, 185, 207–9

Duke University Libraries, 39, 54; Bostock, 39, 54, 82, 187, 192; Perkins, 1, 11, 86, 132, 187, 190, 192; Rubenstein, 192, 220, 221

Duke University Press, 122

DUMAC (Duke Management Company), Inc., 105. See also Duke University: endowment of

Dupree, Jameca, 197–98

Durham, N.C., 85, 127, 128, 134; African Americans and, 128, 213; civil rights movement in, 128; DCRI and, 22; downtown revitalization of, 83, 213–14; Duke faculty research projects in, 48; Duke's relations with, 3, 23, 212–15; economic history of, 213; fairgrounds of, 223; food scene in, 213–14; Google Fiber and, 214; hospitals in, 132; mayor of, 23; as New South city, 212; schools in, 41, 66, 215; student engagement with, 41, 49, 66; Trinity College moves to, 13, 38, 205, 212; West Village, 214

Durham Farmers' Market, 213

Durham Innovation District, 214, 215

Durham Performing Arts Center, 213

Dzau, Victor, 135, 136, 183, 185–86, 209

Economic Opportunity Act (1964), 229

education, 34, 46, 55, 65, 76, 96, 106, 211; charter schools and, 66, 67, 77; cultural differences and, 180–82; democracy and, 169; continuing, 36, 76, 100, 134;

failures of, 33, 177; humanities and, 150, 167; innovation in K–12, 83, 140, 167, 233; as investment, 125; opportunity and, 196; public, 13, 77–78; purposes of, 176, 199–200, 203; real reforms of, 180; segregation in, 86–87, 123, 131–32. See also higher education

Ehrenreich, Barbara, 163

Eikenberry, Karl, 166, 177, 235

Einstein, Albert, 79

Eisenstein, Marcia, 41

Emerson, Ralph Waldo, 36, 114, 232–33

end of life care, 16, 22, 48, 49, 83

engagement, 176, 211, 244; at Duke, 10, 26, 34, 35, 65–70, 76, 93, 117–18, 141, 154, 222, 245

engineering, engineers, 23, 41, 42, 51, 53, 90, 111, 151, 165, 166, 177, 235; biomedical, 16, 24, 25, 238; in China, 108; students of, 66, 67, 141, 220, 238

Engineers without Borders, 49, 79

English Civil War, 7

enterprise, 67, 82–83

entrepreneurship, 49, 51, 82, 83, 189, 214, 244

Equal Opportunity Commission, 196

European Union (EU), 243

Evans, Mutt, 128

Facebook, 75, 145

FACs (First-Year Advisory Counselors), 98, 145, 201

faculty, 21, 24, 40, 51, 87, 97, 182, 227, 237; academic freedom of, 135; African American, 130, 133–34; complimented, 105; expertise of, 187; funding and salaries of, 91, 104, 193; interdisciplinarity and, 57; lacrosse case and, 72–73; named chairs and, 113; recruitment and hiring of, 13, 53, 58, 92–93, 94, 107, 206; strategic planning and, 53; survey of, 133–34

Farmer, Paul (Class of 1982), 25–26, 41, 78

fascism, 61

Faulkner, William, 120, 170; *Absalom, Absalom!*, 20; *Requiem for a Nun*, 120

Fayetteville, N.C., 123, 131

of, 13, 20; hyperinvestment in, 163; pub-
lic, 90–91, 175–76, 232; research universities and, 174; residential, 191; traditional,
231; value of, 156, 162, 163–64, 240–41.
See also liberal arts; universities
high school, 168
Hines, Lewis, 226
Hobbes, Thomas, *Leviathan*, 7, 10
Holmes, Oliver Wendell, Jr., 228
homesickness, 201–2
Honduras, 25
Homan, Jill, 49
Howard Hughes Medical Institute, 15
Howard School (Fayetteville, N.C.), 123,
131–32
Hughes, Charles Evans, 228, 229
humanities, 29, 110, 151; RHB on, 120–21,
125–26, 150, 164–65, 227, 231, 232, 233–34,
235–36; in China, 108; energy of, 236;
federal support of, 170–71; in North
Carolina, 119; technology and, 179.
See also liberal arts; National Endow-
ment for the Humanities
human rights, 110, 157, 178
Humboldt, Wilhelm von, 181–82
Hurricane Katrina, 41–42, 48, 68

India, 87, 107
inequality, 26–27, 45, 62, 132, 174, 215; in
America, 10, 196, 218
information technology: cloud computers and, 172; infrastructure for, 54, 214
innovation, 130, 168, 179; at Duke, 96, 130,
185, 189, 190; in Durham, 214, 215; in
education, 13, 83, 93, 180; entrepreneurial, 51; research universities and, 105,
174, 180
intellectual property, 48
interdisciplinarity, 15–18, 94, 110; of Duke,
16–17, 21–25, 47, 56, 57–58, 93, 95, 108,
179, 235
internationalism and internationalization,
110, 195; at Duke, 25, 54, 93, 105–7, 108,
130
Internet, 61; global impact of, 55–56.
See also social media
iPad, 179

iPhones, 81, 231
iPods, 79; for Duke students, 75
Islamic studies, 24, 50

James, Deborah Lee (Class of 1979),
239–40
James, Henry, 31, 128
jellyfish, 81, 83
Jenson, Deborah, 111
Jobs, Steve, 178, 234, 239
Johns Hopkins Medical School, 13, 206, 210
Johnson, Lyndon B., 225, 226, 230, 231, 233.
See also Great Society program
John Tyler Caldwell Lecture on the
Humanities (2011), 119–26
Jones, Gregory, 40, 109, 204
Jones, Susan, 40
Jonson, Ben, 113
justice, 45, 71, 87

Katz, Lawrence F., and Claudia Goldin, on
"the Human Capital Century," 174
Katz, Sam, 40
Kennedy, John F., 154, 155
Keohane, Nan, 4, 21, 23, 127, 159, 213
Kerr, Clark, 88
Kerry, John, 173
Kidder, Tracy, 25
Kilgo, John Carlisle, 210
King, William, 37
Kluge Prize, 61
Knight, Douglas, 21
knowledge: economy of, 3; social uses of,
18, 23–24
Kornbluth, Sally, 137n1, 184–85
Krzyzewski, Mike (Coach K), 23, 127, 128
Kunshan, China, 98, 172; RHB visits, 99;
Duke and, 95–96, 99, 108–9

lacrosse case, 71–74, 86
Lange, Peter, 44, 52, 109, 135, 183, 184; 2006
strategic plan and, 53
law and legal system, 227–29
Leary, Mark, 202
Lefkowitz, Robert, 154, 155
Levi, David, 227
Lewis, Tracy, 48

women, 66, 71, 158; in Duke Leadership Academy, 134; in Duke leadership positions, 136–37; higher education and, 26, 38, 45, 127

Women-in-Action for the Prevention of Violence and Its Causes, 128

Wood, Wendy, 40

Wordsworth, William: *The Prelude*, 236; "Tintern Abbey," 30

Works Project Administration, 121

Wren, Christopher, 184

Wuhan University, 109, 172

Wynn, Phail, 136

Yale University, 108, 177, 213; RHB at, 2, 3, 19, 26, 27; women at, 26

Yeats, William Butler, 43, 55

Yung Wing, 177–78

Zhejiang University, 180

Zhouzhuang, China, 99